de Gruyter Studies in Organization 16

The State, Trade Unions and Self-Management

de Gruyter Studies in Organization

An international series by internationally known authors presenting current fields of research in organization.

Organizing and organizations are substantial pre-requisites for the viability and future developments of society. Their study and comprehension are indispensable to the quality of human life. Therefore, the series aims to:

- offer to the specialist work material in form of the most important and current problems, methods and results;
- give interested readers access to different subject areas;
- provide aids for decisions on contemporary problems and stimulate ideas.

The series will include monographs, collections of contributed papers, and handbooks.

The State, Trade Unions and Self-Management

Issues of Competence and Control

Editors
György Széll · Paul Blyton · Chris Cornforth

Walter de Gruyter · Berlin · New York 1989

Editors

Dr. György Széll
Professor, Dept. of Social Sciences, Universität Osnabrück, FRG

Dr. Paul Blyton
Senior Lecturer, Cardiff Business School, The University of Wales, Cardiff, Wales

Chris Cornforth
Lecturer, School of Management, Open University, Milton Keynes, England

Library of Congress Cataloging-in-Publication Data

The State, trade unions, and self-management : issues of competence
and control / editors György Széll ... [et al.].
    p. cm. – (De Gruyter studies in organization : 16)
    ISBN 0-89925-475-6 (U.S.)
    1. Management–Employee participation. 2. Trade-unions. 3. Works
councils. I. Széll György. II. Series.
HD 5650.S 665 1988
338.6–dc19   89-1094
                                                                   CIP

Deutsche Bibliothek Cataloging in Publication Data

The state, trade unions, and self-management : issues of
competence and control / ed. György Széll ... – Berlin ; New
York : de Gruyter, 1989
    (De Gruyter studies in organization ; 16)
    ISBN 3-11-011667-7
NE: Széll, György [Hrsg.]; GT

Preface

This volume is one of the outputs of Research Committee 10 of the International Sociological Association, which draws together researchers from various parts of the world with an interest in participation, workers' control, cooperatives, and self-management. Many of the ideas and arguments contained in the following chapters were first raised at a workshop held in Osnabrück, Federal Republic of Germany in 1985, which focused on the role of *competence* as a precondition for increased democratisation of political and work life. This main theme gave rise to a number of sub-themes: how is competence created? What role does education play? What is the significance of technological and industrial change for the development of participatory competence? Do workers' councils, cooperatives, etc. need internal or external experts or advisers if they are to develop successfully? What is the role of trade unions in the democratic workplace? Can external bodies such as trade unions or the state assist in the development of competence?

In the following chapters we address these and related issues, by focusing on such arenas as workers' co-operatives and community organisations, and against such backgrounds as market and non-market economies, and the changing nature of industrial society. Separate sections attempt to shed additional light on the various roles of institutions such as the state, trade unions, and education in the advance of more democratic forms of organisation.

Many of the issues under scrutiny are not new but a re-examination seems timely. The world recession of the early 1980s severely reduced the power of labour and restricted or curtailed many of the initiatives under way in developing more democratic forms of work organisation. However, the current period of economic growth is one in which moves to greater power-sharing could again begin to flourish, bringing forth a new requirement to tackle issues such as creating or maintaining sufficient competence to make the democratic organisation viable in the long term.

Various people helped to make the Osnabrück workshop and this collection possible. In particular thanks to Ute Széll, Susanne Raker, and Wiking Ehlert and our typists Kath Hollister, Wendy Morgan and Penny

Malthouse in Cardiff, and Bernie Lake and Jennie Moffatt at the Open University. Financial help for running the Osnabrück workshop was gratefully received from the University of Osnabrück, the Deutsche Forschungsgemeinschaft (DFG), the Deutsche Stiftung für internationale Entwicklung (DSE), and the State of Niedersachsen.

György Széll
Paul Blyton
Chris Cornforth

Contents

Preface.. V

Introduction

Chapter 1 – The Role of Competence in Participation, Workers' Control, and Self-Management
György Széll.. 1

Part I: Participation and Co-Determination 15

Introduction
Chris Cornforth... 17

Chapter 2 – "Worker Participation" in the United States: A Preliminary Analysis of Quality of Work Life Programs
Bob Barber and Rochelle Towers.............................. 19

Chapter 3 – The Law as a Force for Change
Philippe Bernoux.. 39

Chapter 4 – Co-Determination in the Federal Republic of Germany: An Appraisal of a Secular Experience
Ulrich Briefs.. 63

Chapter 5 – A Political Bargaining Theory of Co-Determination
Ad W. M. Teulings 75

Part II: Worker Co-operatives and Labour-Owned Firms 103

Introduction
Chris Cornforth...105

Chapter 6 – The Role of Support Organisations in Developing Worker Co-operatives: A Model for Promoting Economic and Industrial Democracy?
Chris Cornforth 107

Chapter 7 – Consulting for Second Order Change
Warner Woodworth 125

Chapter 8 – Self-Management in Wales: Trade Union Encouragement of Worker Co-operatives
Paul Blyton 137

Chapter 9 – The Possibilities and Limits of Self-Management in Cameroonian Enterprises: The Case of an Artisanal Co-operative in the Building Trade
Emmanuel Kamdem 149

Part III: Economic Change, Labour, and the Unions 157

Introduction
Paul Blyton 159

Chapter 10 – New Work Processes, Unregulated Capitalism and the Future of Labour
Daniel Drache 163

Chapter 11 – Belgian Unionism and Self-Management
Bob Hancké and Dany Wijgaerts 187

Chapter 12 – Trade Unions and the Challenge of Modernisation and Computerisation in France
Peter Jansen and Leo Kissler 211

Chapter 13 – Technical Change and Informal Participation: The Role of Competence and Control in Administrative Work
Ulrich Heisig and Wolfgang Littek 235

Part IV: The State and Self-Management 253

Introduction
Paul Blyton 255

Chapter 14 – Limited Expertise and Local Autonomy
András Sajó 257

Chapter 15 – Organizations and Society: On Power Relationships
Dusko Sekulić 273

Chapter 16 – The Impact of State Intervention on Workers' Control:
A Case Study of Autogestion in Algeria
Lena Dominelli 289

Part V: Education and Competence 299

Introduction
Paul Blyton 301

Chapter 17 – An Inter-Organizational Analysis of Competence
Veljko Rus 303

Chapter 18 – The Prospects of Industrial Democracy in the Context
of the Proposed New Educational Policy in India
Abha Avasthi 315

Chapter 19 – Cooperation Between Universities and Unions
Edgar Einemann 327

Conclusion 337

Chapter 20 – Competence and Organizational Democracy:
Concluding Reflections
Cornelius Lammers 339
List of Contributors 359

Introduction

Chapter 1
The Role of Competence in Participation, Workers' Control, and Self-Management

György Széll

> "Unwissen ist Ohnmacht!"
> "Ignorance is impotence!"
> (Rosa Luxemburg)

After centuries of struggle for more democracy the question still stands: "Is self-management, the most developed form of democracy, possible?" And if yes: what are its preconditions? How is it affected by the division of labour, the gender division, science, technology, the economic system, the state, trade unions, political parties, education, family, etc.? In this chapter I explore these question in order to identify some of the initiatives that will be necessary to further the development of genuine workers' participation and self-management. In this perspective "competence" and "the trade union movement" have key roles.

The Historical Process

In the immediate aftermath of the American and French revolutions a broad movement for more democracy developed in most Western countries. Socialist utopias spread far in taking the slogan of the bourgeois revolution of "liberté, egalité, fraternité" seriously and not limiting it merely to the political sphere of representative democracy, but rather extending it to all domains of social life: economy, culture, science, religion, etc. The workers' movement *in statu nascendi* developed different strategies ranging from anarchism and Marxism to reformism. Without doubt the trade unions have become the most powerful and widespread self-managed organizations so far. At the same time we find the formation and growth of consumer and producer co-operatives, even including financial self-help institutions.

But soon after their birth these movements were weakened through inherent faults, a lack of analysis of historical conditions, and severe repression by the ruling classes. Nevertheless, for a long time the owners of the means of production had only formal control over the production process. So workers had the opportunity to advance their interests, by means such as strikes, go-slows, and sabotage. The response of the bourgeoisie was a political one: repression; and counter-strategies in the form of "yellow" unions etc. It was through Taylorism and Fordism that the real subsumption of the production process under capital was largely realized at the beginning of this century. The reaction of the workers for more self-determination at the work-place, coming as it did after failed political revolutions in the West after World War I, was answered both by repression and offers of co-operation and integration in the form of workers' councils, full voting rights, and human relations styles of management.

The developments in the Soviet Union were quite different. Although the political base had been the councils (the Soviets), from the very beginning real power lay in the hands of parts of the intelligentsia, who had been transformed into professional revolutionaries. The restructuring and the forced industrialization of the Soviet economy under strong pressure from outside (with the aim of destabilizing the whole regime), was directed as a war economy from above. Revolts like the Kronstadt uprising were suppressed by force (Bahro 1978, Dutschke 1974). For many reasons the Soviet Union of this period can be regarded as an underdeveloped country in the Marxian sense of the development of the productive forces. Indeed, many of the economic, social, and political problems of this society can be better understood against this background. That is, the objective preconditions of a socialist society had not been assembled. The development of the productive forces cannot just be reduced to technology and science, but also includes skills and knowledge held by the producers (Marx 1970: 54). These skills and know-how (defined as competence; Heller 1983) in regard to the production process were very much lacking in the Soviet Union, an agrarian society far behind the technological development of Western Europe at that time. Thus the subjective aspect of the social revolution, the consciousness of at least the then existing proletariat, was there, but not the objective aspect.

The old directors of the companies, leading managers, and even foremen had to be reinstalled to continue production.

Two other important historical events further illustrate my argument: the Commune of Paris in 1871 and the Spanish Civil War of 1936/37. The failure of the Commune de Paris is certainly only to a small degree explainable through lack of competence, and more through physical destruction. Although only a degree of self-organization at the workplace could be realized in the few months of the Commune's existence, it is astonishing how fast the decision processes were restructured in the absence of most of the owners. The low complexity and development of the production sphere no doubt facilitated this take-over by the workers.

Apparently the situation was quite different during the Spanish Civil War, where in some regions the whole production and distribution process was self-managed. But here as well we have a relatively low degree of technological and economic development, which while facilitating the take-over, places limits on further development. The Mondragon experience is a fascinating survival of these initiatives for a whole region (Bradley and Gelb 1983).

After the Second World War we find a number of fascinating examples of participation, workers' control, and self-management. The most important seem to be those in Yugoslavia, Israel, Poland (Solidarnosč), Hungary, Czechoslovakia, China, Cuba, and in the liberated areas of a number of Third World countries in their struggle for independence, (for example there have been periods of greater self-determination in the early history of Algeria, Peru, and Chile). But with all these experiences there is a common denominator: in spite of all orthodox theories it was never in the most developed countries that a political revolution of this kind occurred, and in no case (not even the example of Yugoslavia; see Supek 1978) has a lasting self-managed society been realized. It is our task to look for the reasons for this. In some cases the lack of international competitiveness has been forwarded as a reason for reducing or abandoning self-management practices, as the capitalist countries are far more successful economically and technologically. On the other hand, in a number of capitalist countries we find different degrees of workers' participation in the plant, in worker-owned companies, in the political sphere, etc. Thus, models such as co-determination in West Germany and workers' co-operatives become more prominent even in periods of economic crisis.

The terms "participation, workers' control, and self-management" are understood differently in different societies. For example, whereas in the

Yugoslav context "self-management" means autonomy vis-à-vis the State and "workers' management" refers to the enterprise level, in the Anglo-Saxon world it is often just the opposite. So it is necessary to clarify concepts for international discussion, to avoid different interpretations of the same term. Participation undoubtedly means in every context the weakest form of a democratization process, if we think of a scale. In regard to the political and economic spheres of society a tentative illustration of these concepts is shown in Figure 1.

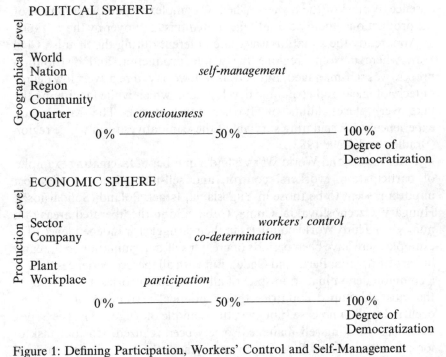

Figure 1: Defining Participation, Workers' Control and Self-Management

The Main Tendencies

In recent decades there has been a constant trend towards centralization in the economic sphere. The internationalization of capital makes democratic control and participation more and more difficult, because it becomes nearly impossible to obtain the necessary information to participate effectively.

The complexity of the structures and relations, and the distance of the centres of decision-making, also hinder any effective intervention by workers' representatives. Coupled with this are increases in the division of labour, which increasingly affects office and administrative work, the services, and the public sector. There are various contrasting theories relevant here, and recently some have spoken of the end of the division of labour (Kern and Schumann 1984). Apparently, there is a degree of reintegration of work taking place in some areas, but nobody could yet hold the thesis that this is a general process. At best there is a process of a polarization occurring. Again the effect of this is to weaken the process of democratization.

The introduction in the work process of the so-called New Technologies have also tended to increase managerial control. Instead of liberating workers and employees from dull work – as promised by the manufacturers – the level of control grows. But that does not mean that I am arguing for a deterministic approach without any possibility of greater autonomy. On the contrary, rising organizational complexity and the level of long-term planning also gives workers new possibilities for intervention. The dependence on loyal and competent workers – as long as the completely automatic factory and administration remains a dream – becomes more and more important in relation to the capital tied up in machinery. These contradictions may give new opportunities for participation to develop and even some degree of workers' control (Briefs 1986, Hartmann 1984).

On the other hand, we find for these same reasons an enormous development of specialization and expertise. The number of people who have a university degree has multiplied over the last decades. It might be controversial to take the percentage of professionals as an indicator of the growing role of experts. Increasingly both private and public sector managers are dependent on the advice of experts both from within and outside their organizations.

The growing role of technology and science has further decreased the role of workers in the control of production management and distribution processes. The percentage of highly qualified personnel inside and outside companies has increased markedly. This does not necessarily mean that these specialists really control the decisions. In Germany the term "Fachidiot" ("specialist idiot") is used quite often. One of the leading managers of the biggest nuclear plant production companies (Klaus Traube), who lost his job recently for this kind of remark, stated that nobody in the company really oversees the technological and economic risks inherent in this kind of technology. One of the biggest firms in the world – General Electric – had to sell its nuclear production department, because it nearly ruined the whole company. The same is true for the second biggest German electrical firm – AEG – which nearly collapsed a few years ago for the same reason.

Over recent years both the internal and external control of companies and administrations has become more and more important. The economic and financial crisis led to the need for savings. The irrationality of many management decisions was potentially fatal in this situation (Jones and Lakin 1982). Counselling bureaux spread, and banks scrutinized the books more intensely. Profit-centres were created, decentralization – which became more easily realizable with the help of computers – began. The optimal plant size for management seems to be a plant with 700 to 1000 employees. This size also has the benefit for management that it is easier to control any strike or sabotage actions by the workers.

To answer the demands of public bureaucracy, more personnel were required in areas such as statistics and accounting. Workers' unrest provoked activities to humanize working life to prevent industrial conflicts and many a psychologist and sociologist found work in this field.

State bureaucracy at all levels started a planning euphoria in the sixties. The welfare state seemed to be in reach. Planning experts in great numbers were sought. Social work, further education, and health services boomed. At the same time participation became *en vogue*: at company level semi-autonomous work groups, organization development, etc. was launched; in public affairs and in urban, social, artistic and education spheres, new initiatives were begun.

In the absence of legitimation for the changes coming from religion or traditional authority, science became the only source of legitimation, and the importance of experts grew. That does not mean – as I pointed out earlier – that these experts necessarily have real influence on decisions such as the siting of a nuclear power station. But since experts in general claim an authority resting on a special knowledge, which the majority of the population do not have, they are generally not contested. On the other hand, it is clear for anybody who knows the business, that to find the "right" expert is a matter of price. There is no expert without counter-expert – if wished.

Trade unions and works councils identified this early and developed their own expert systems: members of the works council were relieved from ordinary work, and the number of full-time paid trade union officials grew at the same pace. Their counter-proposals as well as those of citizens' initiatives were based on scientific data and methods.

An "expert" culture came into life in the seventies. There were even experts on self-management. But is this not a contradiction in terms?

This process of professionalization seemed to be part of a general trend towards a society of services and information, but it did not change the hierarchical structures; on the contrary, it seems that these hierarchies have been strengthened through the use of experts. For the people in power, besides their naked power, now also have the arguments, and sometimes even the knowledge for counter-strategies to prevent unrest and revolt.

In addition, the economic crisis has weakened these counter-strategies through lack of money, neo-conservative politics, and economics.

The Crisis of the Experts

For different reasons along with the general economic, political, social, and ecological crisis, the system and the belief in experts has itself undergone a deep crisis. The economic experts, who did not foresee the extent of worldwide economic recession, and the incredible increase in unemployment, have lost their prestige. The official commission of the federal government in Germany, called the "Five Wise," has in its twenty years of existence never predicted economic developments correctly. Likewise, since Tschernobyl the trust in the infallibility of modern technology (and therefore in technologists) has been considerably weakened. Even the "half-gods in white" – the medical experts – are more and more contested.

Hartmann and Hartmann (1982) have classified the "misery of experts" under four points:
- deprofessionalization through the computer;
- deprofessionalization through declassification;
- degradation to bureaucrats; and
- participation versus professionalism.

The introduction of new technologies in many fields of highly qualified labour, e. g. CAD for engineers, and even Joseph Weizenbaums psycho-analytical program "ELIZA," often replaces the specialized knowledge of human experts. Even software engineers are making themselves redundant by building their own expertise into their programs. Moreover, the increasing number of experts also increases the supply, which in a market economy in turn lowers the price and the status of professional positions and leads to unemployment or jobs lower in the hierarchy. Legislation, jurisdiction, and regulations narrow the field of activity for many professions and experts. Sometimes new professions – such as social workers, economists, and sociologists – emerge and stake their claims in the search for their own professional identity. But it is with the fourth point that we are at the centre of our debate on participation and self-management.

Generally the monopolization of certain knowledge and its restricted use through a social group confers upon that group privileges and even social power, as can clearly be seen within the medical and legal professions. The access to this knowledge is through *numerus clausus* or other restricted operations. Social control of these experts from outside is nearly impossible. The democratization of society is severely handicapped, if these experts occupy central places in society.

The development of the political class as a profession in recent years is perhaps the most evident and dangerous aspect of this process. Expert knowledge and "inside" knowledge is out of control.

The counter movement from citizen groups or from parties such as the Greens have at times questioned not only the nature of industrial society and technology as a whole, but also science and scientific rationality. In some feminist groups this even takes the form of the growth of new cults of witchcraft or other mythical and religious revivals.

But the main part of the contest takes the form of alternative socially useful products and arms conversion. Where the competence of the traditional management has failed and the company has decayed, the traditional response by the workers was to look for another job with another (capitalist) employer. Over the last ten years in all capitalist countries we have seen a revival of co-operatives by the jobless, some involving taking over the old firm. The experience of these groups shows that it is not sufficient to just continue their own work, but that they also have to take new decisions on investments, marketing, and new products. In most cases of organizational crisis, the leading personnel quit first, as they normally have better information and financial strength and are thus more marketable. So the answer is often for the remainder to address themselves to outside experts within trade unions, universities, polytechnics, etc. Trade unions are mostly very hesitant and not prepared for this kind of assistance. They have fought for so long to keep jobs that these old traditions are well embedded. One difficulty in this context is also that in most Western countries there has developed a division of tasks between political parties of the left and trade unions; in this regard the first undertake the political struggle (that means State affairs), and the second the economical struggle. In this situation, where often a whole region – like Liverpool, Inner London, Wallonie, the Ruhr – is depressed, this kind of action is ineffective. The British have found some possible answers where, for example, the Greater London Council established the Greater London Enterprise Board in order to implement its London Industrial Strategy, and there have been other regional enterprise boards established. A precondition for this kind of strategy is a decentralized mode of operation and the concentration of all efforts and competences.

Competence and Control

In summarizing the past arguments I am going to make several points which seem to be essential in this context:

1. Experts are necessary

All self-management initiatives need competent counsellors. But we have to differentiate between internal and external counsellors. (There is a debate around the expression of "expert." Corpet (1984) prefers to use the term "specialist," because for him "expert" means hierarchically privileged knowledge. On the other hand, this could be said also for the "specialist." It depends perhaps on the cultural context, which term has a more "democratic" signification, and once again a literal translation does not help much.)

The social division of labour is so far developed that it is impossible for a single person to be competent in every sphere of production, circulation, and distribution. Marx's fully developed personality will be the dream for the communist society to come. It is important that a new vertical social division of labour is not installed, but rather that any division takes place on horizontal lines. That means that everybody is an expert in his or her field and is counselling and helping others.

The level of social inequality in our societies has resulted in the situation that most of the producers do not use their intellectual, creative, and organizational capacities. They have not learnt to build on their own capabilities and they ask for help without trying to help themselves first. Under these conditions it is necessary to integrate those outside – even the jobless – who are ready to intervene.

2. Experts Are not Allowed to Be "Specialist Idiots"

It is not helpful for those concerned, asking for help, if the "experts" come in with standardized knowledge, not knowing the situation of the company or the sector and thinking they can give help quickly. A central precondition for effective co-operation is a long-lasting and intensive relationship. "Fire-brigade" interventions from outsiders, who come in briefly and who cannot be contacted again later or for which you have to wait for weeks or months, are not very helpful. Also external experts should be at the same place and always in reach. It is important that a relationship of confidence between those concerned and the experts is developed. A necessary precondition is a long-lasting, credible associ-ation with trade unions by the experts. Competence alone is not enough. Its use is often monopolized by the experts and not generalized. And in most cases the solution for problems of a company is not a technical but a political one.

3. The Initiative to Ask for Help from Experts Must Come from Those Directly Concerned

Productive co-operation is not possible if the experts try to explain to the concerned that they have problems and that these problems have to be solved with expert help. A precondition for successful co-operation is a certain problem consciousness by those concerned which leads them to the conclusion that they cannot solve their problems alone and need support. Trade unions are not able to give all this support, because their resources are too restricted. (Even most managements are not able to solve all their problems alone. Industrial chambers, chambers of commerce, consultants, employers' federations in regional and sectoral divisions, etc. are there to help and their resources are at least ten times more extensive than those of workers' associations.)

4. The Aim of the Intervention of Outside Experts Is Help for Self-Help

This means that outside experts have to make themselves redundant as soon as possible, otherwise they themselves become part of the group; the aim must be to help the concerned solve most of their problems themselves – without permanent outside help. Self-management is impossible if there is a permanent dependence on persons or outside institutions. Therefore the aim of co-operation is to establish the capability of self-management by the workers themselves.

5. The Expert in Regard to His Work Is the Worker Himself

The worker is the only one who really knows what his needs at work are and how he reacts to different working conditions. There are no objective criteria for the acceptance of certain work environments or certain conditions. And, finally, work-groups are the only ones who are able to fight for the removal of alienation. Political representation through experts is bound to fail from the beginning, because it represents nothing else than a circulation of elites.

6. The Expert Does not Exist

The danger of asking too much from experts has already been mentioned. But it is clear, although there is a strong inter-relation between economic, technical, and legal questions, that nobody can be an expert in every field. In the field of product- or process-innovation, of micro- or macro-economic problems, within work and social law, and trade and civil law there is such complexity that a single person is overburdened (incidentally, this is also true for any management).

It is important in the context of self-management to develop forms of co-operation which inter-relate and enable decision processes in which all can participate. Therefore counselling teams need to be created which meet regularly to exchange their experiences.

7. A Network of Initiatives Is Necessary for the Broadening of the Self-Management Movement

The stupid competition between traditional and so-called "new" social movements (especially between trade unions and the "alternative" movement), should cease, because it only helps non-democratic forces. The alternative movement can only survive if it renders a substantial contribution to the democratization of society. If not, it will remain in the marginal positions which the conservatives reserve for it. In this context it is important to realize that "State money" for these alternative initiatives does not come from the State, but from tax payers and value creators: the workers! On the other hand, it is evident that the traditional workers' movement is often bureaucratized and that new initiatives from the alternative movements do open new perspectives for them. Thus, in all regions and communities centres should be created to co-ordinate scientific, alternative, and trade union institutions and groups.

8. Self-Management Is Only Possible with Few Experts, if There Is a Broad Competence, Which Allows Control and Which Is Secured Through Permanent Further Education

One of the first steps in the near future is to establish the means for all those who want to acquire the necessary competence to run their own affairs in a self-managed way to do so, so that the old mistakes are not permanently reproduced. This should include networks and federations, where the problematization of experiences can begin. Unfortunately the majority of the groups at the centre of the industrial crisis have still to recognize their common interests. If this first step of educating workers about such management practices as rationalization is reached, the next step for competence development and enlargement can be tackled. The "right consciousness" is not sufficient for participation, workers' control, and self-management.

And here the role of the sociologist comes in once again. Consequently, I am pleading for a deprofessionalization instead of a professionalization of this discipline. We have to make ourselves redundant as soon as possible as a separate profession. That does not mean that our knowledge is obsolete: on the contrary, it is so important that everybody has to participate in it.

But I fear that we still have much, too much, work for the years and decades to come.

References

Bahro, Rudolf (1978): *The Alternative in Eastern Europe*, London: New Left Books.

Bradley, Keith and Alan Gelb (1983): *Cooperation at Work – the Mondragon Experience*, London: Heinemann.

Briefs, Ulrich (ed.) (1986): *Anders produzieren, anders arbeiten, anders leben*, Köln: Pahl Rugenstein Verlag.

Corpet, Olivier (1984): La république des experts, *Autogestions*, Paris, 18, (dec.): 37–42.

Dutschke, Rudi (1974): *Versuch, Lenin auf die Füße zu stellen*, Berlin-West: Wagenbach.

Hartmann, Heinz and Marianne Hartmann (1982): Vom Elend der Experten: Zwischen Akademisierung und Deprofessionalisierung, *Kölner Zeitschrift für Soziologie und Sozialpsychologie*, Köln, 34: 193–223.

Hartmann, Michael (1984): *Rationalisierung im Widerspruch*, Frankfurt/New York: Campus.

Heller, Frank (1983): *The Role of Competence in Democratic Organizations*, London: Tavistock.

Jones, Roger and Chris Lakin (1982): *The Carpetmakers*, London: McGraw-Hill.

Kern, Horst and Michael Schumann (1984): *Das Ende der Arbeitsteilung?* München: Beck.

Marx, Karl (1970): *Das Kapital*, Vol. 1, Berlin-GDR: Dietz.

Supek, Rudi (1978): *Arbeiterselbstverwaltung und sozialistische Demokratie. Beitrag zur geschichtlichen Kontinuität einer Idee*, Hannover: SOAK.

Part I
Participation and Co-Determination

Introduction

Chris Cornforth

This part of the book examines some of the different forms that workers' participation in decision-making takes in both the private and public sectors in four countries. It considers the impact that workers' participation schemes have on the ability of workers and trade unions to influence enterprise decision-making. In any country the forms and degree of workers' participation are greatly influenced by the activities of the State. In the USA there are few legal requirements on companies to introduce workers' participation schemes. As a result, the introduction of workers' participation has usually been a managerial prerogative, limited to the shop-floor level. Barber and Towers' chapter takes a critical look at these schemes, in particular the recent growth of "quality circles." They argue that most are designed to increase managerial control and that they are frequently used to undermine the power of trade unions. They consider the contradictions that organised labour faces in finding an appropriate response to the introduction of quality circles.

In contrast to the United States, many Western European countries have introduced legislation to promote some form of workers' participation in enterprise decision-making. Bernoux' paper examines the impact of some recent French legislation to encourage the formation of "direct expression groups" in companies. The purpose of the law is to give workers a voice in issues concerning the content and organization work. The impact of these groups has been quite modest. Many have ceased to exist after a short period, while in contrast some have developed to allow workers to negotiate with management over a variety issues affecting their work. Crucial to the success of expression groups has been management's willingness to decentralize decision-making and to engage in discussion and negotiation with them. Bernoux' article also shows that legislation will be interpreted and implemented differently in different organizations. This is a theme that is taken up in the next two chapters.

enterprise level. The chapter by Briefs describes this system and its origins and then examines its impact on trade unions. While co-determination is often seen as a system of joint regulation between labour and management, Briefs argues that labour faces much greater constraints than management under the system, which greatly limits labour's ability to influence decision-making. However, the system does also have some advantages for trade unions, for example providing information that they might not otherwise have access to. Briefs also argues that co-determination has affected the competencies of trade unions, increasing knowledge and skills in areas such as legal and technological matters, but at the same time undermining the competencies necessary to mobilize social movements.

The chapter by Teulings focuses on the developments of co-determination in the Netherlands. Based on detailed empirical studies, his chapter examines how co-determination is being put into practice in a cross-section of Dutch organisations. He argues that there is an increasing gap between "leading" works councils, that use the legal provisions effectively to increase workers' influence, and the "followers" which are less effective. He suggests that the support structure and network connecting leading works councils is vital as a means of disseminating good practice. Extending this support structure to include the weaker works councils may be one way of improving their performance.

Chapter 2
"Worker Participation" in the United States: A Preliminary Analysis of Quality of Work Life Programs

Bob Barber and Rochelle Towers

> "Reform is fine, but how can managers be sure that employees do not abuse the system? How can managers assure themselves that the circle members will not just goof off during the hour meeting or plot proposals and schemes that do more to disrupt the system than to improve it? In short, how can you reform the system without losing control of it? First, management must have faith in its employees, second, management does not give away decision-making authority or responsibility in a quality circle process. It simply allows all employees to make responsible inputs. *Ultimately, management retains the right of decision through the mechanism of the management presentation...*" Philip C. Thompson, *Quality Circles: How to Make Them Work in America*, New York: American Management Association, 1982. (Emphasis added.)

Introduction

The current economic crisis in the world economy has had a profound impact on the U.S. economy and on the conditions of the U.S. working class. U.S. capital, faced with the declining competitiveness of its domestic industries, is using new management strategies in its effort to increase the rate of profit and restore U.S. economic hegemony in the world. The U.S. working class now faces an assault which takes a variety of forms – union busting, speed-ups, wage cuts, massive lay offs and unemployment, loss of jobs to the periphery, and forced concessions in contract bargaining. At the same time, capital has devised methods to enlist labor's co-operation in solving the crisis, including selling failing firms to workers and, the topic of this paper, "worker participation" programs, generally referred to as Quality of Work Life programs (QWL).

In this chapter our goal is to demonstrate how QWL programs in the United States are used as a mechanism of intensifying the exploitation of labor. We will argue that behind these programs is the need to increase productivity and product quality, which in turn requires the most efficient utilization of labor as well as capital. Efficient utilization of labor requires that management have not only the power and the freedom to organize and reorganize the labor process at will, but also the benefit of the knowledge held by those closest to the labor process: the workers themselves.

We will also argue that the traditional relationship between managers and the managed does not fundamentally change with these programs. Despite the fact that they appear to lead to workers and managers sharing information, in reality the information flows from the workers to management, thus reinforcing management's control. In addition, we will show how the use of QWL programs is complementary to other anti-working class and anti-union tactics being practiced by capital in the 1980's.

We will also analyze the generally co-operative attitude taken by organized labor to QWL as well as the dangers and difficult contradictions QWL presents, in the context of historical patterns of weakness and collaboration on the part of American unions.

There is a handful of experimental plant designs that in fact grant a great deal of autonomy to work teams to function independent of direct supervision (Whiting 1983). We will not address these developments in this paper but they deserve further investigation.

Perspective and Methodology

The theoretical framework for the paper is provided by the work of Marlene Dixon and others (1978, 1982, 1984a, 1984b) analyzing developments in the capitalist world economy over the past several decades. This work has identified the crisis of accumulation on a transnational scale which is leading to massive realignments in the global world economy, including a relocation of production processes from the core to the periphery of the global economy. Suffering from an excess of productive capacity and finance capital, capital is seeking to increase its rate of profit through the reduction of production costs, primarily through reducing the cost of labor, and through reorganizing domestic industrial production.

It is in this context that the Institute of Contemporary Marxism has initiated an ongoing research project, to examine the history and uses of "worker participation" programs in the United States and to contrast these findings with comparable experiments in other parts of the world. This paper represents the preliminary findings of this project, which will be developed further in the coming period.

The research in this paper is based on a search of the extensive literature on QWL; a review of the work of organizations such as the Work in America Institute (WAI) and the International Association of Quality Circles (IAQC), which study and advocate QWL; data and studies from the U.S. Department of Labor; a review of position papers and resolutions on QWL from unions; and interviews with worker participation experts, union officials, and rank and file members of unions.

The U.S. Economy in Crisis

The world economic crisis has manifested itself at the level of the U.S. national economy in the collapse of the basic industrial economy, stemming from the loss of international competitiveness. Indications of this crisis in the U.S. include the following:

(i) New profit rates in the U.S. fell from above 10.5% in all years between 1961–67 to around 3% in 1974–75 (Frank 1980).

(ii) The U.S. share of world industrial production dropped from 60% in 1950 to 30% in 1980 ("Deepening Crisis of US Capitalism," *Monthly Review*, October 1981).

(iii) At present, only 20% of all jobs in the U.S. economy are in the manufacturing sector (*New York Times*, April 6, 1985). From 1979–84, 5.1 million experienced workers lost their jobs due to plant shutdowns or staff cutbacks (*New York Times*, December 12, 1984).

The Reagan Administration's domestic economic policies are designed to encourage this trend; the President's current "tax reform" plan would abolish investment tax credits and cut back on the accelerated depreciation allowance for new plant and equipment measures that would directly affect heavy manufacturing (*New York Times*, May 26, 1985).

The general approach taken by most unions in response to the economic crisis has been to try to help save the industries which provide them employment. AFL-CIO Secretary Treasurer Thomas Donahue put it this way:

The adversarial role, appropriate to the conflict of collective bargaining, ought to be limited to the period of negotiation. And during the lifetime of a contract so arrived at, it ought to be replaced by a period of co-operation, aimed at maximizing the potential success of the joint enterprise, i.e. the company's business or production. (AFL-CIO, "Labor Looks at Quality of Worklife Programs", *News*, January, 1982).

The degree to which organized labor has made concessions to the needs of industry is evidenced by the Amalgamated Clothing and Textile Workers Union which has put $ 14.5 million into the development of a sewing robot that could potentially displace one third of the union's members! (*The Economist*, London, March 2, 1985). In addition, it is reported that approximately 3 million union members made wage concessions to management between 1982–85 (Ross 1985).

The organized labor movement has suffered major political and bargaining setbacks as well as a continuing loss of membership:

(i)   While unions represent over 20 million workers in the U.S., overall membership is now down to 18.8 % of the American workforce (*New York Times*, February 8, 1985).

(ii)   During the 1970's, about 90 % of all new jobs were added in the service sector, yet less than 10 % of this traditionally unorganized sector is unionized.

(iii)   Between 1972 and 1983, real wages for U.S. workers declined 14 % (Ferguson and Rogers 1984).

(iv)   Since December 1983, average wage increases for unionized workers have lagged behind pay increases for non-union workers (*New York Times*, May 2, 1985, citing U.S. government statistics).

(v)   The AFL-CIO estimates that over $ 100 million goes annually to consulting firms which assist management in resisting, undermining, or preventing unionization (AFL-CIO Committee on the Evolution of Work 1985).

(vi)   In 1982, the last year for which data is available, workers rejected unions in 56 % of federally supervised elections, and decertification elections to expel unions from a workplace succeeded 75 % of the time. Strike activity is at a 38-year low (Ross 1985).

Early in his first term, Ronald Reagan set the tone for American labor relations in the 1980's by firing thousands of government-employed air traffic controllers who had gone on strike, thereby destroying their union. He appointed Raymond Donovan as his Secretary of Labor, a business executive who was forced to resign after his indictment on charges of fraud and larceny involving his construction firm. Enforcement of federal health and safety laws has declined dramatically under Reagan; comparing 1980 with the fiscal year 1983 one finds that on-site inspections generated by worker complaints declined 60%, follow-up inspections declined 86%, and recommendations for penalties declined 66% (Ferguson and Rogers 1984). Reagan also placed the National Labor Relations Board (NLRB), which enforces legislation concerning union organizing, under the control of a former steel industry executive, Donald Dotson. Dotson and the four other Reagan appointees who now sit on the NLRB voted against labor and in favor of management in 60% of all unfair labor practice and union representation cases between September 1983 and August 1984, a dramatic increase over previous years, according to the AFL-CIO (*National Journal*, June 8, 1985).

Domestic Consequences of Global Economic Crisis

The roots of the attack on the U.S. working class are to be found in what Dixon (1982) has identified as three

interrelated aspects of US industry's efforts to re-establish its competitiveness and profitability on the world market:

(a) Relocation of industries producing for the world market from the USA to peripheral and semi-peripheral nations, in order to take advantage of cheap labor forces and other conditions guaranteed by "counter-insurgency states" there.
(b) Employment of immigrant labor forced to seek employment in the U.S. as a result of the impact of the world crisis on the peripheral and semi-peripheral nations.
(c) Reindustrialization schemes (which) seek to address both sources of U.S. industry's crisis of competitiveness, obsolete technology and high labor costs.

Beginning in the mid-1970's and accelerating since, a global attack has been waged by transnational capital against the living standards of the working classes of the world. Under the direction of the U.S. dominated International Monetary Fund, numerous nations have had the purchasing power of their working classes reduced through restrictive monetary and fiscal policies, restrictions on labor's right to strike and organize, incomes policies aimed at reducing the growth of real wages, and other measures. The U. S. also installed dictatorships where it needed to force recalcitrant populations to submit and to ensure an adequate supply of cheap labor for the transnationals. These global tactics on the part of transnational capital have created the conditions for the relocation of industrial production from the core to the periphery and have driven millions of workers into a new migrant transnational labor force available to capital in the core as well as the periphery.

With respect to the core itself, and particularly the United States, Dixon (1982) goes on to point out:

Given the international capitalist crisis, modernisation of obsolete plants in heavy industry was impractical both because of the tremendous costs and because of saturation of the world market for traditional heavy industrial exports. Thus, the most immediate responses of US industrial capital were: first, to relocate to cheap labor areas in the periphery and semi-periphery, and second, to transfer this crisis onto the US working class by lowering wages, in order to restore competitiveness with industries based in other capitalist countries. Lowering labor costs was by far the cheapest "solution" in the short run.

By the early 1980s, however, it had become clear, at least to the more farsighted sectors of the US bourgeoisie (as opposed to the Reaganites and the ideological Far Right), that the attack on the working class and the lowering of wages is by itself no long range answer to the economic crisis. Thus by the 1980's, various sectors of the US bourgeoisie have been pushed to consider a range of options for a restructuring of the US economy or at the very least of its industrial base. Reindustrialization, as currently discussed, has meant a series of projects with different emphases, ranging from proposals to finance the upgrading of obsolescent, failing heavy industries, to Reaganomic supply-side proposals for the creation of domestic "urban enterprise zones," cheap-labor havens much like the free trade zones of the Third World.

In order to carry out this reindustrialization program, new strategies were needed for the management of labor. In particular, American management looked to the "Japanese model" of industrial relations, which focused on highly controlled forms of worker participation in certain aspects of the organization of work, and adapted them to the United States in hopes of controlling the workforce and improving productivity under the conditions of economic crisis. That model had proven successful in Japan in the post-war reconstruction of its economy and had contributed to its rapid expansion. American management hoped to use the lessons in the context not of expansion but of contraction.

The Development of QWL Programs in the United States

By now, QWL programs have become an established fact of American labor management. The term Quality of Work Life encompasses a wide range of programs aimed at improving job satisfaction, and product quality, and reducing unit costs by increasing productivity. QWL-type programs have titles like Quality Control Circles, Workplace Participation, Humanization of Work, Work Improvement Program, Suggestion Systems, Job Redesign, Relations by Objectives and Socio-Technical Systems (International Association of Machinists and Aerospace Workers, *IAM Report*, Winter-Spring 1982). QWL programs cover a range of issues from fresh paint in the employee lounge to safety conditions in the plant, changes in the design of work, the introduction and development of new technology, and new forms of pay and benefit programs.

QWL as a methodology derives generally from behavioral science theories which "in their crudest form are really theories of management developed for managers" (Kochan et al. 1984). Theoretically they draw upon social psychology, social work, and industrial psychology, as well as their derivative application in the "human potential" movement. The emphasis is on small group behavior and methodologies for resolving conflict through personal interaction. Rather than seeing labor and management as opposite poles of a contradictory system, QWL assumes that harmony is realizable through the application of the correct, technocratic, behavioral interventions.

Much of the programmatic development of QWL has taken place in organizations such as the Work in America Institute (WAI) and the International Association of Quality Circles (IAQC). They produce the manuals and the studies which are used to implement these programs on the shop floor. In our previous work (Felice et al. 1977), we analyzed WAI as a key point of collaboration between the transnational ruling class and the U.S. labor movement. Its Board of Directors includes: Thomas Donahue, Secretary-Treasurer, AFL-CIO; James J. Renier, Vice-Chairman, Honeywell; Irving Bluestone, former Vice President, United Auto Workers; and David C. Collier, Vice President and Group Executive, General Motors Corporation. WAI serves as an information clearing house and has an extensive publications program.

The most widely publicized form of QWL is the Quality Circle, which was developed first in Japan and has since become popular in the United States. A Quality Circle (QC) is a group of workers, usually from a single department, led by a foreman or supervisor, which meets about once a week to solve concrete production and quality problems. It is through the development of ideas from workers based on their firsthand knowledge that management hopes to improve productivity and product quality. QC's have no decision-making power and may only recommend changes to management; as IAQC board member Philip Thompson (1982) stated, "ultimately, management retains the right of decision." In some cases, QC's have been associated with making sure that workers do not resist the introduction of new technology. The Quality Circle is usually initiated in a highly controlled fashion, beginning with management training and then training of supervisors and workers.

It is difficult to estimate the actual extent of the wide array of QWL programs, given the lack of commonly agreed on definitions, management self-reporting, and the active promotion of these programs by management consultants. According to the IAQC, in 1983 there were 135,000 Quality Circles involving one million workers in the U.S. (Thompson 1983).

QWL programs are generally concentrated in the competitive manufacturing sector of the economy. A 1982 New York Stock Exchange study of 49,000 U.S. firms found that 58% of the manufacturing firms with human resource management programs had QWL programs as opposed to 27% in non-manufacturing firms. The study also demonstrated that the larger a company is, the more likely it is to utilize QWL (New York Stock Exchange 1982: 26).

Management's Goals in QWL

Management has played the leading role in introducing QWL programs into the workplace. In a major 1982 Work in America Institute study, *Productivity Through Work Innovations*, Rosow and Zager (1986: 26) point out that increasingly, American management is managing the working environment "as deliberately as they manage markets, finances, costs, and assets." They also warn that the failure to adopt work innovations "can only result in a continuation of, perhaps an increase in, the negative behaviors of workers that have plagued many organization in the past."

Hy Kornbluh, Director of the Labor Studies Center, Institute of Labor and Industrial Relations at the University of Michigan, summarizes two major and interrelated management goals in adopting QWL programs:

(1) Dealing with worker alienation in an over-educated workforce that, it is claimed, frequently results in absenteeism, drug abuse, low morale, and other expressions of worker dissatisfaction;
(2) Increasing productivity through enhanced job satisfaction and through harnessing the skills and ideas of those responsible for doing the work (Kornbluh 1984).

Retention of management control is the centerpiece of these programs. One manual, written by a member of the Board of Directors of the IAQC, on how to "install" a quality circle in "your firm" makes very clear the manipulative and divisive nature of QWL programs:

With quality circles, management changes the rules slightly to grant employees just enough power to allow them to participate in the decision-making process on subjects that relate immediately to their immediate work ... as a result of its small size and specific shop focus, as well as the explicit rules of the quality circle process, the "interests" that its members can articulate are limited to their immediate work such things as improved tools, procedural changes, product innovations, safety improvements, and production and cost-saving shortcuts. *With quality circles, the strategy is still divide and conquer, but its application is more subtle and sophisticated.* We divide by small groups rather than by individuals. (Thompson 1982. Emphasis added).

QWL type programs are also used as a form of "union avoidance." This is a very critical issue which, while not discussed in depth in this paper, is central to understanding the overall anti-union thrust of American labor management strategies today. There is a specialized literature on how to use QWL type programs to keep unions out. The California Hospital Personnel Management Association conducts seminars on the use of QWL against unions, the Council on Union-Free Environment publishes a "how-to" on starting "circle" programs (Parker and Hansen 1983). In this regard, we should also note the legal efforts of the IAQC to have the NLRB "relax outmoded legal constraints on employers" who institute QWL programs and join American industry "in moving away from the adversarial atmosphere which has dominated the industrial scene for so many years." These IAQC efforts are designed to remove obstacles to the use of QWL as a company union mechanism (see *Labor Notes*, September 27, 1984 and April, 1985).

Organized Labor in the U.S.: A Legacy of Collaboration

Within the United States, labor unions have been unable to mount an effective counter offensive to the attack on American workers and the labor movement. Since Roosevelt's New Deal, the capitalist ruling class has pursued a strategy of strangling the militancy of organized labor, entangling and constricting unions in a complex web of laws and regulations. The unions' struggle for legal protection, representation, and legitimacy won important concessions from the bourgeoisie such as the Wagner Act of 1935, which recognized the legal right of trade unions to represent workers under collective bargaining agreements. But these same laws increasingly enmeshed unions in legal restrictions set by the state as union organizing came under the regulation and control of the National Labor Relations Board (Dixon et al. 1977).

The strategy of Roosevelt and subsequent administrations was to encourage and compel the top union leadership to adopt policies which advanced overall capitalist interests in return for higher wages for a small segment of the labor force. At the same time, the state conducted a vicious anti-communist campaign which further weakened organized labor by removing its most class-conscious forces. These factors combined to reduce union activity to little more than collective bargaining, thus limiting unions' overall effectiveness in defending workers' rights. This weakness is compounded in the current period of austerity and the resurgence of the Right.

The AFL-CIO recently published a major statement on its own problems and weaknesses, which generally supports the development of more labor management co-operation (AFL-CIO 1985). The AFL-CIO's Committee on the Evolution of Work, which published the study, was advised by a group of academic and corporate management experts. The report concludes that the structure of national labor regulatory legislation has basically disintegrated under Reagan and is no longer any help to labor. At the same time, workers' attitudes towards work, job satisfaction, bosses, and unions have changed, leaving the trade union movement in a position of having to demonstrate and prove its usefulness to workers. Among other things, the report notes that the needs and desires of workers to have a say in their jobs are being met in some cases by union-management co-operation programs, and that "the labor movement should seek to accelerate this development." (There is some union opposition to this prevailing viewpoint about QWL, which we shall comment on later.)

QWL: Unions Face the Contradictions

The attitude of organized labor toward QWL is conditioned by several factors: the overall economic crisis, the blatantly anti-union atmosphere prevailing in the U.S. today, alienation of many workers not only from their jobs but from their unions as well, and the view that unions can only survive if their employers survive. In this context, many unions have, with greater or lesser degrees of enthusiasm, supported and participated in QWL programs. According to an *IAM Research Report*, (Winter-Spring, 1982) as of 1982, unions representing 20% of the nation's organized workers had signed national agreements committing themselves to QWL programs of one type or another. Many more unions have become involved in some type of QWL program including the United Rubber Workers; United Food and Commercial Workers; Bakery, Confectionary, and Tobacco Workers International; International Union of Electrical Workers; International Woodworkers; Oil, Chemical, and Atomic Workers; American Federation of State, County, and Municipal Employees; National Education Association; and some construction unions (Rosow and Zager 1986: 71).

A United Rubber Workers bargaining handbook listed ways in which unions could benefit from participation in QWL programs: higher visibility for unions (lower costs of contract administration, i.e. fewer grievances and arbitration cases), improving the company's chances for successful operation through the avoidance of management mistakes, access to company information for unions, improved public image, and enhanced popularity of union leaders (United Rubber Workers 1982).

The ambivalence that some unions feel toward QWL is rooted in the recognition of the risks involved in taking on such programs. This is reflected in the adoption of a policy of "decentralized neutrality" toward QWL, meaning that the national union and its leadership speak out from time to time on the issue but generally leave it to local unions to decide on their own how to deal with QWL. Often, the national union will provide summaries and background data but not dictate policy (Kochan et al. 1984: 164).

On the other hand, several major national unions have taken a more active role in encouraging local participation in QWL programs and in making QWL an issue with management at the national level. In particular, these include the United Auto Workers, the United Steelworkers, and Communications Workers of America, which together represent almost three million workers.

While a full review of the situation facing the U.S. auto industry is beyond the scope of this paper, the magnitude of the crisis is indicated by the level of concessions demanded from the United Auto Workers (UAW) and the fact that since 1979, the auto industry workforce has been cut more than 40% – a loss of 656,000 jobs (Brown 1985). The first QWL clause to be included in a national labor contract was the one signed by the UAW and General Motors in 1973. Similar agreements were later reached with Ford and Chrysler. UAW Vice President Irving Bluestone became one of the most outspoken proponents of QWL programs.

In the steel industry, also characterized by extensive contract concessions in the last several years, the United Steelworkers have actively promoted a form of QWL called Labor-Management Participation Teams (LMPTs) as a method for improving productivity in firms facing serious economic problems. In preparation for implementing the LMPTs, a joint union-management group travelled to Japan to study Japanese techniques. By 1982, 13 plants had LMPT programs comprising 100 teams (Camens 1982). Overall, however, relations between the Steelworkers and steel management have worsened as companies like US Steel shut down more plants and demanded further concessions after obtaining a 9% wage cut in the 1983 contract negotiations (*Business Week*, February 25, 1985). According to Sam Camens, Assistant to the International President of the United Steelworkers of America and National Coordinator of LMPTs, where there are shutdowns and concessions, morale is low and LMPT stops functioning (Telephone Interview, June 1985). In the communications industry, AT & T management planned the use of QWL as part of its strategy to confront increased competition resulting from the breakup of the monopoly. Communications Workers of America President Glenn Watts says that "through QWL, we are extending our influence into the murky territory of management prerogatives." Further, Watts says,

I don't think it is sufficient to stand on the sidelines and attack management's motives. That strategy puts unions on the defensive and makes management appear more concerned about workers than we are. We can offer our own labor model of a good QWL process as a challenge to management" (Watts, n.d.).

Union Opposition to QWL

There are also pockets of criticism within labor, although they represent a minority opinion. William Winpinsinger, president of the International Association of Machinists is harshly critical of QWL for its potential to bypass union structures and prerogatives. An IAM bulletin stated that its locals "should, in general, oppose these programs as both unnecessary duplication and an effort to undermine the duly elected bargaining agent for the workers" (*IAM Report*, Quality of Work-Life Programs, Winter-Spring, 1982). Nonetheless, the IAM is an active advocate of full joint union-management discussion of the use of new technology (Kochan et al. 1984: 160).

The United Electrical Workers (UE), however, are far more blunt, in a resolution adopted at its 46th Convention, recalling the use of company unions as an anti-union tactic in the 1930's:

Today, the companies are singing the song of company unionism again, to a 1980's beat ... In fact, Quality Circles are better called Quantity Circles ... In sum, Quality Circles are an attempt to create a shop floor structure controlled by management und pushing management's point of view, aimed at undermining the union steward system and bypassing the union. ("Quality Circles," Resolution Adopted by the 46th Convention of the United Electrical, Radio, and Machine Workers of America, undated).

There has been resistance to QWL within the United Auto Workers (UAW). In 1983, the Flint, Michigan UAW Local 659 suspended its QWL program after General Motors announced it would close the plant the following summer. Likewise, Pontiac, Michigan UAW local 594 stopped participating when the company announced the closing of a parts depot and the loss of 200 jobs (*Labor Notes*, November 22, 1983). Some higher level UAW officials have begun to distance themselves from QWL, especially as the turnabout in auto industry profitability led to no change in the automakers' drive for continued work rule concessions and to continued "outsourcing" of jobs, that is, contracting work to non-union firms (*Labor Notes*, Sept. 27, 1983).

At the Wheeling-Pittsburgh Steel Corporation, three steel union officials were fired after they opposed the development of an LMPT at their plant. In April, 1983, Steelworkers Local 2227 voted to cease participating in their LMPT "due to the lack of progressive action by US Steel pertaining to previous Local Union requests and due to the continuing job eliminations and combinations" (*Labor Notes*, July 27, 1983).

To summarize, U.S. labor in the 1980s is in a position of vulnerability and defensiveness. Most unions, especially in the declining industrial sector, have taken the position that they have to co-operate in order to survive. Their other choices are to oppose QWL or ignore it. Both are risky: to oppose it may signify to the rank and file that the union is opposed to the increased participation of workers and that management is more concerned than their union with workers' welfare; to ignore QWL programs means that unions would give up any ability to affect the structure and operation of such programs. Both of these options also leave unions vulnerable to management's use of QWL to organize workers out from under the Union.

The Effects of QWL Programs

There are numerous specific examples of increased productivity and savings being realized through workers' suggestions and proposals. The Work in America Institute notes that:

Innovations in work organization can help achieve substantial productivity improvements. But results are possible only if employers channel the efforts of employees towards the areas that will have the greatest impact on the company's performance. Changes in work organization are often most effective when linked with the introduction of new technology – when, for example, workers can give their opinions on the functioning of a new assembly technique (Rosow and Zager 1982a: 18).

To accomplish this goal and to effectively channel employees' efforts in the direction that will most improve productivity, management must obtain greater flexibility in work rules, job classifications and assignments, and other matters relating to enhancing managerial control of the workforce. In this sense, QWL goes hand in hand with management's general collective bargaining strategy that demands concessions from unions, not only on wage issues but also on work rules and related matters, in order to eliminate that small portion of control or input into the labor process which unions have been able to obtain in the past several decades.

Most unionists stress the need to maintain a clear distinction between those issues which can be dealt with through QWL and those which should remain in the sphere of collective bargaining. This distinction is essential if unions are to survive. The UAW's Irving Bluestone was one notable exception; he argued that while collective bargaining remained a necessity, "this is not to say that collective bargaining agreements cannot be altered to meet mutually desirable objectives of the QWL process, subject of course to the bargaining process and membership ratification" (cited in Kochan et al. 1984: 173). According to Mike Parker (Co-ordinator of Labor Notes QWL Task Force and member of UAW Local 600), the trend under QWL is toward the narrowing of collective bargaining to issues of wages, as union concessions allow greater management control over work rules, and the grievance procedure atrophies in favor of QWL. What hurts the unions the most, he argues, is the cumulative effect of workers becoming accustomed to solving problems and making changes through QWL programs rather than unions, together with the potential to drain the brightest workers out of union structures and into QWL structures.

To the extent that any changes are introduced into the workplace by way of worker input through QWL, these programs may indicate a shift away from the most rigid forms of the Taylorist work simplification approach to the management of labor which has characterized American management practice for most of the century. In this vein, Hy Kornbluh posits a struggle between old-line Taylorists and a newer breed of manager who is more open to change, less defensive about worker participation, more empathetic to workers' needs, etc. (Kornbluh 1984: 92–93).

However, there is no fundamental shift in the basic relationship between the managers and the managed. In particular, management does not give up any control over the appointment of supervisors and foremen. Management also retains ultimate control of the information to be made available to workers as well as the final control over what changes are implemented and what changes are not.

With QWL, management also gains tremendous intelligence about worker attitudes and desires which can be used not only to manipulate workers but also to undercut union negotiating positions. In fact, these programs contribute further to the monopolization of knowledge on the part of management, in the sense that through worker participation all the good ideas that workers have had about how to do the work better get summed up and transferred to management. The UE described the goal as being "to break down workers' natural mistrust of bosses, and then get workers to begin telling the company how jobs can be speeded up and made more 'productive'" (Resolution adopted by the 46th Convention of United Electrical, Radio and Machine Workers of America).

In one particularly blatant example, Ford tried out an approach of removing production quotas, encouraging workers to make quality products at their own pace. Then they used a QWL-type program to have workers share how they organized their work with each other and coach each other on how to do the job. The management objective was described as trying to substitute peer pressure for management pressure. Although assurances from management that QWL programs will not result in speed-up or job loss is considered a prerequisite for a successful joint QWL program, it does not take a Henry Ford to figure out that if a worker can suddenly do the same job more quickly when he or she is motivated, the workers know something that management does not. When increased productivity is the goal, how can management resist utilizing the knowledge they gain about how the job got done faster to speed up the work process? This also increases the divisions between older and younger workers and threatens the security of those who cannot or will not speed up (*Labor Notes*, June 28, 1984).

Another indication of the manipulative character of QWL is that most programs do not last once they are started, presumably once workers understand their superficiality. CWA's president Glenn Watts cites one study showing that 75% of the QC programs in the US fail within a few years (Watts, n. d.). There are a number of reasons for this (which we plan to investigate in future research), beginning with the fact that the opportunity to have input into one's job as a motivating factor to participate in QWL programs will dry up after workers have initially shared what they know. In addition, after the initial experience of some participation where there had been none before, the reality of how little substantive change takes place becomes apparent. Finally, in the industries such as auto and steel where QWL has been most heavily promoted, the existence of these programs has done nothing to stop massive layoffs and plant closures.

Conclusion

This paper represents an initial effort to examine and explain the rise of QWL and related forms of management-inspired programs of worker participation in the United States. From preliminary research, we draw the following conclusions:

(1) QWL is said to be a method by which workers can participate in the

organization of work in today's economy. Even the most extensive programs, however, are not intended to open up key realms of owner and manager decision-making related to the overall control of a business, its investment policies, or its allocation of resources. QWL addresses a narrow sphere of shop floor issues, and within that, only the range of issues which management approves.

(2) QWL represents a concerted effort to eliminate the adversarial aspect of labor-management relations, and replace it with a co-operative model controlled by management. QWL in the United States seeks to roll back gains made by unions since the New Deal and to establish alternative models that can be used in the non-union sector and, potentially, to replace existing unions. With all their problems, unions still represent a form of organization that can fight for workers' rights, and workers' loyalty, and, in essence, intervene to oppose management's point of view. QWL programs provide a more predictable mechanism for conflict management than do unions.

(3) QWL, which has its ideological roots in social psychology and social work, serves both to address and depoliticize the alienation, insubordination, and militancy of workers. By providing management with intelligence from the shop floor, QWL facilitates the cooling out of grievances before they become a source of collective antagonisms. The quality circle has become the modern-day equivalent of the Taylorist stopwatch in controlling and regulating labor.

(4) QWL has been shown to be effective in increasing productivity. However, this productivity increase is not accomplished through democratization of the workplace, but rather through a tightening of managerial control and the further monopolization of knowledge on the part of management.

(5) From the point of view of organized labor, QWL presents serious contradictions. There are risks in participating in QWL, and there are risks in not participating. The overall weakness of labor, coupled with the fact that capital is very much on the offensive, places unions in the position of defensively maneuvering to block QWL's worst aspects and learning to live with its least damaging aspects. In this respect, organized labor is responding to QWL in much the same way that it is responding to the general offensive of capital against labor. The problems of labor are exemplified in the contradictions of QWL, but they are far more structural and pervasive than this single program.

There is no doubt that human beings are capable of – and desirous of – performing productive work in a co-operative manner that utilizes the full range of human intelligence and creativity of the species. Likewise, there is an inherent human desire to be productive and fulfilled in one's work, to control the product of one's labor, and to serve a larger social purpose than the immediate satisfaction of one's own needs. These human characteristics have never been realized under capitalism, nor can they be, since the necessities of the private accumulation of capital dictate everything from what gets produced to how it gets produced. Quality of Work Life programs in the United States, ultimately, are aimed at turning these innate human qualities against themselves, and subordinating them to the larger needs of the capitalist system.

References

AFL-CIO Committee on the Evolution of Work (1985): *The Changing Situation of Workers and Their Unions*, Washington, D.C.: AFL-CIO (February).

Brown, Warren (1985): A New American Pay System May Be in the Making, *The Washington Post National Weekly Edition*, March 4.

Bureau of Labor-Management Relations & Co-operative Programs (1984): *Labor-Management Cooperation: Perspectives from the Labor Movement*, Washington, D.C.: U.S. Department of Labor.

Camens, Sam (1982): Steel – An Industry at the Crossroads, American Productivity Center, Productivity Brief '17, (September).

Dixon, Marlene (1978): Abstract: The Degradation of Waged Labor and Class Formation on an International Scale, *Synthesis*, II, 3 (Spring): 46–53.

Dixon, Marlene (1982): The World Capitalist Crisis and the Rise of the Right, *Contemporary Marxism*, Journal of the Institute for the Study of Labor and Economic Crisis, San Francisco.

Dixon, Marlene (1984a): The Suez Syndrome, *Contemporary Marxism* (Fall), Journal of the Institute for the Study of Labor and Economic Crisis, San Francisco.

Dixon, Marlene (1984b): *Dual Power: Transnational Corporations and The Nation-State* (unpublished version).

Dixon, Marlene and McCaughan, Ed (1982): Reindustrialization and the Transnational Labor Force in the United States Today, *Contemporary Marxism*, (Summer), Journal of the Institute for the Study of Labor and Economic Crisis, San Francisco.

Felice, Stein and Frappier (1977): *Boss und Bureaucrat: Managing Labor's Discontent*, San Francisco: Institute for the Study of Labor and Economic Crisis.

Ferguson, Thomas and Rogers, Joel (1984): Big Labor Is Hurting – Itself, *The Nation*, September 1.

Frank, Andre Gunder (1980): *Crisis: In the World Economy*, New York: Homes and Meier.

Kochan, Thomas et al. (1984): *Worker Participation and American Unions: Threat or Opportunity?* Kalamazoo, Michigan: The W.E. Upjohn Institute for Employment Research.

Kornbluh, Hy (1984): Work Place Democracy and Quality of Work Life Problems and Prospects, *The Annals*, 473, (May): 88–95.

New York Stock Exchange (1982): *People and Productivity: A Challenge to Corporate America*, New York: N.Y. Stock Exchange.

Parker, Mike and Hansen, Dwight (1983): The Circle Game, *The Progressive*, January.

Rosow, Jerome and Zager, Robert (1986): *Productivity Through Work Innovations*, New York: Pergamon Press.

Ross, Irwin (1985): Employers Win Big in the Move to Two-Tier Contracts, *Fortune*, (April 29): 82.

Thompson, Philip (1983): Quality Circles in the U.S.: Growth and Trends, Paper given at the National Convention of Quality Circles.

United Rubber Workers (1982): *Collective Bargaining. Policy Handbook.*

Watts, Glenn (n.d.): QWL and the Union: An Opportunity or a Threat, Presentation to National Labor-Management Conference.

Whiting, Basil (1983): QWL: All or Nothing at All…? Discussion draft, Michigan Quality of Workers Life Council, Troy, Michigan.

Zager, Robert and Rosow, Michael (eds.) (1982): *The Innovative Organization Productivity Programs in Action*, New York: Pergamon Press.

Chapter 3
The Law as a Force for Change

Philippe Bernoux

Why Change?

The organization of firms, and their system of relations, both formal and informal, is undoubtedly undergoing an important transformation. Although it is always difficult to prove such statements, if only because firms function according to multiple models, a certain number of factors indicate that things are incontestably happening in this domain.

In the case of France, where the system of professional relations is highly centralized in the sense that the State takes a lot of the initiative, the analysis of a law voted in 1982 by the Socialist majority in the National Assembly may help to clarify this transformation. Two main factors underlie these changes. Although they interact with each other, it will be helpful to examine them separately.

The Crisis of Taylorism

Since the analyses of Georges Friedmann (1956) at the end of the Second World War, denunciations of the bad effects of Taylorism have become innumerable (see also Walker and Guest 1952), yet it apparently continues to flourish.

The first critiques focused on the inhuman aspects of the division of work, where human beings are reduced to an automaton, whose movements, reduced to the most simple, are repeated endlessly throughout interminable working days. Friedmann represents this current perfectly. A psycho-technician of work, his observations made him pessimistic. In 1963, for the third edition of his work, he wanted the title, "Where is Human Work going?", to be followed by a publicity strip bearing the reply "... to rack and ruin." Human work was becoming more and more inhuman, and Friedmann deplored the fact.

The only answer found to this inhumanity was in the application of the methods advocated by the human relations school of Elton Mayo; the practice of a more open style of command, greater attentiveness to the needs of workers, an amelioration of their salaries (obviously!) and working conditions, and perhaps some action on the organization of the shop floor. Using this model, management tried to improve the fate of the worker, subjugated as he was, or so it was believed, to the iron law of the division of labour. But the division of labour itself was not tampered with.

Things began to change at the start of the 1970s. On the one hand, disputes at work increased in a dramatic fashion during this period. In France, the annual number of working days lost through strikes almost doubled between 1971 and 1977, by comparison with the previous period. It was an important alarm signal. Moreover, it was manual workers who were the instigators of these conflicts. Up to then, this type of worker had been dragged along by their more highly skilled colleagues. But, starting from 1970, one witnessed long and bitter conflicts led by unskilled workers (the strikes at the Renault works, Le Mans, in 1971), by female employees (the strikes at the Credit Lyonnais, in 1976), or by immigrant workers (the strikes of the Parisian dustmen, in 1974). What was known as the feeling of "enough's enough" among the unskilled workers, emerged as a social phenomenon during this period.

The second reason why change occurred is linked to the problem of economic competition and the emergence of problems of quality. The industrial world had come through the post-war period of shortage and inflexible markets. Mass consumption products were selling well because they were in short supply, and because consumers did not have as large and precise a knowledge of the competition as they would subsequently acquire. At the end of the sixties, industrialists became aware that, more than ever, they would have to reduce their costs and, above all, do something about the quality of their products. This became a funda-mental selling point. With production on a very large scale in a Taylorized organization, management put more emphasis on the worker's sub-mission to the norms of the work study office than on his initiative, as a means of rectifying the faults. But these became a more and more serious cause of low sales. It was imperative to reduce them, and one possible way of doing this was by rethinking the organization.

Finally there was an increasing recognition by management of the importance of informal behaviour in the functioning of the shop floor. In fact, this was not new: researchers at Western Electric, in their study during the 1930s, had already pointed it out. What appeared new in its rediscovery by management thirty years later was the link between, on the one hand, this informal activity and, on the other hand, productivity and, most importantly, product quality. Informal activity was seen as a way of rescuing the individual from monotony and disinterest. Management took it seriously only as a way of improving work performance. The day that experience and observation showed that informal activity was indispensable to production, they began to seriously study ways of taking it into account in the organization, from which arose the wave of concrete experimentation launched in firms during the 1970s.

Crisis of Work, Crisis of the Firm

Rousselet's (1974) book "Work Allergy" captured the mood of the time and expresses what was generally meant by the crisis of work. It was a question of disinterest in work, manifested in certain types of behaviour. Absenteeism was the most important; the number of working days lost through absenteeism (short and long periods of illness, diverse absences) was estimated at 300 to 400 million, or ten times more than the number lost through strikes. Staff instability, or turnover, was, during this period, an alarming phenomenon; it reached, for example, 27 % of the workers in an electronics assembly factory, and 25 % in the Ford factories in the United States in 1969 (Durand 1974). Many observers noted the disaffection of the young with regard to industrial work; they no longer wanted to work in factories. And in spite of unemployment, which was already high at the time, many deskilled jobs were not accepted by native workers. It was necessary to bring in foreign labour to fill them.

The Crisis of Authority in the Firm

The confrontation of May 1968, taken up again afterwards, was aimed at the hierarchy and the bosses whose power was challenged on the shop floor. The rejection was not so much of the capitalist system itself but rather of large organizations and institutions. Conflicts would break out on the shop floor if a supervisor was seen to behave excessively. Perhaps there was a slide of power towards the shop floor. We are not convinced of this. But it is certain that, during this period, doubt began to insinuate itself into the administrative categories of the State, the employing class, and the unions; what if, one day, factories were paralysed because no one was any longer prepared to obey commands, or even to work in them? Uncertainty began to take root, reinforced by the fact that certain kinds of production, requiring an unskilled and abundant workforce, were being carried out in the countries of South-East-Asia. As Bunel et al. (1985) suggest, "the behaviour of employees called into question the industrial order, weakening the instruments of social regulation which assured the economic performance of firms..."

The Recognition of These Factors by Employers, Unions, and the State

Faced with this double crisis, entrepreneurs, anxious about acute economic competition, and sensing this threat of disinterest towards work, tried to apply all the formulas that might lead to a better integration of the worker into the firm. This integration was to lead to higher productivity and an improvement in quality, an important factor today. The recipes of Taylorism no longer produced this result, and so other solutions were turned to.

Historically, the domain of social relations in the firm at the start of the 1970s and in the decade which followed, was influenced by motivation theory. The socio-psychologist Frederik Herzberg advocated, among other things, the enrichment of tasks. Frederik Herzberg thought that giving workers more interesting, "richer" tasks would increase job satisfaction, and hence productivity. The theoretical fragility of this thesis results from the vagueness of the theory of needs upon which it is based (Bernoux 1980), from the equal vagueness of the concept of satisfaction (Roustang 1977), and from the confusion between what concerns the individual interests of workers and what concerns the better organization of work. The practical results of the application of Herzberg's theories in industry were disappointing and, for example, the experiments on autonomous groups were abandoned in the form in which they had raised hopes of a renewal of relations within the firm. It seems that they fell foul of the combined hostility of the different protagonists (employers, unions, work study units, management hierarchy), who were unprepared, at the time, to accept this type of change.

Enrichment of tasks and autonomy corresponded to a phase of the employers' policy that one might describe as experimental. The end of the 1970s opened a new period, which may be characterized as that of "participative management." Taking account of previous experiments, influenced by the so-called Japanese model and by a new managerial current (see Archier and Seryiex 1984; Peters and Waterman 1982), many firms launched "progress groups," or "quality circles." The aim of these innovations was to respond to malfunctions in the firms by a new and more participative organization, appealing more to the initiative of the employees while retaining overall control of operations. At the same time, this allowed more flexibility in the management of the workforce. At the moment when a left wing majority came to power, in May 1981, the search was on for a new managerial style. Even if the reasons put forward by the Ministry of Employment in favour of the law were of a political order, there was a convergence in the will to change. In the spirit of the new law, it was a question of making the firm more democratic, so that the citizenship experienced by the worker outside the firm should also be accorded to him within it. The usual rules of company life had to be changed. While remaining a place of conflict, it was to become a place where workers' self-expression would be formally recognised and effectively realized. Workers would be able to express themselves on issues concerning the content and the organization of work, and the conditions of working life.

This evolution was not to be at the expense of efficiency. On the contrary, as one reads in the text of the report, "direct expression" was to promote greater productive efficiency; by allowing the workers to express themselves, one was giving them the opportunity to point out hidden flaws, and to become better integrated into the firm itself. The idea of democracy was linked to that of efficiency, in the mind of the Minister.

These ideas, including the idea of efficiency (if in a diluted form), were included in the union proposals for the creation of shop-floor committees. Here, too, it was a question of making the workers full citizens of the firm, on the basis of humanism and socialism. The workers had a right to speak their mind, they saw things that no one else could see; thus there was a question of efficiency, but also one of democracy. The shop-floor committees were to be based on homogeneous groups, and to be small in size. Within a contractual framework, they were to have decision-making power over the choice of equipment, the organization and the conditions of work, and the role and the purpose of the structures of authority.

The Auroux Act, whose application we shall analyse on the basis of a survey, is comprehensible only in the context of the crisis of Taylorism, of the firm, and of work, and in the light of the objectives of the social protagonists concerned.

The Auroux Act and its Application

The Historical Background and the Content of the Law

Immediately upon its arrival in power, the government which was formed after the elections of May 1981, and which was composed of Socialist and Communist deputies, put forward a law on the reform of the firm. This reform had been on the agenda in France for a long time but had never come to fruition. François Bloch-Lainé's book "Pour une Réforme de l'Entreprise," published in 1963, had had a great deal of success, and had instigated numerous debates. But it did not change anything. Then, in the course of his 1974 electoral campaign, Valery Giscard d'Estaing had promised, if he was elected, to reform the firm (his principal rival at the time was François Mitterrand). When he arrived at the Elysée, he set up a committee charged with looking into this reform and making proposals, which it did (Sudreau 1975), though again, nothing came of it.

The new "left wing" majority owed it to themselves to do something. And they did. The result was the Act of 4 August 1982, called the Auroux Act after the Minister of Employment who supervised its drawing-up.

In the part of the law that we are concerned with here, it is stipulated that workers in firms with a staff of more than 200 should "enjoy a right of direct and collective expression with regard to the content and organization of their work." "Direct" expression signified that it would be without intermediaries, without elections, and would not pass through delegates. "Collective" implied that the employees should come together in groups to express themselves.

The way these rights were to be put into practice was to be negotiated between the employers and the representative union branches in the firms. The negotiations were to be concerned with the organization of meetings, their frequency and duration, the transmission of requests, and the responses of the employer. It was not necessary to come to an agreement; the sole obligation of the law concerned the inauguration of negotiations between employers and unions; these were to be begin within a period of six months. The law said nothing more about them.

This law was supposed to be provisory, the government committing itself to putting before the Parliament, by 30 June 1985, a report on the application of this first law. It did so. A second law, comparable to the first, was voted in in December 1985.

All the firms concerned (those with a staff of more than 200) began negotiations in 1981–82.

Agreements Signed and Offical Assessments[1]

The envisaged negotiations did indeed take place, almost without exception. Almost half (45 %) of the firms with a staff of more than 200 employees came to an agreement on the right of expression.

Most of these agreements allowed for meetings of coherent work units, comprising up to 20 members, of a duration of one to two hours, taking place at least 2 to 4 times per year. It was often specified that the employer would have to reply not only to the questions of the groups (which was obligatory), but also to those of the Works Council and of the Hygiene and Security Council. The running of the meetings, a problem on which the workers' and employers' organizations had come into conflict during the negotiations, was confined, in two thirds of cases, to the executive level.

In the firms, the unions signed agreements in differing proportions, which did not accurately reflect the positions of their confederations. At the national level, the CGT and the CFDT had been the most ardent in defending the Auroux Act, the CGT-FO had rejected it vigorously, the CGC and the CFTC adopting a guarded attitude. The proportion of agreements signed by union branches does not reflect the confederations' stand as can be seen from table 1.

It must, however, be emphasized that the refusal by a union to sign an agreement did not necessarily imply a refusal by the shop stewards of that union to participate in the expression meetings, still less a policy of systematic opposition. The particular situation of each firm, and of the union branches, weighed heavily on the concrete behaviour of the union representatives in the workplace.

Table 1: Percentage of Unions Signing Agreements under the Auroux Act

	Union presence	% Union branches signing agreements
CGT	71 %	76 %
CFDT	57 %	78 %
CGT-FO	41 %	62 %
CGC	48 %	87 %
CFTC	21 %	84 %
Other unions	14 %	89 %

---

[1] This section draws upon the article: "Problèmes humains du travail." *Liaisons sociales*, série R, No 90/85, 2 August 1985.

The effects of the law can be evaluated in different areas such as: internal relations, action on the material conditions of work (often more visible, but which would possibly have occurred even without the expression groups), and the organization and content of work, where change was difficult to observe and to evaluate.

Many reviews mention an improvement in the domain of information and communication. For the employees, it was a matter of getting a better grasp of their function in the production process, and also a better appreciation of economic constraints. Employers, for their part, said that they gained information on the workings of the shop floor and of the other sections.

In the domain of working conditions, the most frequent improvements were in the development of work stations, and in working conditions such as the fitting out of the premises, the modification or the reduction of nuisances, and the improvement of security.

Improvements for the organization were in general a matter of the simplification and greater uniformity of procedures, the rationalization of working time, the reorganization of tasks, and, more generally, a change in the concrete division of work.

The Outcomes of Expression Groups

One must, however, be prudent in estimating the overall outcome of expression groups, since they continue to exist and evolve. When they were established, expression groups did not generate a wave of enthusiasm in firms, neither on the part of the unions which had supported the principle nor on the part of the grass roots. Management was at best reserved, and often hostile; it was only through experience, after a year or two of functioning, that some of them realized the benefits they could derive from the groups, in the sense of more participative management. In this case, there was often a movement of renewal in the functioning of the groups, without union hostility, and with a member-ship that agreed to play the game.

Globally, one cannot call the expression groups a success. The assessment is rather one of a mitigated failure. In most firms, few groups went beyond a total of four meetings. In general, the first two took place within a short interval, the third after a longer period, and the fourth not until well afterwards. In a minority of firms (10 to 15 % approximately), expression groups still exist and play a role in reorganization and change. This result, while not insignificant, is still very limited.

However, in more than a third of the assessments sent by firms, it was stated that the right of expression would be made permanent. Also the right wing political parties which had violently opposed the law at the time of the vote in 1982 have, since then, tacitly recognized its utility. Most of them, during the election campaign of 1986, no longer spoke of its abrogation, but decided that the greater part of it ought to be retained. Such a result demonstrates the value of this law, but also the difficulty of analysing a phenomenon which is difficult to quantify.

The Life History of Expression Groups[2]

A research study was carried out in six firms of the Rhône-Alpes region. The evolution of the groups, at the time of their initial meetings, gave a similar picture, which may be described in the following manner.

A process of observation and testing took place in the first meetings. It was a question of finding out how seriously management took the right of expression, and so responded rapidly and efficaciously to questions. It was also a case of the group testing itself, that is to say assessing its own cohesion, and the willingness of its members to engage in negotiations with management. If the group felt itself to be divided or, on the contrary, if it was relatively united but without strategic resources, or if it felt that the management hierarchy was not very involved, then the groups ran a high risk of not lasting very long.

In this phase of its life, the group looked for an issue that did not commit it too heavily but allowed it to test the will of management. The members of the group did not involve themselves heavily at this stage, as they were not sure either of management, of each other, or of likely external reactions to the group. So the theme of working conditions was chosen, as it suited the idea of combining these double objectives. It could be expressed in the form of demands, but without any hint of a solution, as this would have risked too high an involvement on the part of the

---

[2] At this point, and for the remainder of the chapter, we are working from research carried out under my direction. Cf. Ph. Bernoux, "De l' expression à la negociation. Les Groupes d'Expression Directe dans six entreprises de la région Rhône-Alpes," duplicated report, GLYSI document No 6/85, November 1985. This report is available. In the present article, when we talk of groups, it will be a question of direct expression groups, set up in firms by the Auroux Act.

group. A reply that included a financial commitment was a good test of the will of management. Moreover, a positive reply gave accrued status to the group.

Many groups received no reply, or an inadequate one (too many replies were not immediately positive), or the reply was dilatory. As a result, they scarcely got past the stage of two or three meetings.

Groups which got as far as this in testing their own will to negotiate, and that of management to engage in the process of expression, carried on. They set themselves up progressively as protagonists, that is to say that they became capable of negotiating with the immediate hierarchy, with higher level members of the hierarchy, and also among members. Continuation was only possible if the group possessed sufficient resources to carry on the process of negotiation. This was the case for both blue- and white-collar workers. Our sample included only one firm where the majority of workers were unskilled; these workers had a lot of difficulty in progressing to the second stage (more than two meetings), and in acquiring some autonomy with regard to the hierarchy. For the other firms the groups which felt that they had among themselves – or from outside particularly in their relations with the unions – adequate resources, managed to set themselves up as protagonists.

Expression and Negotiation

As a matter of principle, giving workers the right of expression probably seems like a good thing when they are reputed not to have the right to speak, which was the case for the majority of employees in firms. The law gave a platform to the "voiceless" of the industrial world. One might have imagined that they would have rushed to take advantage of it. But this was not the case. Why?

A strategic analysis shows that to express oneself in a universe where one has no power – the law did not modify the balance of power in the firm – means simply to risk the content of that expression being "hijacked" by others, without those who express themselves, the employees, deriving any benefit from it. Their "expression" runs the risk of becoming expropriated.

Where the blue- and/or white-collar workers in these groups got the impression that they could express themselves, but not negotiate, things came to an abrupt halt. This is the explanation for the slow and progressive way in which the groups took off. They gradually tested managements' willingness to involve themselves with the scheme. It seems to be possible to schematize the approach in the following terms: the groups said, "You suggest that we express ourselves; but you, the management, have you something to say to us?" This led to the first reactions, which were prudent, posing factual, concrete questions, which did not heavily commit the group, but tested the will of management to involve itself. These were questions on the theme of working conditions, or on minor organizational changes. Then the group waited passively, that is to say without intervening or exerting pressure, but nonetheless attentively.

The follow-up might not come, or it might come slowly, very slowly. During this time, nothing would change on the side of management. In concrete terms, after a first meeting, in most cases, the group produced a report that its immediate superior passed on to the echelon above. If nothing happened, at least during the following two or three months, or if a reply was given, but in the conventional form, without any new ground being broken, the group was likely not to want to carry on. Let us say, for example, that it had asked for, among other things, two chairs. A month later, the chairs arrive. What do the employees in the group say? That expression groups, in this respect, are a trifle more effective than the shop steward or the foreman. Was it worthwhile passing a law for such a result? Even if, very conscientiously, management gave numerous other positive replies, but the results, in spite of everything, remained modest, then the group's commitment would be in doubt. To the extent that the same thing was likely to happen again, once demands in the domain of working conditions had been satisfied, there was every reason to think that the members of the group would lose interest. And, as was seen above in the first part, this is in fact what happened.

What was the group to talk about, after the material problems of working conditions had been raised? It was necessary to advance onto a terrain of higher involvement and risk, that of the organization of work, a domain most often reserved for the hierarchy and policy-makers. This was a difficult problem to tackle raising issues concerned with the division of tasks, the distribution of roles, the system of authority, of communication, and of remuneration. A member of the group who posed a problem of organization (from the simplest type, "Why are four copies of such and such form required, when three should be enough?" to the more complicated, "Relations with the maintenance department ought to be looked at") knew that this was likely to affect the way he worked – his share of the division of tasks, his relation to the central organizing departments or to departments closer at hand. He would only do that if he knew that he could discuss and negotiate such changes.

Groups failed to go beyond the stage of the first meetings except where they could be assured that discussion, and the beginnings of negotiation, could take place. The studies done in the six firms bear unanimous witness to this fact; the groups came alive only insofar as they could discuss and negotiate.

It will be helpful, at this juncture, to recall the significance of negotiation. It is not only concerned with the skill of scoring points or gaining advantages (features which are sufficiently emphasized by current propagandists of managerial-type negotiation), but also with social recognition. To negotiate, to be accepted at a bargaining table, is to be recognized, if not as an equal, at least as someone who can be talked to, and thus someone recognized as having resources. In a firm, many employees, even if their work is interesting, their salaries (relatively) good, and the atmosphere in the workplace satisfactory, etc., aspire to a certain degree of social recognition. "Paternalistic" management know this well, and sometimes exploit symbolic rewards, such as the director, in a well-orchestrated public ceremony, shaking hands with this or that worker, who is held up to the others as a model.

In the firm, the most common way of obtaining social recognition, whatever the inequality in the distribution of resources, is by participation in negotiation. Concretely, in our studies, even if the hierarchical superior listened to the group, dealt with such problems as he could, communicated with the higher echelons, received a reply and gave it to the group, this of itself achieved nothing. But if the same person came before the group after having met with other officials, on particular questions or proposals, gave an account of the meeting and of the fact that the official in question had asked for explanations, showed that he had understood the question and that he was dealing with it, the members of the group became more interested. They responded. The negotiating process began to take off. The group would be able to survive.

Three examples will clarify this phenomenon. The first is drawn from the reports of an expression group belonging to a department which felt it was undervalued in relation to the members of another department, with which it was in daily contact; the employees of the second department perceived themselves as being highly valued. The expression groups of the first department were not very animated. We talked about this with an official, who did not understand the reason for it. To make himself clear, he took, at random, the report of a meeting and began to read it. The first two lines, concerned with requests, were written in the same way, "Would [names of members of the other department] kindly inform us...". We asked the official what he had done in response to these requests. He replied, "I studied the question seriously, sent for the head of the department to which the request had been addressed, and we included our reply in the report, giving the group a measure of satisfaction and explaining why it was impossible to go any further than that. The report, with my reply, went to the group." This manner of replying was in conformity with the letter of the law, with the firm's draft agreement on direct expression groups, and with the notes of the personnel management on application of the law. But it neglected the essential point, which had been contained implicitly in the formulation of the question, namely the request for recognition, and the group's expectation of negotiation. This request, and this expectation, could be read into the way the request had been drawn up; a rapid survey of the group confirmed the fact. The members of the group had wanted a meeting with one of the members of the department in question, a meeting which would have conferred on them the recognition that they were seeking. The group ceased to meet after this event.

A second example concerns the expectation for negotiations. Four groups from a department where the machines were similar, if not identical, included in the report of one of their first meetings a request for a modification of the installation. They had not consulted with one another about this in advance. The head of the department, who was responsible for the decision on modification, gave a written reply, which he attached to the reports. The groups were expecting a discussion at least with their direct hierarchical superiors, and doubtless with the head of the department, on this point, which was important for running the machines. They received the written reply, but expressed a feeling of failure on this point, which they spread throughout the expression groups. It became evident to them that the groups were of little value.

From these two examples, it appears that the groups were making an implicit demand for some form of recognition from members of the hierarchy, a demand which could only be made explicit by the presence of the official in charge of the decision. There was a wish to discuss and negotiate change with him. If the only response to this was via the traditional bureaucratic route, the members of the group declared themselves disappointed and no longer wanted to meet.

A third example concerns a difference of approach to technical problems and the resolution of this difference (Amblard 1985: 200–201).

On the shop floor, the members of the different groups frequently posed technical problems in their own language, which was related to operational knowledge. The same problems were analysed differently by the members of management and this lead to difficulties. More than the words, it was the frame of reference which was different. This led management to propose setting up working groups around the supervisory foreman, the member of the hierarchy who was closet to the workers. The foreman could then form a link between the operational knowledge of the workers and the more technical formulations of management. The workers and the members of the hierarchy were thus obliged to formulate the same questions in different ways, according to their particular objectives. Then a working group comprising employees, the supervisory foreman, and members of the functional department studied the problem and put forward alternatives for decision and experimentation. This was discussed again in the expression group. In this way a negotiated decision was arrived at in the framework of the expression group.

The conclusion of this section is, thus, that the vitality of expression groups depends on the extent to which the formal rights of expression accorded to them by the law are transformed into negotiations. These gave the group certain powers, which were then recognized by the hierarchy and management. In this sense, the Auroux Act was an important factor for change.

This change took place when, as we shall see later, management desired change and secured the means of carrying it out, particularly through decentralization. On the groups' side, two conditions were necessary; that their members should have effective cultural resources and negotiating power, and that they should form a sufficiently homogeneous unit to accept collective negotiation. In this chapter, we do not have room to examine these last two conditions, instead, we are going to look at the problems of decentralization and change.

The Conditions for Success: Decentralization and a Desire for Transformation

The vitality of the groups is explained by a willingness to change, by de facto decentralization, and by increased autonomy. Measures need to be taken in the following domains:

- renewal of the worker-hierarchy relationship;
- semi-autonomy of the work group accepted by the hierarchy, in particular in its representation; and
- decentralization.

On the other hand, groups disappear when there is:
- absence of autonomy and of group power;
- absence of autonomy and of hierarchical power;
- no real engagement nor delegation of responsibility, on the part of management;
- too much centralization and hierarchy; and
- no transformation of institutional practices.

The Utopia of Change Emerging from Expression

A certain degree of decentralization is necessary, if groups are to survive, since it is an important, if not a central, element in the transformation of rules and practices. Traditionally, centralization can be defined as the distance between the place where the decision is made and that of the initial request, or of the place of execution. Michel Crozier (1963: 250) points out, moreover, that the logic of centralization is accompanied by a preference "for the stability of the internal 'political' system in terms of the functional objectives of the organization;" a judicious remark, which brings out an additional obstacle, one that management has often been unable to overcome, much as they may have wished to do so, that is to build groups that would function to close the distance between decision and execution, and to reinforce the second pole in relation to the first. The movement to decentralization led, in concrete terms, to a transformation of the system of procedural rules. It was necessary that management and the hierarchy accept this. Groups could function if:
- there was decentralization of decisions,
- which came down to giving more power to the operative echelons, i.e. to the groups themselves,
- which presupposes a major transformation of the organization.

An illusion of the reform of direct expression groups was to believe that it was enough to make promises for transformation to take place. On the contrary, the first necessity was the desire for transformation. Only management and the hierarchy could do that since they possessed the power and authority to set in motion the necessary organizational changes.

This statement can be illustrated by a drawing and a schema (Figures 1 and 2). The former is related to transformation, the latter to decentralization. The drawing below, by the cartoonist Plantu, shows that transformation as a result of the law on its own is an illusion. The bricklayer who is wheeling the barrow, and being vigorously abused, wishes, of course, that this way of going about things would change. The wish that he expresses gives one to understand that change will come the day the Auroux Act is applied; as if the law on expression could, by itself, modify the system of power and, more generally, the organization of the firm. We consider the contrary to be true. The transformation of the principles and practices of power and of the organization of the firm is the only way of giving content to expression meetings. The drawing is not exactly explicit on this point, but it gives the impression – and in that it contributes to the spread of the illusion, or at least reflects it – that the bricklayers' expression meetings are going to shake up the power structure (symbolized by the uniform, the belt and baldric, the halberd, etc.). If the aim of the meetings was a complete change in the system, they would be clandestine and would take place in a different perspective, that of rebellion and social change. Independent of the fact that the role of the hierarchy is satirized in the drawing, it suggests that the voting of the Auroux Act was brought about by the pressure of a social movement. This latter is, in our view, indispensable to genuine reform in the firm, but, at the present time, all observers agree that no such movement exists. The Auroux Act, of itself, implies no major change in the functioning of the firm.

In firms where groups demonstrated a certain vitality, this was possible because it was part of a transformation in the working of the firm, which came essentially from management, not from a labour or social movement.

This fact obviously limits the extent of the change which these groups can bring about in the firm. We will return to this problem in our conclusion. However, the fact of being initiated by management does not signify that the dynamism of groups stops with this decision. It can go well beyond that, and has done so. We would simply say that a necessary, but not sufficient, condition for the life of the groups has been the willingness of management to include them in a process of change in the firm; a process which is often concerned with better economic and technical adaptation. Management is attempting to optimize the potential of workers' knowledge and initiative. To achieve this end it enlarges the employees' capacity for decision-making. From that point on, even if it

Figure 1: The New Rights of the Workers

continues to direct the operation, the groups will suggest changes, improve the functioning of the workshop or the department, and rethink the organization of their work. This is what management hopes for. But these initiatives of the groups are not without their counterpart, as we saw above. As concrete negotiation gets under way in the groups, they sometimes try to obtain quantifiable benefits, which rapidly go beyond the domain specified by the law (for example salaries, hours, hiring, etc., often expressed in the form of "subject outside of the law" in the reports). At the same time, the groups try to negotiate organizational changes: more power, responsibility, redefinition of their domains of action, etc.

The condition for this successful transformation is an enlarging of the decision-making powers of the primary levels of the hierarchy. This process will be termed one of decentralization. These powers may be "given" by management or "won" by the group through negotiation. For example, in a department that is distant from the centre, a participant asks for the solution to a problem which, according to the rules, concerns the stores department. The relevant member of the hierarchy authorizes him to go ahead with the purchase of this small piece of equipment. He refers the matter to his immediate superior (second level of the hierarchy), who takes care of the matter out of his normal budgetary allowance. The latter asks for an increase in the annual budgetary allowance, and thinks he will obtain it.

Another example concerns the re-establishment of a bonus. In an establishment of 1,200 people, the head of the department (5th echelon of the hierarchy) attends a meeting that he has been invited to, and is asked about the re-establishment of a bonus that had been abolished several years before. He replies in vague and imprecise terms. The assistant engineer, hierarchically under the orders of the first, then intervenes to say that he would like to see the bonus brought back. His superior agrees to re-examine the question. Whatever the result, the negotiations are under way; there has been, at the initiative of a subordinate, the questioning of a rule negotiated and implemented by his superior.

The ability of the hierarchical echelons in contact with the employees to acquire decision-making responsibilities, hitherto reserved for the higher echelons, is a condition of the functioning of groups. And this ability can be extended to the group so that the base of the hierarchy negotiates for, and obtains, the enlarging of its decision-making responsibilities; for example, more responsibility is accorded for the maintenance of the machines, a domain previously entrusted to a specialized department.

Resistance to Change

Decentralization can run up against resistance from those who fear that it will lead to a process of deregulation, for example between work study departments and production departments. Typically, work study departments have hierarchical relationships with the shop floor. In general, the know-how of the workers, that is to say the contribution of the knowledge stored up on the shop floor and in the production department, is not taken account of through negotiation. The work study department attempts to utilize this know-how without modifying the usual hierarchical relations. From this position expression groups can only appear as a potential source of "overall deregulation". Once again the same resistances can surface that occurred during the time of the semi-autonomous groups of the 1970s, and which were enough to slow down and, finally, to bring about the failure of the movement.

To help overcome this resistance, top management must formulate a strategy of support, involving the whole hierarchical chain of command whose goal should be that the requests emanating from the groups are discussed without delay, and receive speedy replies. Groups only function when replies are made relatively swiftly and are accompanied by explanations which make sense to their members. A good way of "sinking" groups is through dragging out replies, or giving mainly negative answers. When an organization is very centralized, this type of blockage easily occurs. It was noticed that in the case of the bank, the groups composed of administrative workers, grouped together in one building and relating according to a hierarchical and centralized model, functioned badly, while the direct expression groups of the counter staff, far from the centre, and composed partly of commercial and partly of administrative staff, functioned much more satisfactorily.

Figure 2 illustrates two models encountered during a survey, of how expression groups may fit into organizational structures based on two industrial establishments. In model A, the group communicates directly only with itself. In model B, it is open to communication with the rest of the hierarchy.

Represented in this figure are the different hierarchical levels, from the employees brought together in expression groups, to the manager of the factory, plus the engineer in charge of a department. (Maintenance has been taken as an example. Any of the other departments or production workshops would have done equally well.)

Legally, the expression group is limited to the group itself plus the head

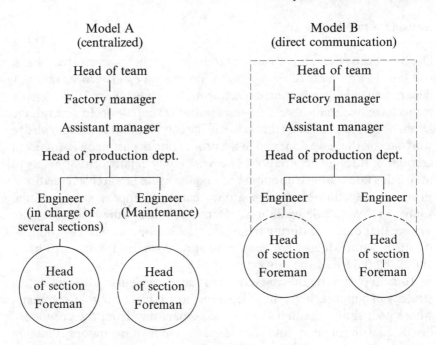

Figure 2: Two different models of communication applied to the same hierarchical model

of the team, or the hierarchical supervisor. The presence of the latter is not stipulated by the law. The bill specifies, however (statute of 18 November 1982 – article 2,1,3,d), that the executive staff are "naturally part of the expression groups corresponding to the work units which they supervise." In fact, no agreement in a firm has excluded them (in the sole case of the mutual insurance union, they were present during the last quarter of the meeting only). In the figure above, the limits of the expression group has been shown by a circle.

In model A, this limit cannot be, and has not been, traversed. In fact, the groups never met, nor had any exchanges, nor negotiated with a member of the hierarchy other than that which dealt with supervision. The reports were passed on through hierarchical channels, going to the foreman, then the head of the section, the engineer, etc., perhaps going to the engineer of the department concerned, then coming back down the same way. It is easy to understand why the groups rapidly withered away in this firm.

It is a different story in model B. All the members of the hierarchical chain, at whatever level, came to see the group at its request, when a question concerned them directly. Thus not only did these questions receive a reply, but the policy of the firm, its strategy, its constraints, its margins of manœuvre, and uncertainties in which it found itself were brought out and debated more or less widely. The members of the expression group understood better the process in which the firm was engaged, and its system of relations. They saw their place in this process and could negotiate certain aspects of it, or modify them, etc. In some firms, the presence of members of different levels of the hierarchy constituted, in itself, an important transformation. But this only took place because, previously, management had envisaged and accepted it in principle. In other words, the acceptance of possible evolution preceded the fact of this evolution.

Where the model A type mode of functioning exists, expression groups cannot flourish. It can be seen from this figure that a single member of the hierarchical chain can block, or slow down, communication by keeping information or reports on hold, and finally giving the members of the group the feeling that management "doesn't believe in it." An in-depth analysis of the real functioning of the firm is thus necessary if the reactions of the group members are to be understood.

Groups were often concerned to consider flexibility and the definition of functions. This area in the working of an organization affects the professional capacities of the employees. It is of extreme importance. Many group members became discouraged and annoyed by non-replies, or deferred replies, to questions bearing upon these points. More than working conditions – even than the organization of work – they involved the credibility of management as to its willingness to introduce change into the firm. In agreeing to discuss and negotiate the content of tasks, they were focussing on the place of the individual and of the group within the firm. It was an essential transformation, which determined the credibility of management and the vitality of the expression groups.

The Lessons of the Firms Studied

All case studies of the firms come to virtually identical conclusions: the elements which were most important for the vitality and the evolution of the direct expression groups can be summed up in terms of the decentralization of decision-making and the transformation of institutional practices, one being linked to the other.

Conclusions: Have Direct Expression Groups Actually Changed Anything?

It is not possible in a short conclusion to have a general discussion on the theoretical concept of change, or theories of social change[3]. Nonetheless it is also evident that in order to know if anything has changed, it is necessary to have a fairly precise idea of what one means by change. Rather than attempt to define it a priori, let us take an example.

The example is Taylorism or, more precisely, its introduction. From the perspective of the organization of the firm, the introduction of Taylorist principles and their application must be described as change. To sum up briefly, it can be said that the model of the professional worker was exchanged for that of the unskilled worker. In the first, the worker is relatively autonomous and is charged with organizing his own work. He negotiates with the employer, not about his salary, scarcely about his rates, but about the amount of time necessary for the execution of the task. In the second, the work is prepared by specialized departments (work study and design offices) and the organization is taken care of by management. The worker has nothing left to negotiate, and even his salary level is laid down for him (Mottez 1966: 121). This constitutes an upheaval in the organization, which Taylor, arguing for the principles of scientific management, clearly foresaw, and which all the numerous commentators insist on at great length. In this sense, Taylorism is a real change, even if it remains within the logic of capitalism.

This change appears, however, relatively small to anyone who looks at social evolution (Touraine et al. 1984) and notably to anyone who has observed the changes that have taken place in France in the domain of work in 1906 (the Charter of Amiens), 1919, 1936, 1945, or 1968. Taylorism did not trigger off any social movement, and the workers movement reacted to the constraints of Taylorism rather than being caused by them. In other words, the social movement fed off this new form of organization rather than being its driving force. It grafted itself onto it. Alain Touraine said that professional protection, having suffered at the hands of Taylorist organization, was the place where workers' consciousness was born. Taylorism is a mode of employer domination, and the workers' consciousness was born out of resistance to that domination.

---

[3] For a recent synthesis and a good overall view, see the article "Changement social," In: R. Boudon/F. Bourricaud, (1982): *Dictionnaire critique de la sociologie*, Paris: P.U.F.

If one transposes this reasoning to the law on expression, we see that the more dynamic expression groups have produced an important change in the organization of the firm or, more precisely, have been one of the instruments of organizational change. As has been seen, they have thrived only where they have been part of wider organizational changes. At this level, undoubtedly, they constitute a change. Not only are they part of a movement towards participative management, which would not be negligible in itself, but they also transform it. Thanks to them, not only does the worker "no longer leave his brain in the changing room" but, in putting it to use, he becomes an interlocutor who can – and does – promote change in the organization of the shop floor. At this level, we may conclude by saying that, in proportion to their vitality, expression groups constitute a change, albeit a modest one, since it remains limited to the organization of work.

Initially the majority of managements of firms were hostile to the Socialist's Auroux Acts. The success of the direct expression groups, when it occurred, can be explained by a reversal of this attitude when certain employers began to realize that it could be in their interests. From then on, the direct expression groups were used for managerial ends. But they are not mere tools in the hands of the employers. They may set in motion a dynamic of negotiation, where the workers have a voice – and our survey proves that they are prepared to use it – in the workings of the firm, and may also cause it to evolve in line with workers' interests.

Does this herald social change? The reply to this question escapes us for the following reasons. First, our research remained at the level of the organization. At no time did the researchers attempt to interpret it in terms of social movements. Second, the enquiry focussed on relations between organizational factors and the way in which expression groups developed. If workers' consciousness grows out of opposition to the organization of work, this opposition rarely takes clear and direct forms. The machine-breaking by the English textile industry workers at the start of the 19th century was first of all a reaction against new technology. In the relation between workers' consciousness and the organization, it can be said that the latter has to be confronted on the way to developing the former. The organization is in effect the place where power relations are worked out. But this process rarely takes place, unless it is carried along by a social movement. That has been the case with the law on expression.

Furthermore, one would need to be clairvoyant to know if a social movement has a chance of even one day setting itself up in opposition to this new mode of organization. The workers' reaction against Taylorism seemed rapid (strikes in the factories of the Nord, then at the Renault factories, in 1912–13). But it is difficult to know when its concrete applications began. For the moment, and apart from the principled stance of the CGT-FO, which is hostile to the law, one notes the provisional support of the other confederations, and an interest on the part of the CGC. As to the workers, their response as we have seen has been largely passive. Thus nothing, for the moment, permits us to establish a relationship between a social movement, if it exists, and the application of the law on expression.

Without having created the movement, in our opinion, the Auroux Act may stimulate it towards more fundamental changes. But these can only come from outside the expression groups. Some expression groups have been accompanied by changes in their organizations, and the members of expression groups have helped to shape these changes in particular ways. The result is not negligible. In itself, it defines its own frontiers.

References

Amblard, H. (1985): *Une expression en quête d'acteurs*, duplicated report: University of Lyon 2, Lyon: Glysi.

Archier, G. and Seryiex, H. (1984): *L'entreprise du troisième type*, Paris: Seuil.

Bernoux, P. (1980): Sociologie du travail, Supplément à la grande Encyclopédie Larousse, Paris: Larousse.

Bloch-Lainé, F. (1963): *Pour une réforme de l'entreprise*, Paris: Seuil.

Bunel, J. et al. (1985): *Le triangle de l'entreprise*, duplicated report, Lyon: Glysi.

Crozier, M. (1963): *Le phénomène bureaucratique*, Paris: Seuil.

Durand, C. (1974): *Le travail enchaîné*, Paris: Seuil.

Friedmann, G. (1950): *Le travail en miettes*, Paris: Gallimard.

Mottez, B. (1966): *Systèmes de salaires et politiques patronales*, Paris: Ed. du CNRS.

Peters, T. and Waterman, R.H. Jr. (1982): *In Search of Excellence*, New York: Harper & Row.

Roustang, G. (1977): Enquêtes sur la satisfaction au travail ou analyse directe des conditions de travail, *Revue Internationale du Travail*, 115, 3.

Rousselet, J. (1974): *L'allergie au travail*, Paris: Seuil.

Sudreau, P. (1975): *La réforme de l'entreprise*, Paris: Collection 10/18.

Touraine, A. et al. (1984): *Le mouvement ouvrier*, Paris: Fayard.

Walker, C.R. and Guest, R.H. (1952): *The Mass of the Assembly Line*, Cambridge, MA: Harvard University Press.

Chapter 4
Co-Determination in the Federal Republic of Germany – An Appraisal of a Secular Experience

Ulrich Briefs

What Is Co-Determination in Reality?

The concept of co-determination was shaped in the 1920s, especially as a reaction to the "soviet" movement, which was relatively strong in Germany in the failed revolution of 1918 and in the political debate discussion afterwards.

Essentially, co-determination means:
- the participation of workers' representatives and trade unions in the decision-making of firms, principally in supervisory boards and boards of directors; and
- the existence of workers' or works councils in firms as a counterweight to managerial institutions of decision-making.

Co-determination, from the point of view of institutional logic, thus combines participative and autonomous elements in the representation of workers' interests.

This specific system for representing workers' interests operates under the following important conditions:
- the private ownership of the means of production;
- a competitive "market economy" with its anarchic structures;
- extremely far-reaching juridical restrictions, e. g. the abrogation of the right to strike as a means to solve conflicts on the shop floor and in plants;
- rapid technological change, especially with the beginning of the "computerization" of work processes. This technological change introduces new intensities and qualities of interaction between management and workers.

To summarize then, co-determination is a system of very limited and partial joint regulation of some decisions at the plant and enterprise levels of decision-making, which operates within the existing capitalist mode of production and its institutions and structures.

The original idea of the trade unions in Germany to establish co-determination as a general economic and political principle has not been realized. The current of economic democracy as it was conceived was that workers' interests should be represented at all levels of the economy[1,2] (see Figure 1). At present, institutions for co-determination only exist at plant and enterprise level, there is nothing at shop-floor or workplace level and nothing at levels above the enterprise, although there has been a revival of demands for participation beyond the enterprise level within the DBG (Deutscher Gewerkschaftsbund – German Federation of Unions) in the last ten years.

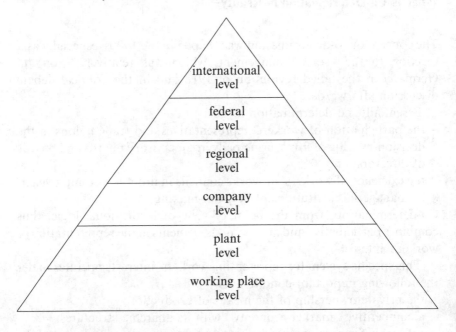

Figure 1: Levels of decision-making for which co-determination model may
         be realized

---

[1] The concept of "Wirtschaftsdemokratie" was shaped by the ADGB (Allgemeiner Deutscher Gewerkschaftsbund) and especially by Fritz Naphtali in the second half of the 1920s, cf. Naphtali, F. (1966).
[2] This was a concession to the ideas of the "soviet" movement in Germany (soviet = council); Deppe, F. (1969).

Different Forms of Co-Determination – Different Forms of Restrictions

The prevailing system of co-determination contains different forms of institutional arrangements:
1. Works councils are a main pillar of co-determination affecting 15 million workers out of 21 million in total in the FRG.
2. Co-determination according to the 1976 "Co-determination Law" affects roughly 4.5 million workers in about 480 major companies (with more than 2000 workers).
3. The "classical" (and, according to trade union understanding, the most advanced) form of co-determination, the so-called "qualified" or "paritarian" co-determination in the steel and coal mining industries affects roughly half a million workers.[3]
4. A specific form of sub-paritarian co-determination in joint stock companies with more than 500 and less than 2000 workers affects another half a million workers.
5. "Personnel councils" operate in the public services with about 3.6 million workers and civil servants and are affected by a corresponding federal law and 10 regional laws.

About 2.5 million workers – especially in very small firms – have no form of co-determination. All the workers affected by the forms of co-determination mentioned under points 2–4 are included within the total of workers mentioned in point 1 above. About 9.5 million workers only have representation in the form of works councils, which is by far the most important element of the co-determination system in West-Germany.

There are several other forms of co-determination embedded in this system, especially as part of the total mentioned under point 1. For example, in the printing industry a specifically restricted form of works councils operates in order to protect entrepreneurs from any interference by workers in their publications policy.

The works councils are exclusively composed of workers' representatives from the firms. These representatives are elected every three years by all workers of the firm (only superior executives are excluded from the right to vote).

The "qualified" co-determination in the steel and coal mining industries has two pillars:

---

[3] The historical background for the demand for co-determination in the coal mining and steel industries was that these two sectors were the most reactionary factions of German capital and deeply involved in the Nazi regime.

1. Representation on the supervisory board, on the basis of parity; among these representatives may be several trade union representatives and experts from outside the firm.
2. A "works director" who is a regular member of the board of management with the full rights and obligations of a director – his functions usually comprise personnel administration and personnel planning as well as social matters (e. g. health and safety services and company restaurants).[4]

In the event of a split vote on the supervisory board (e.g. the 10 workers' representatives vote against the 10 representatives of capital owners), the casting vote is held by a so-called "neutral man."[5] This "neutral man" in the steel industry is usually proposed by the workers' representatives, whereas capital's representatives usually propose the presidency of the supervisory boards. The president in the West German supervisory board has by legal stipulation a very important and prominent role.

The West German joint stock company system is a two-tier system with a management board running the company and shaping its business policy. The supervisory board, usually holding four sessions a year, is an institution located outside the company with limited rights. The main instrument to exercise control is the right to nominate the members of the management board and to approve investments of more than 100.000 or 500.000 DMs. This latter right of control exists only if the statutes of the corporation – voted by the shareholders' meeting – contain such a stipulation (the amount is fixed as well by the shareholders' meeting).

The supervisory board – this is especially the experience in the joint stock corporations owned by the trade unions themselves – is dependent upon the information supplied by the board of management, which it has to control. The works director has a substantive additional role in evaluating intra-company information for the workers' representatives on the supervisory board.

The supervisory board, by its construction, is still basically a shareholders' committee created to exercise financial control in order to

---

[4] In some companies personnel administration for executives is excluded from the works directors responsibility.
[5] To give an impression of the functioning of the co-determination system: the neutral man nominated by the workers' representatives in the supervisory board is, for example, in some of the steel corporations a member of the board of directors of one of the publicly-owned banks; cf. WSI-Projektgruppe, Mitbestimmung in Unternehmen und Betrieb – Handbuch der Mitbestimmung (1981).

safeguard shareholders' property interests in the company. It is not a body designed to control management in view of the much more complicated interests of workers (e.g. job security, safety, working conditions, etc).

Co-determination according to the 1976 law deviates from this classical co-determination system in several aspects:

1. It does not have a "neutral man" but instead confers on the president of the supervisory board a second vote in case of a split vote.
2. It determines that the president must always be a representative of capital.
3. Among the workers' representatives must be a senior executive, i.e. an executive from the inner circle around the directors with a considerable share in managerial power, hence someone dependent on the board of management which nevertheless he or she is expected to control.[6]
4. The works director post under the 1976 law is nominated and elected by the supervisory board rather than by the union. The supervisory board formally has a ten to ten distribution of votes between workers' representatives and capital's representatives, but in reality has a 12 to 9 distribution of votes in favour of capital given the stipulations mentioned in points 1–3 above.

It is thus not surprising that the co-determination law of 1976 is not considered by the trade unions as a fulfilment of the demand for general co-determination. Some voices in the DGB even called the '76 law an Anti-DGB law, this in view of certain tendencies to promote non-DGB-Unions.

Co-determination in the public services falls behind the rights conveyed to works councils.

The Main Element of the Co-Determination System: The Works Councils

Works councils are the nearly universal means for the representation of workers' interests in firms and have a legal basis in the Works Constitution Law, promulgated in 1952 and renewed in 1972. Workers have a basic set of rights to information, consultation, and "co-

---

[6] This is a break with the principle of the separation of control and execution inherent in the two-tier system.

determination," delineated in this law. In practice, the use of these rights is subject permanently to legal procedures. This has largely contributed to making the co-determination system an extremely "juridical" system.[7] In these juridical procedures the works council usually tries to claim or to extend its rights while, management tries to abrogate or confine them.

Of course, the rights of the works councils do not go so far that they can prevent dismissals, shut-downs, and similar actions.[8] They have no right to initiate or prevent investments or the sale of a company or of a part of the company. Neither have they any right to conclude collective agreements on wages, working time, etc. They can, however, conclude company agreements on, for example, social matters, indemnities in case of dismissals, technological issues, etc.

Figure 2 shows in diagrammatic form the rights of works councils on various issues. In general, the more important the matter for the company as a whole, the weaker the rights of the works councils. Nevertheless, the right to information on economic matters has proven to be an important achievement – but it is clearly not a right to "co-determination" in the generally understood sense, and it is even less a real right to control.

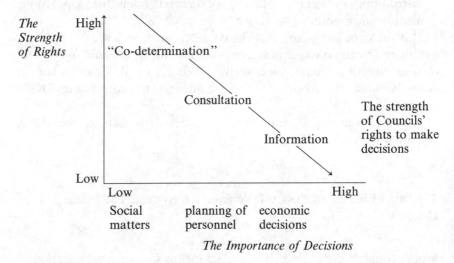

Figure 2: The Rights of Works Councils

---

[7] The German term is: "Verrechtliches System".
[8] It certainly has not changed the hierarchical character of the "Legal system of work" (Arbeitsrecht); but it nevertheless gives workers and workers' representatives some important rights – but no veto rights as for instance in the socialist countries – in cases of dismissals.

The right to "co-determination" means the right to hand the decision over to an arbitration body, later on eventually to a works-court (a special but regular court system for work differences). The arbitration body usually is headed by a professional judge from one of the works-courts. It is this judge who has the decisive vote in the arbitration body. Hence co-determination means finally an objectivizing procedure removing the disagreement from the realm of conflictual processes.

The intricacies of the co-determination system become even more explicit if one analyses the rights to information. The importance of different categories of information and the availability of this information for the works council is shown in Figure 3.

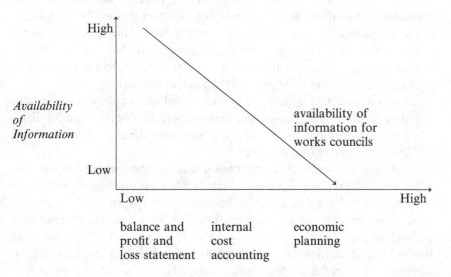

Importance of Information for Works Councils

Figure 3: The Availability of Information to Works Councils

The deficiencies in the works councils' rights to information clearly show how limited and partial this form of joint regulation is. Nevertheless, these limited rights have contributed to making the works councils and their activities an element of the industrial relations system in West Germany which is clearly welcomed by workers. It has, furthermore, by providing information and insight into economic mechanisms given trade unions a much better foothold with regard to other aspects of their activities. But the limitations and also the features of the system which constrain workers and trade unions must not be overlooked. The detrimental aspects of the co-determination system will be dealt with in the next sections.

The Impact of the Co-Determination System on Trade Union Structures and Activities

It is obvious from the preceding analysis that the co-determination system has not fundamentally changed the mode of operation of firms or the capitalist system in West Germany, as was the hope of protagonists of economic democracy in the 1920s. The apparent successes of West German capital point to this as well. In addition it must be seen that:
- the co-determination system has not altered the usual economic structures and strategies of management, it has merely forced management to supplement its usual strategies by certain strategies towards works councils and workers' representatives;
- it has not reduced hierarchy in firms, instead it has established a certain but very limited counter-weight to managerial authority, and has itself adopted certain basic hierarchical features on the side of workers and workers' representatives; and
- it has not led to more stable conditions for the pursuit of workers' interests; the chaotic structure of the capitalist economic system is also imposing its "laws" on the co-determination system.

It has also brought severe repercussions for the trade unions and their policies and activities in West Germany. The most important aspect of this is that it has led to a dual system of representation of workers' interest. In particular, the works councils are a second means of representing workers' interests besides the "classical" system of collective bargaining and the trade union structures oriented towards collective bargaining. Initially the works councils were deliberately designed – in the 1950s, under the conservative Adenauer Government – to create competition or a counter-weight against the trade unions, who at that time were markedly and in the majority socialist unions opposing the forces of capitalist restoration in post-war West Germany. This is why the works councils were conceived as being elected in a universal poll by all workers and not only by unionized workers. This is also one of the reasons why from the beginning the right to strike was abrogated. It is only afterwards and against the ideas of the ruling political forces, that the trade unions of the DGB succeeded in making the works councils and the overall co-determination system one of their main domains. Now they usually obtain about 80 % of the seats in works councils' elections.

Apart from the loss of the local plant-based right to strike, trade unions had to pay a substantive price; a shift in intra-union weight away from the shop stewards to the works councils and the increasing influence of workers' representatives from works councils in collective bargaining. Although collective bargaining is a formally separate activity of the trade unions – works councils are not formally entitled to interfere with collective bargaining matters and collective agreements are always superior to company agreements – the information and insights gained by works councils members, of course, enter in many forms into intra-union processes and thus also into collective bargaining.

During the 1960s and most of the 1970s, in the absence of major unemployment problems and with the rapid growth of production in many companies, a spirit of social partnership was developed and spread in the co-determination system. This spirit also penetrated into general trade union activities and trade union consciousness and hence also into collective bargaining.

On the other hand, it is the sobering experience of the recession by many works councils throughout the last 10–12 years which has led trade unions to change their attitude to collective bargaining, an example of which was the strike for the 35 hours week in 1984 (the largest strike in the post-war period).

The introduction of new technology in firms with significant job losses, deskilling of jobs, and new forms of control, etc. has contributed to changing the relationships between works councils and collective bargaining bodies in certain unions at least, vis-à-vis technological change.

To summarize, the five major problems that co-determination presents trade unions with are:

1. the dual system of representation of workers' interest;
2. the spirit of social partnership promoted by the co-determination system;
3. the abrogation of the right to strike on shop floor, plant, and local matters;
4. the subjection of trade union activities in plants to juridical procedures; and
5. the mediative functioning of the basic mechanisms of co-determination (the appeasement function of co-determination in the fight for interests).

Co-Determination and Competence within Trade Unions

Co-determination has had a marked impact as well on the creation and distribution of competence within trade union organizations. First, co-determination has created new spheres of competence within trade unions. The West German co-determination system is extremely reliant on juridical action and interaction and on juridical confrontation with capital in firms. In addition to juridical competence, quite a few areas of intra-firm economic and technological knowledge have to be dealt with by the co-determinators and hence by trade unions. This has led to a considerable shift in trade union training programs where co-determinators are now the primary target group for training in most trade unions.

Secondly, on the other hand, there is to be observed a relative decline in the importance of traditional trade union competencies, for example in mobilizing trade union members, in campaigning, and in organizing strike actions. Shop stewards and shop steward committees have lost ground and momentum substantively in intra-union structures and processes. In West German unions competencies associated with formal institutions and bureaucracies have become much more important to the detriment of competencies associated with social movements.

Thirdly, in view of the complicated juridical, social, economic, technological, and ergonomic matters, which have to be handled by the co-determinators, support by staff from the trade unions has become of great importance. This has also led in many cases – especially in the case of the steel and coal-mining industries – to the close interaction of co-determinators with management staff and especially with the staff of the works director.

The frequent involvement of co-determinators in intra-firm training programs is another result of the co-determination system. In addition to this, co-determination has led to a close interaction of co-determinators and trade union bureaucracies. In recent years the trade union bureaucracies have organized quite a few research projects to support co-determination processes.

Fourthly, within co-determination structures the necessity to create a countervailing competence to that of management has led to tendencies towards the professionalization of members of works councils. It has induced certain pattern of specialization and also contributed to creating a layer of long-term professional co-determinators. The control of works councils by shop stewards and trade union members in a firm is not facilitated by these conditions.

Fifthly, in some unions, as a result, the presidents of the works councils of large companies are imposing their ideas and concepts onto the unions.

Other features of the co-determination system have been operating in favour of trade union activities and policies: the availability of company information, knowledge of the economic context and about business strategies, etc. The fact is, however, that this knowledge and the corresponding competencies can best be used in formal organizations and their procedures; in many cases, it is not of so much value if conditions of social confrontation and unrest prevail.[9]

The competencies of co-determinators is, of course, aligned and delimited by the real opportunities for action and they are, as we have seen, very restricted. Also, co-determination has weakened rather than strengthened "social" competencies within the trade unions.

If the trade unions in West Germany were to take the knowledge and competencies available among co-determinators in order to systematically denounce and challenge the existing economic and social order, then this new knowledge and competencies could play a much more important role than it ever has done in West Germany throughout the long history of co-determination. This, of course, would run against the logic of co-determination and would demand a tremendous change in trade union policy in West Germany. On the other hand, the deterioration of objective economic and social conditions in West Germany throughout the last fifteen years has already led to a remarkable re-orientation in some unions towards the policy of collective bargaining and to a much more sober evaluation of co-determination than in the three previous decades. New concepts of participation and especially of autonomous participation of workers are emerging only slowly – perhaps too slowly? – in the West German trade unions.

---

[9] In cases of conflict the works council is dependent upon management's provision of information, information which in situations of open and accentuated conflict is considered – rightly in most cases – with distrust.

References

Deppe, F. (1969): *Kritik der Mitbestimmung, Partnerschaft oder Klassenkampf?* Frankfurt/M.: I.M.S.F
Handbuch der Mitbestimmung (1981): Köln: Bund-Verlag.
Naphtali, F. (1966): *Wirtschaftsdemokratie*, Frankfurt/M.: Europäische Verlagsanstalt (Neuauflage).

Chapter 5
A Political Bargaining Theory of Co-Determination*

Ad W.M. Teulings

Changes and Adjustments in the System of Industrial Democracy

The works council occupies a central position in the Dutch system of industrial democracy. Its centrality has been increasing in recent years in relation to other elements of this system such as work consultation, work structuring and humanization projects, shop steward organization, collective bargaining, trade union intervention, worker directors, appeals bodies, complaints procedure, and direct forms of action.

The specific significance of the works council within this system is in its relatively greater strategic capacity of involvement and control of the central decision-making processes of management and its greater tactical capacity of being able to move between the alternatives of (limited) participation in or (limited) control over the formation of managerial power.

Several developments have increased the resources available to the works council in this respect, for example:
- the works council's increase in legal powers and autonomy under the revision of the WOR (law on works councils) since 1979, the ARBO law (on working conditions, health, and safety) in 1983, and the new EEC directive in 1984 (Geersing and Van der Heijden 1983, Mulder 1978);
- the further development since 1980 of the CAO (collective bargaining agreements) as an alternative and more flexible instrument of substantive regulation besides the WOR, which also encourages an increase in the works council's formal powers (Looise 1984);

* I wish to thank Martin Smit and Reinald Heddema (SORU) for their part in the design and field work of this study and their comments on a first version of this article.

– the extension since 1982 of the domain where works councils are
  compulsory institutions to include smaller firms (35–100 employees)
  and the public sector (De Johng 1984);
– the trend towards decentralized collective bargaining on work sharing
  and working hours, whereby the works council may develop a
  delegated responsibility as a negotiating partner (Van Zuthem 1984);
– the ending, at the end of the 1970s, of the strategic and tactical
  competition between various elements of industrial democratization,
  especially management-controlled work consultation and union-
  controlled shop steward organization (Teulings et al. 1981, Vaas 1984);
  and
– the marketing, commercialization, and professionalization of works
  council activities (Teulings 1984b).

In the past few years there have been various ways in which the works
council has been able to develop into an established, mature institution.
If, however, we look at the workings of the works councils individually,
then they do not in any way present an even picture in practice. The
opportunities mentioned above are far from being fully used, and
developments even seem to have passed by a considerable number of
works councils. The quick succession of external events has produced a
picture of leading trend-setting works councils and those which follow far
behind. The distance between the leaders and followers has increased
sharply in the past five years. Nevertheless, the pattern of development is
determined by a new type of works council which has flapped its wings,
discovered its outonomous powers, and has grasped the opportunities
afforded by a developing network of supportive institutions within the
system of industrial democracy (Teulings 1986).

The differential capacity of the works councils to cope with the
turbulent environment of this decade can be regarded as a process of
social, natural selection (Aldrich 1979, Hannan and Freeman 1977).
Works councils which were inadequately equipped to meet these changes,
which did not themselves develop the necessary resources of support, and
– last but not least – which lacked adequate strategy, were left straggling
behind. The law (WOR) which makes the existence of a works council
compulsory prevented the stragglers from dying a natural death.

The distance between the leaders and followers, in this social selection
model, should be measured by a central yardstick of effectiveness. For
works councils that is the measure to which they are involved in and
exercise influence upon the managerial decision-making process, representing the collective interests of employees in the organization. This

differentiation in the organizational effectiveness of works councils and of their organizational characteristics is the main subject of this chapter, based on an empirical study of 63 Dutch works councils.

To a certain extent this study is a replication of a previous study, "Works Council Politics in the Netherlands," the fieldwork for which was done in 1980, when the autonomous works councils had only been operating for a very short time. The replication study deals not only with the works councils' use of the instruments of power and the conditions for differential practice in the use of power, but also with different practices in the implementation of legal rights and competencies. Finally this study covers the works councils' practice in dealing with financial and economic information. The results of the latter are published elsewhere on the theme "Opening up the books" (Smit 1984, Teulings et al. 1984a and b).

The Exercise of Co-Determination as Part of a Political Bargaining Process

If the works council aims at influencing the strategic issues of managerial decision-making, then it must take part in a political bargaining process, characterized by a dual rationality. This decision-making, insofar as it is based on rational premises, is affected by industrial and economic considerations and market conformity as well as by a realistic assessment of the conflicting interests involved, the balance of power, and political feasibility (Bacharach and Lawler 1980, Pfeffer 1981). The process of managerial decision-making in a context of co-determination can therefore be divided into a number of stages:

(a) the *"reconnaissance"* phase, including an early check upon possible politically sensitive issues affected by the proposed course of action, allowing the dominant initiator to steer the decision-making process towards feasible and "satisfying" solutions;

(b) the *informal bargaining* phase, generating the "bedrock" arguments pro and contra possible solutions; searching for compromises, internalizing advantages to the dominant coalition, and externalizing disadvantages or costs to parties excluded from the inner circle of decision-makers;

(c) the *external presentation* phase, where a favoured solution is "translated" into a formal *"plan"* or *"proposed decision,"* with "objective," "universalistic," and "public" criteria attached (such as competitiveness, innovation, long-term employment) that may serve to reduce social resistance and increase legitimation; and

(d) the *operational implementation* phase, where external critique, non-compliance, and unpredicted consequences are integrated by allowing changes in the procedure or speed of implementation (Enderud 1980, Koopman et al. 1984).

The position of the works council can then be described in relation to the stage at which it is capable of intervening in this bargaining process or to participate in it. The later the works council becomes involved in this process, the greater, in general, the power distance between the works council and executive management.

It may also happen that the works council is totally excluded from a strategic decision-making process or overlooked as an interested party. In view of the considerable differences in power between top management and the works council, that is not an unlikely event (Bacharach and Baratz 1962, Hövels and Nas 1976, Teulings 1981, Teulings et al. 1984). But mostly, at some phase of the management decision-making process the works council will enter the arena, by means of a formal meeting with management. This entrance is to be expected, if only because the law obliges management to reveal most of its planned decisions to the works council meeting. Consequently, we may distinguish four degrees of possible works council involvement, apart from the works council's total exclusion from the political bargaining process. We may also call these the managerial decision-making functions of the works council.

1. The Works Council's Adjustment Function

The top management of an organization often has good reasons to wait as long as possible before involving the works council in the process of political bargaining (Teulings et al. 1984) and only propose to meet in the fourth stage. In that case the role of the works council does not need to be negligible, as it is feasible, and in practice not unusual, that management anticipates the possible reaction of the works council in an earlier stage. The "preventive effect" of the works council then comes into operation (Koopman et al. 1984: 167). However, in management's eyes the "real" decision-making takes place in the boardroom. Consultation with the works council will then lead only to changes in the form and timing of the decisions' implementation. For management, once a planned decision is put on the agenda of the joint meeting, the final implementation stage has started at last, whereas for the works council this very moment may be viewed as a first step of "reconnaissance." Reconciling these two completely different time perspectives is often the first issue of a political bargaining process.

2. The Works Council's Legitimation Function

In a more favourable situation the works council enters the arena one stage earlier. This may occur when the council is perceived as an additional instrument for the legitimation of strategic decisions taken by management. In addition to or as a more palatable substitute for economic, financial, marketing, and other managerial considerations, the works council is often presented with other, social justifications – sometimes emerging from a pilot discussion with the works council. These legitimations may stand a better chance of being accepted by the workforce-at-large (here the works council representatives are used as a *pars pro toto*). This legitimation stage is seen as particulary necessary with announcements of "bad news" to employees. Establishing a price for compliance with this role is often the second major issue of political bargaining between the two parties.

3. The Works Council's Review Function

A political bargaining process only comes into existence if the works council is able to roll back the managerial decision-making process into its second stage, converting internal and informal bargaining into formal, external, and therefore political bargaining. Here, the law does provide the instruments for entering the arena, and to re-open the second stage of managerial decision-making. To mould the possibility of legal intervention into a key to formal bargaining with management requires, however, considerable know-how and experience. The leverage required is contained in such actions as a formal rejection of the council's intervention, or the original definiton of the situation is abandoned and the nature of the problem to be solved is redefined, and rational and feasible solutions have to be sought in other directions. Although this may look like a case where counter-expertise available to the works council is brought into play, this is not very likely, and certainly not a necessary requirement. It may well be that asking the right questions may trigger off a process of reorientation by management itself.

The Central Issue of Political Bargaining: The Capacity to Create "Negative Dilemmas"

Only the last two cases imply a form of active intervention on the part of the works council with substantive consequences for managerial decision-making. What makes this intervention work? Achieving compliance with a proposed decision is, in this analysis, defined by management as the very last "stumbling block," just before implementation. Any formal intervention by the works council is bound to be perceived as a delay and as an inroad into managerial autonomy. For the works council, however, the proposed "final" decision, presented by management in a joint meeting, is looked at quite differently. The final stage of managerial decision-making will be the first stage of decision-making for the works council (and perhaps the only stage). The works council can only penetrate *ex post facto* the previous decision-making stages by submitting time-consuming counter-proposals and additional conditions.

From management's point of view these delays do inflict costs. But it is precisely the capacity, based in law, of putting a spoke in the wheel of the intended course of decision-making that often provides the works council with a serious sanction which can force management to reconsider its propositions. The legal capacity of the works council to delay implementation by producing "negative advice" or a "counter-proposal" places management in a position where they have no other choice than between two "evils": a *procedural* fight over the right of the works council to intervene (which may last several months); or the acceptance of a *substantive* ("political") bargaining process, allowing some degree of works council influence upon strategic managerial decision-making (which may be less time-consuming and less costly). The legal instrument of works council intervention is in this respect very similar to the collective bargaining instrument of a strike or work stoppage to a trade union negotiator. The costs of interrupted production have to be compared with the costs of renegotiating over working conditions, accepting a certain increase in wage costs. Rational works council politics imply the design of a similar negative dilemma for management, where possible procedural costs exceed the expected costs of substantive influence by reconsidering the intended decision(s).

This political bargaining model of co-determination obviously contrasts with co-management and participation models. In co-management models it is assumed that employee influence is ultimately based upon some form of "expert power" of workers or their representatives. The political bargaining approach does not exclude the possibility of untapped workers' expertise, but the capacity for works council's influence is not made dependent on it. The capacity to create negative dilemmas for management is seen as a necessary precondition for gaining access to the managerial decision-making process on strategic policy issues.

The works council is thereby a formal participant in the labour process of management (Teulings 1986). In participation models of co-determination the assumption is that the influence of workers' representatives is related to, or even founded upon, workers' control. The political bargaining approach does not deny the relevance of grass roots support, but again, the capacity for works council's influence is not made dependent on it. Organized employee power and trade union power may determine the level of formal rules and rights available to the works council. Once established, and legally or contractually binding, these rules and rights do create an autonomous source of works council power provided they have the "professional" know-how and experience to use them.

This capacity does not bring company affairs to a long-lasting halt; the "legal" hand of the works council is not strong enough for that. The works council also has other ways, in addition to the legal instruments, of wielding influence (Teulings 1981).

Right and Might: Instruments of Co-Determination Open to the Works Council

The Dutch works council has several legal instruments available for breaking into management's decision-making process. We consider the use of these as an essential condition for starting the process of political bargaining with the management (Mintzberg 1983: 23). Only in this way is the works council able to roll back the process of managerial decision-making. In order to proceed with our outline of a political bargaining theory, a further distinction has to be made here between two kinds of instruments: legal interventions and legitimate instruments of power. What follows is a short description of each of them.

1. Legal Interventions

The law on works councils opens up a number of forms of legal intervention by the works council vis-à-vis management:

- The exercise of temporary veto rights or advisory rights. Management is obliged to request the works council's permission or consent on most strategic decisions as listed in the WOR. The latter can reply with rejection, with negative advice, or with conditional advice, i. e. counter-proposals. In the case of positive advice, the works council has admittedly been formally consulted, but in terms of a political bargaining approach we can only talk of participation in the process of legitimation. If the works council decides to give a negative advice, binds positive advice to conditions, or submits counter-proposals, the road towards implementation of a decision is blocked for some time.
- Actual exercise of the right of initiative. In exercising this right, management is obliged to respond to the works council initiative with "all information and data in sufficient time which the latter may reasonably require to fulfil its duties." Again, the use of this article can be regarded as indicative of an attempt to exert influence.

The statutory rights of the works council and the legality of the collective interests of the workers are at stake here. Legal interventions, however, deal only with the acquisition of *access to power*.

2. Legitimate Instruments of Power

The issue of legitimate power arises when this access fails to bring about substantive influence, in other words, as soon as management refuses to follow up these interventions and to reconsider the issue(s) at stake. In such a clash of interests the works council can look for other extra-statutory but nonetheless legitimate instruments of power open to it to reinforce its bargaining position.

A distinction can be made between four kinds of instruments of power which are used in practice to a greater or lesser extent by works councils to exert pressure on management when further consultation fails (Teulings 1981: 68):

a. Forms of Consultation Boycott

By this we mean instruments such as suspending consultation (temporary boycott), or in a much stronger form, collective with-drawal from the works council.

b. Forms of Mobilizing "Public" Support

By this we mean instruments such as publishing an internal statement and informing the daily press, with a view to obtaining public support.

c. Intervention of Third Parties

This includes instruments such as involving the shareholder representatives ("Council of Commissioners"), the bi-partite Industrial Commission, or in the final instance the cantonal judge or Industrial Court.

d. Mobilization by Union Action

The works council can mobilize the support of the (organized) workers in the organization which may result in demonstrations, a suspension of work, or finally by a local strike or sit-in.

We speak of instruments of power because the works council can resort to them when it considers further talks in the joint consultation meeting to be useless; they are aimed at changing a (planned) decision contrary to management's preferences.

The use of these instruments does not automatically produce substantive influence in the decision-making process. The reconsideration of a decision to make it more favourable to workers' collective interests can also mean that the decision itself is not changed, but that other ways are found of compensating workers.

Managerial Effectiveness of the Works Council

The result of the works council's attempts to exert influence, either by formal legal intervention or by using specific instruments of power, should be apparent in a certain degree of influence on the companies' decision-making. That is, after all, the final criterion for managerial effectiveness of the works council.

In our empirical analysis we will therefore relate the differential use of the works council's capacity for legal intervention and legitimate power to the degree or level of influence on decision-making, within the domain of decisions to which the works council is legally entitled.

The empirical analysis is based on two simple hypotheses:

1. The works council's involvement with strategic, managerial decision-making increases in proportion to the number of legal interventions and/or instruments of power used.

In other words: the works council must actively intervene in order to gain access to management's decision-making procedures, thereby creating a margin for negotiation with management and thus producing chances of a more even balance between workers' collective interests and business interests.

2. The use of instruments of power determines the extent to which the works council actually influences the decision-making in the organization.

This study uses a method of estimating actual influence, according to the conventional Tannenbaum technique (Tannenbaum 1968). The method is not without objections but has a reasonable validity for use in comparative studies. Two subjective estimates of the works council's influence were employed, one at the start and one at the conclusion of the interviews. This second assessment is more conservative due to the presentation of various evaluation criteria during the interview. Both estimates, however, produce the same correlations so that we can talk of a consistent, albeit subjective, judgment. The latter estimate is employed as a criterion by which the effectiveness of legal interventions and the use of legitimate instruments of power by the works councils is compared. The model of this empirical analysis is summarized in Figure 1.

Research Design

The study was carried out under a multi-annual research programme *"Differentiation in the system of industrial democracy in the Netherlands,"* by the Sociology of Organizations Research Unit of the University of Amsterdam. The present study had two parts: (a) a follow-up of the 1980 study "Works council politics in the Netherlands" (Teulings 1981), and (b) a study of the employers' practice of disclosure of financial and economic information and the use by works councils of information, advisory and veto rights. The aim of this second part was to reveal by empirical comparison of works councils' practices the actual variety in scope for exerting employee influence and to predict what external contingencies could restrict or widen this scope. This chapter deals mainly with the results of the replication study.

Model of Analysis

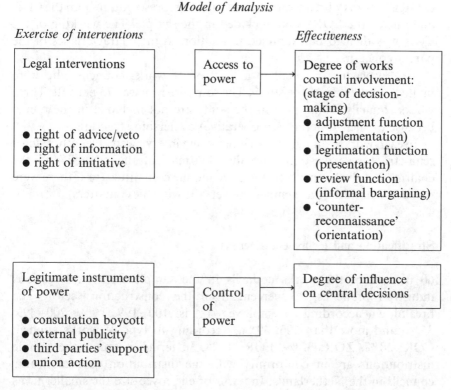

Figure 1: Works council's influence on strategic managerial decision-making

Population and Sampling

A model of stratified random sampling was chosen to cover as wide as possible a variation in environmental contingency factors. Twelve industrial and four services branches of industry were selected from a population of 1500 listed businesses operating in the Netherlands. Then three companies per branch of industry were drawn: the largest firm in terms of staff, a medium-sized (approx. 500 employees), and smaller (approx. 150 employees) firm. The 48 businesses chosen were divided according to the structure of the corporate firm. Firms may have a stratified structure with a central works council (COR), an intermediate (divisional) level, and a number of local works councils (LOR). An organization with a simple structure only has one single works council

(ZOR). In firms with a stratified structure of representation both the COR and one of the LORs were included in the sample. The working of the COR was then to be examined in relation to the characteristics of the parent concern.

This procedure resulted in a total of 91 works councils who were invited to take part in the study. The response rate was 73 percent. Three works councils taking part in the study are not included in the report because of their different (co-operative) ownership structure.

In each works council two members were interviewed at length, using a semi-structured questionnaire: the chairman of the council and the chairman of the council's financial/economic committee (or if there were no such committee, a member conversant with these matters).

Stratification and Representativeness

60 percent of the works councils in the sample were from various industrial branches, 13 percent from the construction sector. The breakdown according to employee size is: 100–199: 16%, 200–499: 35%, and more than 500: 49%. According to type of works council: COR: 28%, ZOR: 32%, LOR: 40%. In terms of sector the sample distributions are in conformity with the distribution over all works councils in the Netherlands. In terms of employee size the smaller firms are (deliberately) under-represented; similarly the COR is strongly over-represented.

Some Empirical Results

The statutory availability of legal powers and rights does not automatically mean that these will be used to influence decision-making in the firm. The manager, for example, can fail to bring a decision on which formal advice must be sought to the attention of the works council (deviating from standard procedure). Or, the works council can limit itself to a formal dutiful discussion of a planned decision submitted to it (ritualism). Management's failure to consult and the works council's perfunctory discussion are frequently observed phenomena (Teulings et al. 1984: 47).

With regard to the right of formal advice, generally speaking, a real effort to exert influence – as explained earlier – only exists when the works council proposes conditions, counter-proposals, or some form of negotiation which can lead to a re-evaluation of employee interests.

This interventionist use of exercising formal rights implies that the works council makes a deliberate effort to influence. The substantive effectiveness of such an effort has yet to be established; the attempt alone again does not automatically mean that decision-making is substantively affected. The frequency of formally legal attempts to exert influence and the effectiveness of such attempts can vary greatly from one works council to another. Table 1 shows the average outcomes of the 63 works councils in our sample.

Table 1: Use and Effectiveness of Legal Interventions under the Law on Works Councils

Influencing attempts	Use	Effectiveness (in percentages)	
a. *Right of formal advice* gives negative or conditional advice	[1]	[2]	[3]
– single or first attempt	38	30	54
– second attempt	33	38	44
– third attempt	11	45	86
lays down conditions/submits counter-proposals on	[4]	[5]	
– general company state of affaires	15	10-6	
– annual accounts	2	7-6	
– multi-annual plan	15	19-19	
b. *Right of initiative*	[6]	[7]	
	3	100	
c. *Right to information*		[8]	
	16	50	

[1] frequency of intervention: percentage of works councils giving negative or conditional formal advice (the total number of works councils in the sample = 63, in 1983/84).

[2] *"counter-reconnaissance"* effectiveness: percentage of an interventions where the works council could exert influence at the orientation phase of management decision-making.

[3] *review-effectiveness*: percentage of interventions where conditions/counter-proposals were partly or totally taken into account.

[4] frequency of intervention: percentage of all requests for formal advice, where works council laid down conditions or submitted counter-proposals.

[5] over-all effectiveness: percentage of interventions which *"considerably influenced"* the outcome of managerial decision-making; the first percentage indicates the subjective measure of influence before the interview, the second percentage at the end of the interview.

[6] right of initiative or right to information exercised by preparing written documents (once or several times).

[7] effectiveness: percentage of interventions with "considerable influence."

[8] percentage of requests for further information granted.

Use and Effectiveness of Formal Right of Advice

Compared with other available forms of legal intervention, the formal
right of advice is used most frequently as a method of changing the
planned policy of management. More than one third (38 percent) of the
works councils studies had used this form of intervention at least once
with management during its present term of office. In 33 percent of the
works councils this happened twice, and 11 percent of the works councils
intervened on at last three different occasions (Table 1, column 1). The
effectiveness of these interventions, based on the right of advice, is
established in two ways. Firstly (column 2) by calculating the influential
interventions (as perceived by the works council representatives). This we
referred to earlier as a *counter-connaissance* function. In 30 percent of
these works council interventions there follows a process of reorientation
by management. A striking feature is that this type of influence increases
with the frequency with which works councils intervene. The success rate
rises from 30 percent at one intervention to 45 percent with frequent use
(during the term of office). Recurrent resort to legal intervention does
seem to increase the chance that a works council may actually have a
steering function. We may define an instrument of influence as being
effective if it produces results in 50 percent of the cases where it is used.
Using that criterion, it is not generally effective in producing a
reorientation in management decision-making.

However, legal interventions based on the formal right of advice do
seem to be more effective in reopening the subsequent decision-making
stage of *informal bargaining*; in more than half of the cases where it *does*
intervene (Table 1, column 3), the works council manages to introduce a
partial review of planned decisions and convince or force management to
open a discussion with the works council about weights attached to
alternatives, previously the prerogative of informal bargaining within
management itself. Planned externalization of costs, in particular those
bearing upon the employees, are partly re-internalized. On that basis we
may consider legal intervention, based on the formal right of advice, an
effective review instrument, as it tends to strengthen the bargaining
function and negotiating scope of the works council, especially when used
recurrently.

Use and Effectiveness of the Right to Information and the Right of Initiative

In the disclosure of the "general company state of affairs" in the annual accounts or the multiannual plan which the WOR (art. 31) makes compulsory, subjects may be brought up under article 25 of the right of advice such as issues concerning the transfer of control, participation in the assets of another undertaking, reorganization, or investments. Here, too, the works council is entitled to make written proposals or lay down conditions. 15 percent of works councils used this facility (only 2 percent in discussing the annual accounts). The perceived effects of this type of intervention is very limited; in one out of ten, or at most one in five, cases it had a "considerable" influence on decision-making. The striking difference in effectiveness, as compared with the right of formal advice (Table 1 (a)) may be due to the fact that in the first case management is formally obliged to request advice, whereas in the second case the works council gives its advice without being asked. In the first case management may well anticipate possible opposition from the works council. This may well explain the difference in resistance. Another explanation is that the works council is less well equipped to deal with the more complex financial issues at stake here.

There is also seldom a request (16 percent) for further information under the right to information. However, when used it is a fairly effective instrument. The right of initiative is hardly ever used.

Summarizing, we may conclude that in practice the works council generally has no independent initiating and steering function in the managerial decision-making process with respect to strategic decisions. But this does make the few works councils who deviate from this general tendency all the more interesting. In general, however, works council influence is mostly exercised through making occasional inroads into the informal bargaining process of management and may act as a counterbalance of their interests. We may conclude that works councils are able to exercise power by using the legal means available. Little else could be expected; the works council, after all, is not an instrument of determination, but an organ of co-determination and cannot be judged according to criteria of power equalization or counter-management.

Use and Effectiveness of Instruments of Power: Changes in Trends due to the Economic Crises

Despite the economic crises and resulting weakened position of the trade unions, the works councils surveyed here often used additional instruments of power in situations where further consultation and the use of formal legal means showed no signs of progress.

A study in 1980 showed that 68 percent of works councils had used one or more instruments of power; the present study (1983/84) revealed an almost identical percentage, namely 70 percent.

Sampling differences, however, could affect this figure: instruments of power are generally used more in larger firms and in those with a higher union density among works council representatives, especially of the FNV, the major federation of of Dutch trade unions (Teulings 1981). Although the present replication study covers more large concerns and firms, the average union density is about the same as compared to 68 percent in the 1980 study. The percentage of FNV members in the works councils is 47 percent; in the 1980 study it was 43 percent. The FNV has a stronger position in the follow-up study; this is even more apparent in the number of works councils with an FNV-majority: in no fewer than 53 percent of works councils the FNV group forms a majority as against 35 percent in 1980. A breakdown of these figures does suggest that this difference can only partly be explained by sample variations. The increase in works councils with an FNV majority does seem to reflect a recent trend; the position of the FNV and CNV groups in works councils was considerably strengthened in the period 1980–1984, at the cost particularly of unorganized labour but also of smaller clerical unions (MHP and Unie BLP). An important explanation could be that more of the unorganized workers do not complete their term of office and more easily stand down as a member of the works council when the business is going through an economic crisis. Another explanation is offered by a slightly falling interest in works council elections, according to the turn-out figures. Falling interest is particularly prevalent in firms with a large number of unorganized labour. A slight drop is seen in firms with a high degree of FNV/CNV organization.

Although the use of instruments of power did not drop in the serious economic crisis of 1980–84, there has nonetheless been a remarkable shift since 1980 in the choice of instrument. This shift could be seen against the background of a gradually *increasing differentiation* in the way in which works councils function. The number of works councils that make no use whatsoever of instruments of power when consultation fails remained about the same (30 percent now, 32 percent in 1980). The number of works councils that did resort to one or more instruments also remained the same, but their degree of "militantism" changed: the number of power instruments brought into operation has increased. Works councils as a whole have not become more militant, but the militant councils have often been more active: *"militant" and "non-militant" works councils have moved further apart.*

The most striking change, however, is in the *type* of instrument used. Table 2 compares the use of various instruments in 1980 and 1983/84. Despite the increase in the number of works councils with a FNV majority in the 1983/84 study, fewer *unionist instruments of power* (1, 6, 7, 9, 12, 14)

Table 2: Changes in Trends in the Use by Works Councils of Legitimate Instruments of Power, 1980–1984 (in Percentages)

Instruments applied	national random sample (1980	follow-up study (1983/84)	difference (1980–84)
1. calling in trade union officials	43	38	− 5
2. suspending meetings with management	39	30	− 9
3. strongly worded statement in staff paper (house journal)	33	64	+ 31
4. calling in external consultants	26	34	+ 8
5. appeal to the council of commissioners	18	35	+ 17
6. supporting demonstration during lunch time	12	10	− 2
7. supporting short work stoppage	11	5	− 6
8. publication in daily press	10	10	0
9. publication in trade union paper	10	5	− 5
10. appeal to Industry Commission	9	25	+ 16
11. collective withdrawal from council	4	10	+ 6
12. supporting strike action	3	5	+ 2
13. addressing the Parliament	3	12	+ 9
14. supporting a sit-in	1	2	+ 1
15. appeal to cantonal judge	1	5	+ 4

are used. There is admittedly a slight increase in strikes and sit-ins, but as the 1983/84 study covers a larger proportion of big firms (where the FNV generally has a stronger position in the works council), one could expect a higher level of industrial action such as work stoppages, strikes, and sit-ins from 1980 to 1984. A breakdown of these figures by firm size confirms this view.

Under the category of *public support* methods there has been a similar change: the use of the "weaker" form of internal public support (3) increased considerably, but the stronger counterpart of seeking external public support (8, 9) did not.

Recourse to "third parties" (4, 5, 10, 13, 15) is quite a common phenomenon in the 1983/84 study. A clear increase is seen in recourse to the bi-partite Industry Commission and to the Council of Commissioners. This figure may be affected, however, by the larger proportion of works councils from larger concerns in the second survey.

Overall, these changes may well be interpreted as reflecting an adaptation by works councils to crisis conditions: works councils think twice before calling for trade union action, become more "introverted" when looking for support, but especially more often seek the support of authoritative third parties besides the trade unions.

The use of instruments of power may not in itself lead to results in the sense of actually changing the substantive outcome of decision-making. The effectiveness of the instruments mentioned above varies. We consider instruments effective if they produce results in at least 50 percent of the cases used, measured as a perceived "(very) considerable influence" on management's policy (Teulings 1981: 132).

Here, too, we should expect that the worsening economic crisis from 1980–1984 has lead management to be less receptive to pressure from the works council and so to a drop in the effectiveness of instruments of power. Table 3 gives a clear indication of this. The general picture is that the changes in effectiveness are much greater than in the use of the instruments (as shown in Table 2). *The economic crisis does not affect so much the use of the instruments of power as their effectiveness.*

The number of effective instruments has dropped. The effect of a *work stoppage*, *strike*, or *sit-in* has dropped dramatically, as has incidentally the effect of political pressure (recourse to the Parliament) or corporative procedure (appeal to the Industry Commission with its parity structure). Typically, union action is on average at best marginally effective.

On the other hand, the effectiveness of calling in external consultants has increased sharply, as has recourse to other external parties such as the

Table 3: Changes in Trends in the Effectiveness of Instruments Used, 1980–1984 (in Percentages)

Instruments applied	Degree of effectiveness[1]		
	national random sample (1980)	follow-up study (1983/84)	difference (1980–84)
1. calling in trade union officials	53*	67*	+ 14
2. suspending consultation	51*	58*	+ 7
3. strongly worded statement in staff paper	48	4	− 6
4. calling in external consultants	50*	80*	+ 30
5. appeal to the council of commissioners	56*	70*	+ 14
6. demonstration during lunch time	50*	100*	+ 50
7. supporting short work stoppage	64*	33	− 31
8. publication in daily press	50*	50*	0
9. publication in trade union paper	30	33	+ 3
10. appeal to Industry Commission	56*	37	− 19
11. collective withdrawal from council	100*	43	− 57
12. supporting strike action	75*	50*	− 25
13. addressing the Parliament	33	17	− 16
14. supporting a sit-in	75*	50*	− 25
15. appeal to cantonal judge	50*	62*	+ 12

[1] Effectiveness = in the opinion of the works council concerned the use of this instrument had a "(very) considerable influence" on management's decision-making.
* "Effective instruments": more than 50 % chance of positive outcome ("(very) considerable influence").

Council of Commissioners, the trade union officials, and to a lesser extent the cantonal judge. If the effect of trade union action and political pressure seems to have diminished in favour of external support, the demonstration forms an exception to the rule; the effect of this form of symbolic action (where the firm does not suffer any economic danger) has increased in the opinion of those concerned.

This exception may explain why other forms of union action are (seen as) less effective: the use of heavy economic sanctions at a time of crisis may seem to be a double-edged weapon. At any rate, economic sanctions are less frequently applied, and when used it is less likely that the desired outcome is achieved.

The changes in trends observed in the use and effectiveness of instruments of power in times of a serious economic crisis (1980–1984) all point in the same direction to an increased gap between the "followers" and the "leaders":

– the relative size of the two types of works councils may remain the same, but the followers are becoming more amenable and the leaders often more militant;
– there is no decreasing propensity to use power but an increasing preference to use "milder" forms: mass mobilization by union action is resorted to less quickly. Workers and their representatives tend to become more "selective" in their choice of instruments which are examined more carefully for their aim and possible effect. The fact that various forms of mass mobilization have not produced such obvious results in recent times will further constrain the decision to use them again;
– support is sought often from "authoritative" third parties, such as external consultants, the cantonal judge, and the Council of Commissioners. Recent experience has also shown that these latter instruments are fairly effective, in view of the prevailing economic situation.

Studies into the effects of the economic crisis on consciousness and militantism of union members have produced a similar picture (Teulings 1983).

The more "selective" choice of instruments of power could be described as a fairly rational, calculative approach to the use of power instruments. A high degree of rationality in this choice is also evident from a more detailed "issue-analysis" (see Teulings 1982: 151). Although according to the present studies, instruments of power are used especially when consultation on "strategic policy decisions" fails (41 percent of the works councils use one or more instruments in this case), some instruments are used in response to specific issues, suggesting a rational reflection on the substance of the contentious policy. The works council brings pressure to bear in financial and economic matters, particularly by bringing in external consultants, issuing strongly worded statements in the staff paper, calling in the trade union officals, appealing to the council of commissioners, and taking it to The Hague. The industrial sit-in is only used by the works council with respect to factory closure and mass redundancies. Decisions concerning personnel policy and employment conditions are met with one or more instruments of power by 43 percent of the works councils. The particular means used in this domain are: involving trade union officials and issuing strongly worded statements in the staff paper. Strike action is only used in an attempt to influence wages and working conditions.

At present, economic decisions and policies on employment conditions form the main areas of intervention for the works councils. On these issues they are inclined to resort to instruments of power, and several (different) instruments are used. This is the practice of a good 40 percent of the works councils studied. As compared with the situation some 10–15 years ago, this is an astounding growth and development in the quality of works council functioning (Hövels and Nas 1976). Against this the other work councils in our survey hardly intervene at all. This is another illustration of the differentiation in works council functioning in the Netherlands, despite their common legal basis.

Discussion

Right and Might of the Works Council

In analytical terms, but also in the view of many works council members, a distinction has to be made between forms of legal intervention as covered by the law (WOR) and forms of exercising power. This distinction formed the starting point in the presentation of the results of this study. That distinction, however, reinforces a false impression met in many studies on works councils, namely that there is an open choice in voluntaristic terms, between complying with the law and excercising its own power. Or between opting for "the legal way" and rejecting the exercise of power as illegal or illegitimate, or placing power above the law. Such a juxtaposition would, however, in view of the actual practice of works councils as observed in this study, be quite wrong. Legal interventions are found to also contain forms of exercising power which bear direct sanctions for the entrepreneur. But legal interventions do normally imply formal, legal sanctions: only occasionally is management obliged to change its decision after an appeal body has been called in. The real nature of the sanctions under the WOR are social and economic. A dispute with the works council may damage the public prestige of management, who may be quite sensitive to this. Confrontation with the works council may decrease the legitimacy of the decision: pushing through a decision whose legitimacy has been called into question can lead to a greater divergence between the original aim and final outcome of the decision, and so be detrimental to the effectiveness of management. But the major factor at stake may be management efficiency in purely economic terms: intervention by the works council can lead to a costly suspension of the decision-making process, i.e. a *stoppage of the labour process of management*. In view of a prolonged conflict, management may feel more inclined to allow some degree of substantive influence to the workers' representatives. Both choices bring about costs; their balance will determine whether to proceed forward into procedural conflict, or "backward" into renewed political bargaining and substantive compromise.

Stripped of its idealistic connotations of co-determination, legal intervention by the works council is on a par with a *stoppage of the operational labour process* at the implementation stage. A work stoppage also forces a decision between two "evils": renegotiation losses versus production losses.

Table 4: Relation Between the Frequency of Legal Intervention and Legitimate Exercise of Power

Legal interventions	Legitimate exercise of power
a. Right of formal advice (art. 25 WOR)	
– once	0
– twice	+ +
– three times	+ +
b. Right to information (art. 31a WOR)	
– discussion on general state of affairs	+ + +
– annual accounts	0
– multi-annual plan	+ + +
c. Right of initiative (art. 23 para. 4 WOR)	+ +
d. General right of information (art. 31 WOR)	+ + +

Notes:
Test: tau-b in the table (almost) significant relations are indicated by corresponding p-values:

+: .05 < p < .10
++: .01 < p < .05
+++: .001 < p < .01

Theoretically there is therefore no difference between legal interventions and the use of other legitimate instruments of power. And in empirical terms the use of legal interventions and of legitimate instruments of power are correlated. Works councils, for example, which exercise their right of formal advice in an active way also tend to use more instruments of power. The same is true of the right to information and the right of initiative (Table 4).

An Empirical Typology of Works Council Functioning

A significant correlation does not inform us about the direction of that relationship. Is the propensity to use instruments of power a *precondition* for exercising one's legal rights, or is it the other way round: are instruments of power only used when the works council actually tries to put these formal legal rights into practice? A further elaboration of our results does seem to point to the first conclusion (as shown in Table 4).

Legal interventions to exert influence do not take place in works councils which refrain from using instruments of power. On the other hand, instruments of power *are* used in works councils which do not make any attempt to exert influence by legal means. This applies not only to the use of the legal right of formal advice but equally to the right of initiative and the right to information.

This conditional relationship becomes stronger if the particular form of legal intervention is more exceptional, that is, the proportion of works councils practicing this form of intervention drops. Thus legal intervention to influence decision-making concerning the annual accounts or the multi-annual planning and use of the right of initiative only occurs in works councils which have used more than two "strong" instruments of power. This suggests a curvilinear relationship. It suggests that four types of works councils should be distinguished with respect to their orientation towards strategic decision-making:

1. The "Traditional" Works Council

This is the council that prefers to have nothing to do with instruments of power and therefore shies away from actually using legal rights as an instrument for exerting influence on the company policy. This orientation reminds us of the compliant atmosphere of the 1950's with its "joint consultation" without actual co-determination.

2. The "Radical" Works Council

This council is like the type first developed at the beginning of the 1970's: as the outpost of the shop steward organization in the company policy-making process. Within this orientation works councils make little or no use of formal legal interventions but do resort to various instruments of power, in particular "unionist" interventions, to influence decision-making.

3. The "Rationally Political" Works Council

This type of works council increased in importance at the beginning of the eighties. Where necessary, they use instruments of power in addition to legal interventions if normal consultation fails to produce desired outcomes.

In our sample of 63 firms we did *not* meet a "legalistic" works council, i.e. one which would use its legal rights to exert influence on management's decision-making but then *refrain* from using instruments of power. There is, however, a remaining category which can best be typified as follows:

4. The "Ritualistic" Works Council

This council, when presented by management with proposed decisions for a formal advice, does not commit itself to any intervention designed to influence such decisions: the decisions are discussed, questions are asked and answered, but positive advice is always the outcome. One may suggest, of course, that these works councils are always presented with decisions that are favourable to the interests of the workforce. But this is unlikely. In their own opinion these works councils – compared with other councils (which actively use power and/or rights) – exert the least influence on decision-making. Giving positive formal advice is therefore more of a bureaucratic gesture, a ritual act.

Leading Works Councils and Followers

The 1979 Law on Works Councils is itself a retarded product of the political and social situation of the seventies which favoured organized labour. They were almost immediately put to a hard test in a period of economic crisis with considerably less favourable circumstances for labour. The crisis often caused the path toward the gradual accession of new rights and obligations for management and works councils to be cut off. Many a council felt it had been thrown in at the deep end and faced with responsibilities it would have preferred to avoid. The potentially divisive problems and subjects for decisions in these times of crisis and restructuring encouraged the development of political bargaining strategies even by those works councils who considered these strategies as less undesirable and somewhat daunting. For the "leading" works councils in the Netherlands, however, the developing practice became to use instruments of power to supplement active legal intervention.

On the one hand, the economic crisis may have strengthened the need for the works councils to use instruments of power, on the other hand – as has been shown –, it affected both the choice between various available instruments of power and their effectiveness. The reduced effectiveness can be explained in the decreasing effectiveness of union action. But another important factor has been the increased "weight" of the issues at stake in meetings with management. The more important or strategic a decision is, the smaller the works council's *chances* are of actually influencing it, not only because of greater opposition by management to changes from the council, but also because of the constraints, perceived by both parties, from the "market," the "competition," and "technology." Management may feel its hands tied under these "imperative" conditions. The greater the perceived constraints, the more limited the room for managerial choice, and the smaller the opportunities for influence.

Growing external constraints will therefore increase the differences in the way the works councils operate. There is a growing gap between leading councils who know how to use the opportunities available to exert pressure and are willing to do so, despite the limitations, and the followers who often yield to the pressure of circumstances in an early stage and refrain from action. Leading works councils engage in "radical" and "rationally political" co-determination. They play a pioneering role in the system of industrial democracy because their activities often come to be seen as an example by others. Their role is widely published through the external network of trade unions, consultants, works council training centres, the press, and appeal bodies.

The real stragglers are those works councils which are isolated from this external network and so miss the opportunity of learning from the experience of others.

References

Abrahamsson, B. (1980): *The Rights of Labor*, Beverly Hills: Sage Publications.

Aldrich, H. (1979): *Organizations and Environments*, Englewood Cliffs, N.J.: Prentice-Hall.

Andriessen, J.H.T.J. et al. (1984): *Medezeggenschap in Nederlandse bedrijven*, Amsterdam: Noord-Hollandsche Uitgevers Maatschappij.

Bacharach, P. and Baratz, M.S. (1962): Two Faces of Power, *American Political Science Review*, 56: 947–952.

Bacharach, P. and Lawler, E.J. (1980): *Power and Politics in Oganization*: San Francisco/London: Jossey-Bass Inc.

Enderud, H. (1980): Administrative Leadership in Organized Anarchies, *Int. Journal of Management in Higher Education*, 12 (2): 235–253.

Geersing, B. and Heijden, P.F. van der (1983): *Rechtspraak Medezeggenschapsrecht 1971–1981*, Alphen aan den Rijn: Samsom.

Hannan, M.T. and Freeman, J. (1977): The Population Ecology of Organization, *American Journal of Sociology*, 82: 929–946.

Hövels, B.W.M. and Nas, P. (1976): *Ondernemingsraad en Medezeggenschap*, Alphen aan den Rijn: Samsom.

Jongh, J. de (1984): De voorsprong van de achterstand: medezeggenschap bij de overheid, *M & O*, (6): 501–509.

Koopman, P.L. et al. (1984): Rationaliteit bij reallocatie, *M & O*, 38 (2): 151–170.

Looise, J.C. (1984): *CAO en Medezeggenschap*, Enschede: TH Twente afd. Bedrijfskunde (report).

Mintzberg, S. (1983): *Power in and around Organizations*, Englewood Cliffs, N.J.: Prentice-Hall.

Mulder, M. (1978): *De zelfstandige ondernemingsraad*, Leiden: Stenfert Kroese.

Pfeffer, J. (1981): *Power in Organizations*, Boston/London: Pitman.

Sainsaulieu, R. et al. (1983): *La démocratie en organisation*, Paris: Librairie des Méridiens.

Smit, M. (1984): *Ondernemingsraad en Bedrijfsinformatie*, Amsterdam: Universiteit van Amsterdam, SORU (report).

Tannenbaum, A.S. (1968): *Control in Organizations*, New York: McGraw-Hill.

Teulings, A.W.M. (1981): *Ondernemingsraadpolitiek in Nederland*, Amsterdam: Van Gennep.

Teulings, A.W.M. (1983): *Strijd en Zekerheid, een onderzoek naar ledenverlies en ledenbinding van de vakbeweging in crisistijd*, Amsterdam: Univ. van Amsterdam, SORU (report).

Teulings, A.W.M. (1984a): The Social, Cultural, and Political Setting of Industrial Democracy, In: Bernhard Sorge (eds.), *International Perspectives on Organizational Democracy*, Chichester: John Wiley.

Teulings, A.W.M. (1984b): Vijf jaar WOR, optimisme gerechtvaardigt, *Or-Informatie*, 10 (7/8): 22–28.72

Teulings, A.W.M. (1985): *Ontwikkelingen in het Systeem van Industriele Democratie*, Amsterdam: Univ. von Amsterdam, SORU (report).

Teulings, A.W.M. (1986): Managerial Labour Processes in Organised Capitalism; the Power of Corporate Management and the Powerlessness of the Manager,

In: D. Knights and H. Willmott (eds.), *Managing the Labour Process*, Aldershot: Gower.

Teulings, A.W.M. et al. (1981): *De Nieuwe Vakbondstrategie*, Alphen aan den Rijn: Samsom.

Teulings, A.W.M. et al. (1984): Opening van de Boeken, *Or-Informatie*, 10 (9): 43–49 and (10): 13–20, 47.

Vaas, F. (1984): Van zelfbestuur als ideaal, *M & O*, 38 (6): 522–530.

Zuthem, H.J. van (1984): Uitzicht en uitbouw van medezeggenschap, *M & O*, 38 (6): 541–550.

Part II
Worker Co-operatives and Labour-Owned Firms

Introduction

Chris Cornforth

As we saw in Part I, most forms of workers' participation or co-determination in the West still give workers little real influence over the key decisions affecting the enterprise. Control rests firmly in the hands of the owners, or management as their representatives. As a result, some advocates of greater industrial democracy have been attracted to worker co-operatives and labour-owned firms where, in theory at least, workers have the ultimate control over the firm.

During these last fifteen years the number of worker co-operatives and labour-owned firms in most Western countries has increased rapidly. A number of factors have influenced this growth. Some co-operatives have arisen out of the alternative and youth movements of the 1960's and the early 1970's. They were formed by people seeking more democratic and less alienating forms of work where they could produce goods or services that they thought were socially useful. Others were promoted by activists on the "left" as a means of increasing workers' control of the economy. Often these firms were taken over by workers after they had failed. Increasingly since the late 1970's many co-operatives have been set up for more pragmatic reasons to create jobs for their members.

The degree of control that workers in co-operatives can exert over the enterprise has been the topic of some debate. Although workers have the right to make decisions concerning their enterprise, any organisation is constrained by external factors, such as the product and labour markets in which they operate. Given that the vast majority of co-operatives are small businesses, these constraints can be very severe. As a result some critics of co-operatives on the "left" have gone so far as to suggest that the choices left open to workers will be minimal and that co-operatives will inevitably degenerate into capitalist businesses. Others (see Cornforth et al. 1988) argue that degeneration is not inevitable and that the internal and external barriers to co-operative development can be overcome. In particular there is a good deal of theory and empirical evidence to suggest that co-operatives are better able to resist these pressures towards degeneration if they are linked together and have their own support structure.

Three of the chapters in Part II are concerned in one way or another with support structures for co-operatives and labour-owned firms. The chapter by Cornforth examines in more detail the barriers to development that co-operatives face and the functions a support structure will need to perform to help overcome these. In addition, drawing on the experience of the UK, he examines some of main dilemmas that co-operative support organisations are likely to face in practice. Woodworth's chapter suggests that the relationship between consultants, or workers in support organisations, and labour-owned firms will have to be very different from the conventional model of management consultancy. Based on his work with one labour-owned firm, he begins to outline a new model for consultancy that is designed to empower workers. Blyton's chapter examines the role of a centre established by the Wales Trades Union Congress to promote and assist co-operative development in Wales. He suggests that over-ambitious objectives and the failure to develop good relationships with other local bodies supporting co-operatives may have limited the centre's success. Again he highlights the problems co-operatives face because they are small businesses, and suggests that co-operatives researchers could learn more from the expanding field of small business research.

Kamdem's chapter looks at the difficulties of pursuing self-management in a Third World country, Cameroon. He argues that self-management in the private and public sectors is not possible. He suggests that worker co-operatives offer the best possibility of self-management. However, his case study of one successful worker co-operative shows that it is dominated by a handful of members who refuse to allow other workers into membership, demonstrating how without constitutional safeguards and an appropriate support structure and sympathetic culture, co-operatives are likely to degenerate.

References

Cornforth, C., Thomas, A., Lewis, J. and Spear, R. (1988): *Developing Successful Worker Co-operatives*, London: Sage.

Chapter 6
The Role of Support Organisations in Developing Worker Co-operatives: A Model for Promoting Economic and Industrial Democracy?

Chris Cornforth

Introduction

During the last fifteen years there has been a considerable expansion in the number of worker co-operatives in most Western industrialised countries (Jacklin and Levin 1984, Paton et al. 1987, Thornley 1981). This growth has been particularly apparent in the UK since the mid-1970s. After nearly 70 years in which the sector gradually declined new co-operatives again began to be formed. From a low point of about 30 co-operatives in the early 1970s their numbers have grown steadily to over 1200 at the end of 1986 (Cornforth et al. 1988). This growth has been accompanied by the formation of approximately 80 funded local co-operative support organisations (CSOs) whose job is to promote and assist the development of worker co-operatives (Cornforth and Lewis 1985, Cornforth et al. 1988). This new period of co-operative growth has been stimulated by dislocations in the social and economic fabric of society. One important influence was the development of the "alternative" movement during the 1960s and 1970s. Many people, influenced by the hippy and youth cultures of the 1960s, were concerned by what they saw as the damaging social and ecological consequences of modern industry and commerce, and by the hierarchial and authoritarian nature of many organisations. As a result, some people became involved in collectives, communes and co-operatives as a way of trying to put their beliefs into practice. From the late 1970s the economic recession and record levels of unemployment became the main spur to co-operative formation, as people and government looked for new ways of creating jobs.

In the UK one of the most important factors in the continued revival of the sector has been the establishment of local CSOs. This is in line with various theoretical arguments (Cornforth 1988, Horvat 1982, Vanek 1970) and empirical studies of countries such as France, Spain, and Italy which have better developed co-operative sectors (Earle 1986, Oakeshott 1978, Thornley 1981, Weiner and Oakeshott 1987). The purpose of this paper is to examine the role of co-operative support organisations and some of the dilemmas that need to be faced in developing an effective support structure for co-operatives.

The paper adopts the position that a support structure is necessary to overcome various barriers to co-operative development. The paper begins by describing these barriers in more detail. It goes on to describe the functions that any support structure will need to perform to overcome these barriers. Then we look at some of the operational dilemmas that will have to be addressed if a support structure is to be effective.

Barriers to Co-operative Development

There has been a wide-ranging theoretical debate concerning the comparative economic performance of worker co-operatives with capitalist firms. On the one hand, it is argued that the financial and organisational structure of co-operatives will lead to difficulties of raising finance, under-investment, and poor management and discipline which will lead to co-operatives having inferior performance to capitalist businesses (see Fanning and McCarthy 1986: 23–29). There are important differences between authors as to the cause of these problems. At one end of the spectrum there are those that see these problems as stemming inherently from the organisational structure of co-operatives (e.g. Alchian and Demsetz 1972), while at the other end of the spectrum there are those that see the problems arising because co-operatives have to operate in a hostile capitalist environment (e.g. Mandel 1975). It was problems like these that led Beatrice and Sydney Webb (1920, 1921) to conclude that co-operatives would either fail or degenerate into capitalist businesses, and this has been the orthodox view of co-operatives on the left. More recently this view has been challenged by writers such as Horvat and Vanek, who stress the importance of developing a co-operative support structure to overcome these problems.

On the other hand, it is argued that co-operation will lead to increased worker motivation and commitment, reducing the need for vertical supervision and leading to greater efficiency (see Abell (1983: 75–77) for a more detailed summary). Although it is often difficult to make meaningful comparisons of the performance of co-operatives with capitalist businesses, the results of empirical research so far do not appear to suggest a strong difference in performance either way (Abell 1983, Cornforth et al. 1988, Jones and Svejnar 1982). However, two important points do stand out. First, the formation rate of worker co-operatives is very low in comparison to that of small businesses in general. Second, there are very few large co-operatives that would compare with large capitalist firms. As Abell (1983: 85) has suggested, the absence of large co-operatives could be explained purely on probablistic grounds given the relatively small size of the population of worker co-operatives.

The view taken here is that there are a variety of barriers to the formation and growth of co-operatives. First, co-operatives do not appeal to many potential entrepreneurs. Secondly, the legal structure of co-operatives places important constraints on how finance can be raised. Thirdly, co-operatives frequently experience problems developing managerial and specialist competences within the co-operative. Fourthly, there are internal limits to growth stemming from members' orientations and co-operatives' democratic goals. Fifthly, there are problems of discrimination against co-operatives. Sixthly, it is difficult for co-operatives to grow through take-overs. Finally, in common with other small businesses, co-operatives are constrained by their position in the economy. Each of these barriers to co-operative development will be examined in more detail below.

Co-operative Formation – The Entrepreneurial Problem

The majority of investigators of worker co-operatives have concentrated on examining the performance of established co-operatives. However, recently a number of authors have suggested that the formation process of co-operatives requires greater attention, arguing that it is the low rate of co-operative formation, rather than poor performance, that explains the relatively small size of the co-operative sectors in capitalist economies (Abell 1983, Aldrich and Stern 1983). They argue that the co-operative form of organisation will not appeal to the majority of potential entrepreneurs in societies that are dominated by materialistic and individualistic values.

The essence of Abell's argument is that it will not be in the material interests of a potential entrepreneur to establish a co-operative in preference to some other form of private enterprise. If an entrepreneur chooses a co-operative, then, among other things, he will have to share control of the enterprise; the return on his capital will be limited; and the right to redeem his share of the business will be restricted. Abell concludes that only in "exceptional circumstances where individuals are roughly equal in capital endowment and hold a marketable idea in common will a co-operative begin to prove at all attractive" (Abell 1983: 88).

Aldrich and Stern reach similar conclusions to Abell. They suggest that co-operatives are most likely to be materially attractive to workers when they lack other opportunities to realise the gains from their labour, for instance during periods of industrial restructuring or as a tactic during strikes. In addition, they suggest that co-operatives may be formed when "purposive" and "solidarity" incentives (Clark and Wilson 1961) are considered more important than material incentives.

If people are committed to co-operation as an ideal, or if they believe co-operation is a means to some larger political objective, they might be willing to ignore the obvious disincentives involved in creating co-operatives and instead provide the resources required (Aldrich and Stern 1983: 387).

This analysis suggests that not only will the formation rate of co-operatives be low but that many of those wanting to form a co-operative will be "pushed" into it because of industrial restructuring or recession. In the UK this process has been encouraged by many CSOs with their goal of job creation. It is not surprising then that, like many new small businesses, worker co-operatives are frequently established in very competitive, low capital intensive, marginal sectors of the economy. As a result, their potential for growth is often limited.

Finance

Co-operative principles impose important constraints on how co-operatives can raise finance. The most important principles in this respect are "limited return on capital" and "majority control by worker members." This means that strictly speaking co-operative shares cannot appreciate in value, must pay a limited rate of interest, and the issue of external voting shares is restricted. Common ownership principles are even stricter: membership is restricted to workers only, and ownership is entirely collective apart from a nominal share held by each member. Common ownership co-operatives have to rely entirely on loans or credit if they want to raise external finance.

As a consequence of these constraints the majority of co-operatives are reliant on external or members' loans and reinvested profits for investment. As a result, co-operatives may suffer from high gearing making it difficult to raise loans, or if they are successful in doing this then leaving the co-operative with a large debt to service. However, this may not put them at a disadvantage against other small businesses, as many small businesses are reluctant to issue external equity. Other factors do come into play though. Many new co-operators, coming as they often do from the ranks of the unemployed, have little to invest and few personal assets to secure bank loans. Perhaps as a result, many co-operatives start under-capitalised. It is probably when co-operatives start to grow that the inability to raise capital through issuing equity becomes a greater constraint. It effectively excludes co-operatives from the growing venture capital market, and saddles many with large debts that have to be serviced.

Managerial and Specialist Competencies

It is commonly acknowledged that many small businesses suffer from a shortage of management skills. Very few small business owners have received any formal management training. In particular, weaknesses in financial management and marketing strategy and techniques are common. Before trading, and with no basic appreciation of management techniques, many do not see the relevance of management training and advice. Once they start trading and experience problems, it is difficult to take time off for training.

Many worker co-operatives share these typical problems, although the origins and orientation of different co-operatives affect how these problems manifest themselves and their extent. The ideology behind some "radical" or "alternative" co-operatives has led some to deny the legitimacy of management and to undervalue management skills. However, once management functions are seen to be necessary the members of these co-operatives have often been quick to acquire the new skills. Management functions are frequently shared quite widely between members in these co-operatives, giving them greater strength and flexibility (Cornforth et al. 1988).

In co-operatives started to create jobs, those involved often have no previous experience of running or managing a business. Rescue and phoenix co-operatives can face similar problems, when managerial staff from the failing enterprise are able to obtain work elsewhere. The problem may be exacerbated by the fact that rescue and phoenix co-operatives often have to be established very quickly. As a consequence, there is little time for workers' leaders to acquire management skills.

Some co-operatives have tried to resolve the problem by recruiting managers or specialists externally, but this has often proved difficult for a number of reasons. First, the wages that they can offer, at least initially, are low because the business is not yet established, is in a marginal sector, or is under-financed. Secondly, most small businesses require people with general management skills. Many of the people most likely to have these skills are running their own businesses anyway, and the financial incentives are greater for such individuals to establish their own businesses. Thirdly, a co-operative has no guarantee of the loyalty of a manager. There have been a number of examples where a manager has tried to take over a co-operative, or has used the experience to go on and establish his or her own business with detrimental consequences for the co-operative (Cornforth et al. 1988).

Successful and expanding co-operatives are also not without problems in recruiting managerial and/or specialist staff. First, in many countries the co-operative sector is so small that a labour market for "co-operative managers" has not yet developed. As a result, potential staff will not usually have experience of co-operative working. Second, many co-operatives because of their size and commitment to low wage differentials do not offer the same incentives as private firms.

Internal Limits to Growth

There is a certain amount of evidence from case studies that many members of co-operatives value the informal atmosphere and close contacts that come with small size. In this respect they are probably not much different from many small business owners who often show an ambivalent attitude towards growth (Curran 1986: 27, Goffee and Scase 1980). However, co-operatives do face additional constraints on growth. There are not the same financial incentives for growth, where the rewards are spread among the workforce as a whole rather than concentrated in the hands of few owners. A commitment to democracy may also inhibit growth. Co-operatives committed to direct democracy have to remain very small in order to make decision-making workable (Rothschild-Whitt 1976). Even in those co-operatives that have introduced representative democracy and a professional management structure there is often a feeling that the sense of "community" would break down if they got too large. After a strike at its largest co-operative (which had 3200 employees at the time) the Mondragon Group decided to limit the size of co-operatives in the future (Thomas and Logan 1982: 35).

Discrimination

Co-operatives may also be discriminated against. This may be active discrimination, or just that their interests and needs are not considered because they are a minority. Various writers see discrimination as a major problem, for example Vanek (1970: 38) argues:

... The majority of those who hold power, whether in capitalist industry, modern large corporations, or in labor unions will see in labor management a threat to their positions. For bankers, in a perfectly liberal environment, it is possible to discriminate in extending credit; for suppliers it is possible to withhold supplies; for intermediate-goods buyers it is possible to discriminate in the selection of sources of supply. Factual examples of all this certainly are not lacking. Nor can it be contested that social pressure can be exercised by, say, the business community on those possessing advanced managerial or technical talent not to join a labor-managed firm.

The legal system and business infra-structure has developed largely to meet the needs of capitalist forms of enterprises and is often not suitable to meet the needs of co-operatives. In Britain the main piece of legislation for co-operatives is the Industrial and Provident Societies Acts which was designed largely to meet the needs of friendly societies and consumer co-operatives. Various authors have suggested how the law could be improved to meet the needs of worker co-operatives (Ellerman 1988, Munro 1987, Snaith 1988). As yet there is no sign that the law will be reformed. The taxation system has also often discriminated against co-operatives although some of these anomalies have recently been removed. Perhaps most importantly, as we have discussed above, the financial system has evolved to meet the needs of large private companies.

Constraints on Take-overs

Successful capitalist firms often grow through acquisition and take-overs. Worker co-operatives face additional constraints in taking over other firms. Bennett (1984) suggested that this was a major factor in the demise of some of the older producer co-operatives in the UK. She carried out a comparative study of 32 co-operatives that were members of the Co-operative Productive Federation (CPF) between 1950 and 1979. She tried to explain their performance relative to capitalist businesses by examining the structural changes in the industrial sectors in which they were located. She argues that in those sectors where co-operatives did poorly it was not because they were inefficient but because they got squeezed out of the market by larger competitors:

The evidence presented earlier suggests that co-operatives have not failed because of their inefficiency. Rather they have been squeezed out of the market because their potential outlets have been acquired by competitors, and because they are unable to grow to a sufficient size (being unable to acquire other firms) either to (i) set up their own outlets, (ii) have the strength to obtain a decent bargain with monopolistic buyers, (iii) provide the range and flexibility of production available from large competitors (p. 25).

Bennett overstates the case in suggesting that co-operatives cannot take over other firms but they do face added difficulties. They cannot raise capital by issuing new shares or offering a share exchange, a common feature in take-overs. In addition, any co-operative is likely to experience problems absorbing a lot of new members from the firm taken over, who may know nothing about co-operatives and have little commitment to co-operative principles (see McMonnies (1984) for an example of the problems that can arise).

The Place of Co-operatives in the Economy

Co-operatives have to survive within the economy in which they are located, be it capitalist or socialist. In the West today co-operatives are being formed at a time when capital is highly concentrated, and decisions over how this capital is allocated are dominated by large corporations, Government, and financial institutions. This is perhaps particularly true of Britain, whose small firms sector is relatively small compared with many other Western countries. Small firms tend to be restricted to sectors dominated by large firms, or those which serve fragmented highly competitive markets. In either case their control over market conditions is quite limited. The chances of breaking out of the small firms sector through growth are low. Even those firms that do grow are likely to be taken over by large firms.

As we will see, much can be done to expand the role of co-operatives in the small firms sector. However, if policy-makers wish co-operatives to gain a more significant position in any industrial sector then more radical action will be required. In Italy and France this has been achieved in the construction industry where some degree of market protection has been provided for co-operatives by the government. This does not imply that co-operatives have to be subsidised. In France, Government legislation ensures that a quota of public building work is temporarily reserved for co-operatives at the average price for the job (Thornley 1981: 146). One of the most significant actions Government could take to improve the position of worker co-operatives (or small firms in general) would be to improve their access to the market through some form of quota system.

Co-operatives and their advisers can also take some action to try to avoid establishing business in the most dependent or least profitable areas. There are often quite wide variations of profitability within sectors. For example, in the clothing industry profit margins are often better for firms in sub-sectors producing high quality or specialist garments. In addition, small firms may be able to find new market niches that have not been exploited. Careful analysis of different markets and how they are changing should guide the choice of business for new co-operatives, not forgetting the possibilities for developing business ideals from links with different social movements.

The Functions of a Support Structure

The functions of a support structure for co-operatives can be divided into three areas: those that are directed towards improving the environment in which co-operatives operate; those that are internally directed towards servicing the co-operative sector; and those that are concerned with maintaining and extending the support structure itself. We will consider the first two of these in more detail below.

"External" Functions

There are three main external functions. The first is to develop a strong worker co-operative movement with links to other social movements, the community, and political organisations that share similar ideals. This will be necessary in order to mobilise resources for investment in co-operatives and co-operative development. In addition, it will also be important as a means of attracting people to form and work in co-operatives. This is particularly important given the lack of appeal that co-operatives have to many entrepreneurs. Rothschild-Whitt (1976) has also suggested that co-operatives that maintain connections with broader social movements that share similar values are less likely to degenerate, i.e. give up their original goals and adopt capitalist forms of organisation.

The second function is to ensure that co-operatives receive fair treatment from other organisations. At a local level this might entail working with banks, local governments, etc. to see that co-operatives are not discriminated against. At a national level the main role will be to advise and lobby national bodies to make sure that the interests of co-operatives are better taken into account. In particular, to work with Government to ensure that co-operatives receive fair treatment in legislation. Given the position of co-operatives in the economy and the additional constraints on growth that they face, then the support structure may need to press Government for some form of market protection if the sector is to become a significant force in the economy (Bennett 1984).

The third function is to promote the idea of co-operation more widely in society. Co-operative principles are still poorly understood by many people, and few have direct experience of co-operative working (O'Brien 1982). Perhaps the most important objective is to get co-operation established as part of the curriculum, particularly in business and management courses.

"Internal" Functions

There are a number of important functions that CSOs must carry out in order to service the co-operative sector. The first is to provide advice and assistance to existing co-operatives and those in the process of formation. This is particularly important as many of the people forming co-operatives have little or no experience of working in a co-operative or of running their own business. A parallel can be drawn with a small business advisory service or management consultancy, although the style of operation and expertise would need to be adopted to fit co-operative practices (see the next chapter by Woodworth for an example). We will also consider this point further in the next section when we look at some of the dilemmas of co-operative development work.

A second function is to identify gaps in training provision for co-operatives and to try to ensure that these needs are met. This might involve CSOs putting on courses themselves or arranging for other bodies such as local colleges to put on courses.

The third function is to encourage and facilitate collaboration between co-operatives. As we have seen, co-operatives face considerable constraints on their own growth. Consequently, it may be more difficult for co-operatives to achieve the economies of scale or market power of large capitalist businesses. In part this problem can be alleviated by establishing joint ventures and collaborative agreements between co-operatives. In Italy it is common for co-operatives (and small businesses for that matter) to form consortia in order to centralise functions such as buying raw materials and marketing finished goods, negotiating contracts and finance, and providing specialist expertise (Thornley 1981: 60). In Mondragon the co-operatives are joined together as part of a group, and also are linked in small local federations. Some of the local federations pool a percentage of profits which can then be used by the federation as a whole (Weiner and Oakeshott 1987). These collaborative ventures have the additional benefit of providing some protection from wider market forces. The support structure may provide the lead in encouraging and giving coherence to these initiatives and in helping to plan the development of an integrated co-operative sector. Vanek (1970: 326) goes further and evisages a major role for the support structure when he suggests that the principal task in this area is "to study trends within the entire economy in order to facilitate optimal entry and production decisions by member firms." As we will discuss later, one of the dilemmas facing support organisations concerns the extent to which they should attempt to plan the sector versus providing a responsive service.

The fourth major function of the support structure is to help provide appropriate forms of finance for co-operatives. This will include improving access to conventional sources of finance, for example from banks and government. However, given the special needs of co-operatives and their heavy reliance on loan finance, it is important that co-operatives have access to their own bank or loan funds. Clearly this has been a vital

ingredient in the success of the Mondragon Group of Co-operatives
(Thomas and Logan 1982, Weiner and Oakeshott 1987).

Some Dilemmas of Support Organisations

In carrying out these functions, CSOs face a number of important
dilemmas. It is important that these dilemmas are recognised and
strategies developed to manage the conflicting pressures they create if
CSOs are to be successful in encouraging co-operative development. We
will examine some of these dilemmas drawing primarily on the experience
of CSOs in the UK.

"Top-Down" vs. "Bottom-Up" Approaches Towards Development

Co-operative development workers in the UK commonly distinguish
between two approaches towards co-operative development, what they
call "top-down" and "bottom-up." This distinction concerns the
relationship between the development worker and the co-operative they
are working with. Although the terms are not formally defined, their main
characteristics can be captured on three dimensions as shown in Table 1.
In "top-down" development the idea for forming a co-operative comes
from the development worker, who then takes a direct role in developing
the co-operative, attracting people to it, providing missing skills, acting as
an initiator, and working with leaders in the co-operative to eventually
take over the development worker's role.

Table 1: Styles of Development Work: Three Dimensions

"Top Down"	vs. "Bottom-Up"
1. Idea for the co-operative comes from the development worker	Idea for the co-operative comes from the potential co-operators
2. Role of the development worker is to "initiate" and supply missing skills	Role of the development worker is to "facilitate" and help group develop skills
3. The development worker works with the co-operatives' leaders	The development worker works with the whole group

In contrast, in "bottom-up" development work the initiative comes from the potential members of the co-operative, the development worker acts as a facilitator in developing the co-operative, working with the whole group so that they develop the necessary skills to run their business.

The dominant philosophy among development workers in the UK favours the "bottom-up" approach towards development work. It is argued that the success of a co-operative depends vitally on the commitment and involvement of its members, and that this is not likely to develop if a co-operative results mainly from the initiative and actions of the development worker. Equally, it is argued that it is difficult to build up democratic practices within the group of co-operators if the development worker is making many of the important decisions. The failure of a number of "top-down" co-operatives has reinforced this view (Thornley 1981, Tynan 1980a, 1980b). In practice, it may not always be possible or desirable to maintain a pure "bottom-up" style of development work. There are often considerable pressures towards a top-down approach. For example, if time is very short, as it often is in the formation of "rescue" co-operatives, the development worker may have to play a direct role in planning the development of the co-operative and negotiating with external bodies.

The line between guiding the group and shaping or making decisions for them is a difficult one to tread, the potential co-operatives may themselves put pressure on development workers to take more of a direct role in the process of forming or running their co-operative. The dilemma then for the development worker is to provide useful advice and assistance, without taking the initiative for forming the co-operative from the potential group of co-operators and without the co-operators becoming too dependent on the development worker.

Ad hoc, Responsive Development vs. Planned, Selective Development

In the UK to date the main strategy pursued by CSOs has been to provide a responsive service to groups wanting to form co-operatives. This has come about for two main reasons. First, the emphasis on "bottom-up" development work has led development workers to promote the idea of co-operatives and then to wait for groups to approach them for help. Secondly, because they are usually publicly funded they often feel that they have a duty to help all those who ask for help. Given the decentralised nature of co-operative development in the UK and the limited resources each CSO has to offer, this strategy has led to the ad hoc development of many small co-operatives in a variety of different sectors. Like many small businesses, these co-operatives are often only just viable and vulnerable to changes in their environment.

As has been argued earlier in the paper, a co-operative sector is more likely to survive if it is integrated. The dilemma facing CSOs in the UK is how to develop an integrated sector, which will require planning and co-ordination, given their small size and decentralisation and without incurring the problems previously associated with "top-down" development work.

There appear to be a number of ways in which this dilemma can be resolved. The first is to promote the idea of co-operatives within selected sectors that are thought to be particularly suitable, for example wholefoods and printing, rather than general promotion. The second strategy is to try to build up trading links between co-operatives that already exist in the sectors where they have a reasonable concentration. There are some signs that this is beginning to happen in the UK; for example, the Greater London Enterprise Board (GLEB) encouraged a number of printing co-operatives in London to form a federation and funded a marketing person for the federation so that they could tender for work that would be too large for them to take on individually. A third strategy is to try to build up informal links between co-operatives perhaps through social links, or by concentrating co-operatives in particular localities so that mutual assistance and trading links have a better chance to develop. A fourth strategy, adopted by the Mondragon group of co-operatives in Spain, takes this further and has institutionalised co-operation between co-operatives through a contractual relationship between each co-operative and the central bank (Weiner and Oakeshott 1987).

Decentralised vs. Centralised Development

Co-operative support in the UK is highly decentralised. This has arisen because the resources available to fund CSOs have come predominantly from local government. However, it has also been supported by the philosophy of "bottom-up" development. This system has a number of advantages and disadvantages. On the positive side, it means that support is available in a large number of areas, and that development workers can work closely with potential co-operatives and build up local knowledge and contacts that are useful in the development process. On the negative side, it means that local CSOs seldom have the number of staff, the depth of skills, or the financial resources to help develop large co-operatives. In addition, there are seldom enough co-operatives in any one industrial sector in their area to develop an economically integrated sector.

One way of resolving this problem is to develop regional support organisations in order to complement and assist the work of local CSOs. This strategy was adopted by the GLEB in London with some success and by some other metropolitan authorities. However, the abolition of the metropolitan authorities and the lack of a regional tier of local government has limited the opportunities to develop a regional support structure.

Co-operative Interests vs. Government/Community Interests

Co-operative support organisations usually have to serve more than one set of interests. In the Mondragon co-operatives, for example, the bank not only has to serve the interests of the co-operatives, but the interests of the members of the community that invests in it. In order to protect the interests of the community, the bank regularly monitors the performance of the member co-operatives. In the UK the two main interests that CSOs have to serve are those of their local co-operatives and those of the state. The interests of the state have to be respected because they provide the majority of funding. In some areas development workers have felt under a lot of pressure to create jobs which has conflicted with the interests of the co-operative movement (Cornforth and Stott 1984). They felt that these pressures were leading to some co-operatives being set up before they were ready, or when they were only marginally viable.

Over time another common tension that is likely to arise is between the interests of existing co-operatives and potential co-operatives that might be formed. As the number of co-operatives has grown, CSOs have often found that they have to spend more time servicing their needs. Unless their resources increase correspondingly, this will mean that they have less time to help groups wanting to form new co-operatives.

Conclusions

A worker co-operative sector in capitalist economies faces various barriers to development. Some of these arise because the existing business and legal infra-structure has not evolved to meet the needs of worker co-operatives or because they face discrimination. Others arise because of internal barriers to growth, for example members may wish to keep their co-operative small. As importantly, the principles underlying co-operation are often at odds with the individualistic and materalistic values that dominate Western society. As a result, a large and healthy co-operative sector is only likely to develop if it has its own support structure which can meet the sector's particular needs, encourage mutual support between co-operatives, and help mobilize wider public and political support.

There remain important questions about how a support structure for worker co-operatives can be developed. In countries with a small co-operative sector it is unlikely that the sector itself will be able to finance its own support structure. As a result, state finance for CSOs is likely to be necessary. However, there is a danger that the state will impose its own priorities on the co-operative movement. In the longer term it is vital that the co-operative movement develops and maintains its own support structure.

The experience of the co-operative sector has important lessons for other new initiatives to further economic and industrial democracy such as employee share ownership plans. It is likely that these new initiatives will also face similar barriers to development: discrimination and suspicion, lack of knowledge and competencies, and difficulties in obtaining resources. As a result, it is vital that they, too, develop their own support structures and organisations. The structures and organisations that have been developed in various countries to support co-operatives could provide a model for initiatives in other areas.

References

Abell, P. (1983): The Viability of Industrial Producer Co-operation, In Crouch, C. and Heller, F. (eds.), *International Yearbook of Organisational Democracy*, London: John Wiley & Sons.

Alchian, A. and Demsetz, H. (1972): Production, Information Costs, and Economic Organisation, *American Economic Review*, 62: 777–795.

Aldrich, H. and Stern, R. (1983): Resource Mobilisation and the Creation of US Producer's Co-operatives, 1835–1935, *Economic and Industrial Democracy*, 4, 3: 371–406.

Bennett, J. (1984): *Producer Co-operatives: A Case for Market Protection*, Occasional paper, Centre for Research in Industrial Democracy and Particip-ation, Univ. of Glasgow.

Clark, P. and Wilson, J. (1961): Incentive Systems: A Theory of Organisations, *Administrative Science Quarterly*, 6: 129–166.

Cornforth, C. and Lewis, J. (1985): *The Role and Impact of Co-operative Support Organisations*, Co-operative Research Unit, Open University, Milton Keynes.

Cornforth, C. and Stott, M. (1984): *A Co-operative Approach to Local Economic Development*, Co-operatives Research Unit, Open University, Milton Keynes.

Cornforth, C. et al. (1988): *Developing Successful Worker Co-operatives*, London: Sage Pubs.

Curran, J. (1986): *Bolton Fifteen Years On: A Review and Analysis of Small Business Research in Britain 1971–1986*, London: Small Business Research Trust.

Earle, J. (1986): *The Italian Co-operative Movement: A Portrait of Lega Nazionalle delle Co-operative & Mutue*, London: Allen and Unwin.

Ellerman, D. (1988): Worker Ownership Legislation in America, In: *Yearbook of Co-operative Enterprise*, Oxford: Plunkett Foundation of Co-operative Studies.

Fanning, C. and McCarthy, T. (1986): A Survey of Economic Hypotheses Concerning the Viability of Labour-Directed Firms, In Jansson, S. and Hellmark, A. (eds.), *Labor-Owned Firms and Workers' Co-operatives*, Alder-shot: Gower.

Goffee, R. and Scase, R. (1980): *The Real World of the Small Business Owner*, London: Croom Helm.

Horvat, B. (1982): *The Political Economy of Socialism: A Marxist Social Theory*, Oxford: Martin Robertson.

Jacklin, R. and Levin, H. (1984): *Worker Co-operatives in America*, Berkeley, CA: Univ. of California Press.

Jones, D. and Svejnar, J. (eds.) (1982): *Participatory and Self-Managed Firms*, Lexington, Mass.: Lexington Books.

Mandel, E. (1975): Self-Management – Dangers and Possibilities, *International*, 2/3: 3–9.

McMonnies, D. (1984): *Trade Unions and Co-ops?: The Scott Bader-Synthetic Resins Saga*, Occasional Paper, Dept. of Political Theory and Institutions, Univ. of Liverpool.

Munro, C. (1987): *The Financing of Worker Co-operatives: A Comparison with Conventional Businesses and Evaluation of Proposed Mechanisms for Invest-ment*, MBA Thesis, Polytechnic of Central London.

Oakeshott, R. (1978): *The Case for Workers' Co-ops*, London: Routledge and Kegan Paul.

O'Brien, T. (1982): *Motivational Research into Worker Co-operatives*, London: Focus Marketing Research Ltd. 87 Regent Street, London W1R.

Paton, R. et al. (1987): *Analysis of the Experiences of and Problems Encountered by Worker Take-overs of Companies in Difficulty or Bankrupt*, Luxembourg: Office for Official Publications of the European Communities.

Rothschild-Whitt, J. (1976): Conditions Facilitating Participatory Democratic Organisation, *Sociological Inquiry*, 46: 75–86.

Snaith, I. (1988): U.K. Co-operative Legislation in the 1980's: A Decade of Neglect, In: *Yearbook of Co-operative Enterprise*, Oxford: Plunkett Foundation of Co-operative Studies.

Thomas, H. and Logan, C. (1982): *Mondragon: An Economic Analysis*, London: Allen and Unwin.

Thornley, J. (1981): *Workers' Co-operatives: Jobs and Dreams*, London: Heinemann Educational Books.

Tynan, E. (1980a): *Sunderlandia*, Co-operatives Research Unit, Open University, Milton Keynes.

Tynan, E. (1980b): *Unit 58*, Co-operatives Research Unit, Open University, Milton Keynes.

Vanek, J. (1970): *The General Theory of Labour-Managed Market Economies*, Ithaca, N.Y.: Cornell University Press.

Vanek, J. (ed.) (1975): *Self Management: Economic Liberation of Man*, London: Penguin.

Webb, S. and Webb, B. (1920): *A Constitution for the Socialist Commonwealth of Great Britain*, London: Longmans.

Webb, S. and Webb, B. (1921): *Consumers' Co-operative Movement*, (published by the Authors).

Weiner, H. and Oakeshott, R. (1987): *Mondragon Revisited*, London: Anglo-German Foundation.

Chapter 7
Consulting for Second Order Change

Warner Woodworth

Little has been written in the United States on the role of external "experts" as they assist trade unions in the movement toward self-managed organizations. However, there is an abundance of literature on the process of consulting or practicing organizational development in conventional enterprises. The paradigm which undergirds this traditional approach is characterized by ground rules such as the need to work in a top-down manner with corporate executives, the importance of creating better patterns of communication, the use of small groups as a vehicle to solving inter-personal problems, and so on. Key variables stressed are human relations, trust, integration of personal and organizational objectives, and consensus (Beckard 1969, Bennis 1969, French and Bell 1973).

In the past decade, a number of researchers have begun to question this traditional method, arguing it is managerially-biased in favor of elites, leading to limited organizational change, and reflecting poor social science methods which only masquerade as "objective," while preserving the status quo (Nord 1974). Woodworth (1974) criticizes this mainstream practice of consulting for ignoring the issues of conflict and dissensus, and Abrahamsson (1977) notes that this paradigm does not adequately deal with the problem of organizational power.

Increasingly, such criticisms seem to be acknowledged as valid indications of an essentially upper-class ideology with matching behavioral science practice. However, when questions are raised about what an alternative model for the process of consulting might look like, there is a paucity of literature about such an alternative. The present paper attempts to address this deficiency by outlining several elements of an alternative – not *the* model, but a few characteristics of a different approach.

A Self-Managed Context

The setting from which this consulting model emerged is a large U.S. company which shifted to worker ownership beginning in 1979. Two consultants worked part-time for three years helping make the transition from a conventional business to an enterprise that was somewhat self-managed.

The blood, sweat, and tears of this effort included considerable sacrifice of time and energy, thousands of miles of travel each month, costly long-distance phone discussions during the interim, and major problems over which we had no control. As of present, the company's future is somewhat in doubt due to severe financial and market factors.

What follows is an explanation of interventions which suggest the beginning of an unusual consulting strategy. The lines of demarcation between the traditional model and this alternative approach are not always neat and clean. In some instances, the point is mostly a matter of emphasis, while at other times, the two methods are clearly differentiated.

Important dimensions of the role of external providers of technical assistance are discussed in the sections below.

Labor-Oriented Change

Typically, organizational consultants in the U.S. gain entry to the company through the executive suite. They often work behind the scenes, collecting data for management and creating schemes which reflect the goals of those at the top of the corporate pyramid. Indeed, much consulting work is openly admitted to be anti-union in nature and methods. In contrast, our approach began through contacts with leaders of the local union. Initial meetings explored the background of the conversion to worker-ownership, who the key managers were and how they tended to operate, which parties were most resistant to change, who was competent, and so on. Over time, not only was an organizational diagnosis beginning to take shape, but a level of trust was established between the union and the consultants. The fact that entry began through the union and that the initial inquiry was framed from a labor agenda set the tone for all future work. It made clear the fact that we were functioning as labor advocates, not as management consultants.

In no way was our independence from management manifest more clearly than in the question of funding. In conventional practice, external agents are hired by executives, the problem often being that reports are prepared and recommendations stated so as to "kiss the hand that feeds." In the present case, however, the union financed the consultants with travel assistance and a modest consulting fee. Later, a grant was obtained from the federal government's Economic Development Administration to support external services. Thus, the government provided funds as a third party to the worker takeover, facilitating the reduction of economic costs to the union, while avoiding dependence on corporate executives.

Beyond entry and funding, the other critical aspect of a labor-oriented approach is that the major thrust of the entire process was a bottom-up strategy for change rather than the usual rule of top-down. The consultants worked with management, true, but they were not, as Baritz (1960) put it about the traditional practice, "the servants of power." The union proposed initial meetings between the consultants and company executives to legitimize our involvement and open up needed sources of information. But the values were clear from the beginning: that the consultants operated from working-class interests, that maximizing corporate profits was not as important as retaining jobs and community economic security, and that the fundamental objective was to empower rank and file workers.

Institutional Restructuring of Power

Most organizational development efforts tend to either tiptoe around the question of power, or leave it alone completely. Historically, in the company under discussion, it was assumed that the manager's job was to manage and the employee's role was to do the work, getting the product out the door each day. Decision-making was management's job, which gave them information, responsibility, and initiative, leaving workers to be mere cogs in the corporate machine. As consultants, our agenda included creating new mechanisms for a potentially unique form of workers' control in America. Differences between the old system and the new innovations that were designed and implemented as the workers took over are highlighted in Figure 1.

Basically, a three tiered structure was developed by consultants and labor leaders which gave the union the right to appoint 10 out of 16 seats

Figure 1: A Comparison Between the "Old" and "New" Management Systems in the Firm

Old Management System	New Workers' System
Management controlled board of directors	Union appointed board majority
Executives made decisions	Labor input to decisions
No long-range planning function	Union/management strategic planning committee
Management controller telling workers what to do	Joint labor/management steering committee ran the plant
Adversarial industrial relations	Complementary system of co-operation
Pattern was that management made decisions, union reacted post facto	Union became pro-active, getting in on decision process

on the board. At a middle level, a steering committee was designed as a new vehicle created to co-ordinate and monitor the movement toward a co-operative, problem-solving approach in the plant. Finally, at the shop floor level, action research teams were formed to deal with problems in the day-to-day running of the plant.

These mechanisms were intended to give the union a voice at each level of corporate governance, from the shop floor to the boardroom. Meetings were co-chaired by labor and management representatives rather than management having the usual control of agenda, discussion, and preparation of the minutes. A written charter specifying equity in participation and execution of decisions helped ensure that not only were the symbols changed, but the essence of power was indeed tilted towards workers.

Management's response to these interventions was replete with smoldering resentment, foot-dragging resistance, and, in some instances, outright sabotage. Information was blocked, falsehoods were common, workers were set up to fail at times, and agreements were not carried out. For some managers, the sharing of power was too painful and they sought employment elsewhere. Others were so intransigent and unwilling to change that they were forceably terminated against their will. A few opened up to the shift willingly, seeing advantages in redistributing organizational power and the attendant sense of commitment and responsibility. Some executives reasoned that if all else fails, turning the company over to the workers was not a bad strategy. They reasoned that new ideas and fresh decisions may be just what the firm needed.

The fundamental lesson for consultants about the redistribution of power is that power is not easily given up, nor can it simply be seized by those from below. To effectively change the system of power requires a restructuring, opening up new avenues to power, and establishing new processes for making organizational decisions.

The Democratization of Management

Much of the consulting practice in America has recently emphasized what is euphemistically called "participative management." The central idea, as expounded in earlier empirical work (Likert 1967) and popularized in current national beststellers (Ouchi 1981, Peters and Waterman 1982), is that managers begin to involve workers in the on-going administration of the business. The problem with these notions is that participation is viewed as a managerial prerogative – the right to participate is conferred by executives (often in condescending fashion), clear limits are spelled out to preserve the feudal nature of corporate authority, and the bottom line of most participative management schemes is simply human relations.

Democratic management, in contrast, moves beyond merely placating workers so they "feel" involved to creating a new organizational culture of genuine democracy. Such a culture includes full access to information, having a voice in corporate actions at all levels of the organization, and both direct and indirect avenues to power. As consultants, our work centered on attempting to help managers "unlearn" the authoritarian styles and provincial attitutes which had dominated in the past. In Lewin's (1951) logic, our goal was to thaw the field of forces which had led to rigid executive methods, change to a more humane and democratic style, and then refreeze the system in a new constellation of forces. Thus, new norms of self-management would prevail as the organization moved into the future.

The task of achieving managerial democratization is not easy. In the present case, it meant as consultants we had to help executives take a critical look at their old methods, reflecting on its inadequacies and human costs. The point had to be made that managers should not seek worker participation simply to improve communications. Instead, good managers need to listen to their subordinates in order to get better ideas, to improve organizational functioning.

During a year of extensive management education, a fairly high degree of change occurred, especially at the top and middle levels of the company hierarchy. A new language had evolved, emphasizing terms such as "consensus," "joint action," "equality," and so on. While we, as consultants, felt frustrated at times at the gap between rhetoric and reality, over time we began to see that this discrepancy, when articulated, pushed behavior to be more consistent with the jargon of democracy. We concluded that as verbal symbols gained widespread use, actions often rose to be congruent with the new language.

Expectations of more democratic management eventually began to be institutionalized. This was powerfully evident in an experience which occurred shortly after the arrival of a new company president hired form outside the firm. The union had pushed for a year to replace the chief executive officer and now a new CEO had been hired. He was invited to attend a labor/management steering committee meeting, his first opportunity to see how the process of democratic management was functioning. He stated, at the outset of the meeting, that he believed workers should be able to participate and make suggestions, but that he would reserve the final decision-making authority for himself. At that point, the newly developed system of genuine organizational democracy was strongly tested. Basically, the rest of the group, union and management, told him he was CEO but would not make unilateral decisions. The steering committee members all possessed equal authority and he was simply a group member. One of the group reflected on the traditional, authoritarian management of most American companies and said, "That's just not the way we operate and you'd better understand this up front." It was a powerful episode in which the collective system of self-management that had been created over past months was challenged and found able to withstand the top executive's pressure to revert to the past.

Blue-Collar Research

The generic model of organizational research reported in mainstream journals is typified by a process which assumes the researcher is the expert, while the population to be studied are mere subjects (or objects) of research. Usually interviews are conducted or written surveys administered, the data are hauled off by the social scientists who do their analysis from secluded offices, high in their ivory towers, far removed from the realities of organizational life. Computers aid in the crunching of numbers, after which the results are written up for publication in some abstract, professional journal. Such activities are largely irrelevant, academic exercises which seem based on a premise that workers are simply passive respondents to a research agenda.

In contrast, our approach attempted to generate a blue-collar strategy for research. Organizational members were enjoined to participate collectively in self-study – formulating questions, developing concrete hypotheses, designing instruments for data collection, learning how to analyze issues from a worker-owner perspective, reporting results of various studies, and formulating action plans to soon be implemented.

The emphasis was on creating a culture of learning, exploring questions, and trying things out. Risk was to be encouraged. If things did not succeed, they were tossed aside and other efforts were attempted. People at all levels of the organization were encouraged to experiment, to test out new ideas and approaches. At the upper level, for instance, consultants linked top union officials with the chief financial officer of the company in order to research the flow of capital through the firm. For the first time in their lives, these labor leaders began to learn how finance was used and how to read a profit and loss statement. They began to ask tough new questions. Studies were formulated and, with reports in hand, workers' representatives were able to start influencing corporate policy and strategy.

Similarly, down at the shop floor level, worker study groups were initiated. In contrast to quality circle groups in Japan or quality of working life teams in the United States, most of which are launched by management, in this case, workers proposed the start up. Mostly meeting after hours, the teams studied absenteeism, productivity, product quality, new markets, and problems of alienation and job satisfaction. Over twenty action research teams attempted to mix analysis with implementation, a movement which grew to include hundreds of workers volunteering thousands of hours, saving millions of dollars. A maintenance department team studied the problem of work imbalances and ended up installing a new system which saved $ 300,000 annually. Two teams in one area of the plant improved yields by 200 percent. Absenteeism, once investigated as to its cause, resulted in changed procedures, cutting the problem from 12 percent to only 4 percent. Another team studied the patterns of energy consumption, recommending changes which reduced energy costs by 10 percent annually.

For the first time in most of these workers' lives, they were given the tools to really assess how things worked in their company. The result was that they not only learned more about the firm and how to improve it, they also learned more about themselves.

Facilitating the Emergence of New Skills and Values

For consulting to significantly alter people and organizations, the change process must lead to client independence and to the creation of self-managing skills and attitudes. It was interesting to video-tape a group of union leaders early in the buyout effort and ask them to predict their future, especially as labor officials. The clear opinion of the majority, as one of them put it, was: "Nothing is going to change. We'll just keep doing what we've been doing in the past."

Four years later, this same group agreed that as they moved toward self-management, it became apparent that, "Nothing will ever be the same again." How had they changed? No longer were they traditional labor leaders worried primarily about grievances, a labor contract, and upcoming negotiations. Instead, they were overseers of a complex $ 500 million-a-year business, with workers owning 60 percent of the corporation's stock.

By what means had they changed? The informal forces operating during the buyout transition impelled a certain degree of change – workers at their jobs discovering the meaning of ownership in their plant and so on. Formally, a series of training programs were jointly designed by consultants and workers. These were not the conventional training designs, often pre-packaged, which are mostly stand up presentations by the "experts." Rather, they were experientially-based and practical. Role playing and exercises facilitated personal growth and the application of new concepts to one's skill repertoire. Skills grew in areas like communication, consensus decision-making, problem solving, research design, questionnaire construction, organizational diagnosis, effective meeting dynamics, and handling conflicts. Some sessions were exclusively for union workers, some for managers, and others for mixed groups. There was a hands-on emphasis in practice as well as feedback and critique.

The other dimension of education was akin to Freire's (1971) notion of generative themes and *conscientização*. In this case, the context was not one of "illiterate" peasants in north-east Brazil, but economically illiterate workers who were now struggling to understand business realities and worker-ownership. Thus, the consultants attempted to teach them value-loaded terms which would enable workers to discern power, control, profits, and other concepts historically not part of one's everyday language in the workplace.

It became surprisingly apparent that the concept of self-managed work is by no means inherent in the average worker's consciousness. This was strikingly illustrated as a consultant met with a group of workers who had volunteered to be a part of the first autonomous, self-managed team in the plant. The team of eleven workers was to launch production of a whole new product line. Other workers had explored the market, studied and recommended the purchase of new equipment, advised where to locate the new line and how it should be structured. They had proposed that a team of eleven could operate independently, without supervision, and learn each others' jobs so as to rotate regularly. The new process would save considerable dollars, cut out supervisory overhead, and fulfull higher level human needs for meaningful, responsible work.

It was, as one person put it, "A great plan everyone will support." However, those who had the seniority to bid for jobs on the new line, did not like the idea. At the first meeting of the prospective new team, it became clear that some of the older workers resisted innovative change. As one of them heard the self-managed concept explained by the consultant, he yelled out: "What in the hell are you talking about? I don't want to be a part of an autonomous team of workers! I've been working in this plant 30 years and I've always had a boss. I have a right to have a supervisor over me. I demand a boss!"

The incident was a classic case of collision between the historical dependency relationships of workers and management versus the dynamics of worker ownership and blue-collar entrepreneurism. Over time, with considerable education, debate, and efforts to risk change, many workers (and managers) did change. Not only were new technical and interpersonal skills acquired, but, more importantly, new ideologies developed. At the outset of the workers' takeover, the overwhelming objective shared by all was to imply save their jobs. It was a very pragmatic goal. Within several years, however, a new orientation arose in the rank and file mentality – a humanistic vision about equality, economic democracy, and workers' control.

First Order Vs. Second Order Change

The preceding case description suggests new elements in the role of external consultants and researchers as they work with self-managed systems. The conventional approach is inadequate to the task of facilitating substantive change. Top-down, management-oriented intervention tends to produce a minimal degree of change. The difference between such an approach and the model herein described may be a useful extension of Watzlawick's (1974) distinction between first and second order change in psychology. Essentially, he suggests that in many cases, solutions are simply "more of the same," adding to the problem rather than bringing about a resolution. Change is simply a tinkering around with no real breakthrough. One can generalize that most participative management and consulting tactics are illustrative of this first order change.

Second order change is different, more dramatic, indeed revolutionary. It involves not only doing things differently, but doing different things. It may violate existing theory and involves reframing the entire situation. In the case of this worker-owned company, the central issue was not simply profits, but an overthrowing of conventional business assumptions. The problem was reframed to emphasize worker power and participatory structures for corporate decision-making.

Not only did the organization move significantly toward a self-managed enterprise. The consulting process itself changed radically, becoming labor-oriented, altering the power structure, democratizing management, initiating blue-collar research, and developing new grass-roots skills and values. These elements may only form a starting point for an alternative, peoples' approach to external assistance. These interventions may not be professional. In fact, they may be anti-professional. But in the end, they may lead to a more liberating consulting practice which not only empowers workers, but frees the consultants as well.

References

Abrahamsson, Bengt (1977): *Bureaucracy or Participation*, Beverly Hills: Sage Publications.
Baritz, Loren (1960): *The Servants of Power*, Middletown, CT: Wesleyan University.

Beckard, Richard (1969): *Organizational Development: Strategies and Models*, Reading, MA: Addison-Wesley.

Bennis, Warren G. (1969): *Organizational Development: Its Nature, Origins and Prospects*, Reading, MA: Addison-Wesley.

Freire, Paulo (1971): *Pedagogy of the Oppressed*, New York: Herder and Herder.

French, Wendell L. and Bell, Cecil H. (1973): *Organization Development*, Englewood Cliffs, NJ: Prentice-Hall.

Lewin, Kurt (1951): *Field Theory in Social Science*, New York: Harper and Row.

Likert, Rensis (1967): *The Human Organization*, New York: McGraw-Hill.

Nord, Walter R. (1976): Economic and Cultural Barriers to Humanizing Organizations, In: H. Meltzer and F. R. Wickert (eds.), *Humanizing Organizational Behavior*, New York: Charles C. Thomas Pub.

Ouchi, William G. (1981): *Theory Z*, New York: Avon.

Peters, Thomas J. and Waterman, Robert H. (1982): *In Search of Excellence*, New York: Harper and Row.

Watzlawick, Paul et al. (1974): *Change: Principles of Problem Formation and Problem Resolution*, New York: W. W. Norton.

Woodworth, Warner (1974): *The Politics of Intervention Theory: Ideology in Social Science*, Ann Arbor, MI: The University of Michigan, Ph. D. dissertation.

Chapter 8
Self-Management in Wales: Trade Union Encouragement of Worker Co-operatives

Paul Blyton

Introduction

It is now well established that the number of worker co-operatives operating in the UK has grown considerably over the last decade, from very small numbers in the early 1970s to around 300 co-operatives in 1980, 700 in 1984, and approximately 1200 by 1986 (Cornforth et al. 1988). In recent years the principality of Wales, with its population of just under three million, has figured increasingly in the development of co-operatives. As Table 1 shows, the recent increase in the number of registered co-operatives has been rapid, though the total numbers of workers involved remains comparatively small.

The recent increase in the number of co-operatives in Wales coincides with the establishment (in April 1983) by the Welsh Trades Union Congress of a Co-operative Development and Training Centre (CDTC) to facilitate the growth of co-operatives, primarily as a means of job creation. Prior to the Centre's establishment, a feasibility study had been

Table 1: Workers Co-ops in Wales

	1980	1982	1983	1984	1985	1986	1987
No. of Co-ops registered	11	23	28	59	65	81	95
Full time jobs	n/a	n/a	96	221	295	n/a	575
Part time jobs	n/a	n/a	88	126	156	n/a	135
Total jobs	n/a	n/a	184	347	452	n/a	710

n/a = not available
Source: (Mainly) Wales Co-operative Centre, *Annual Reports 1983–84 and 1986*

conducted (see Logan and Gregory 1982, also Gregory and Logan 1982). This had identified not only the importance of trade union support for worker co-operatives (a point also emphasized by Cornforth 1982) but also the importance of a resource centre providing professional and managerial skills to assist co-operative start-ups, and an investment fund to provide capital for new cooperatives. In part these conclusions (particularly the last) followed an evaluation of the factors bringing about success in the Mondragon co-operative enterprise and in particular the pivotal role of the banking and other services provided by the Caja Laboral Popular (see Thomas and Logan 1982).

This union-backed centre has now been in operation for over five years. Yet, despite the growth in the number of co-operatives registered in Wales, the CTDC can claim only some of the *direct* credits for this expansion. Various factors appear to have acted to limit its role. These include the nature of the centre's original objective (to create jobs as quickly as possible), an uncertain relationship initially with existing bodies promoting worker co-operatives (such as local Co-operative Development Agencies) and major difficulties (as yet unresolved) in establishing an investment fund or facilitating financial assistance for co-operative groups. Broader problems include the response of the wider trade union movement in Wales to the co-operatives and, perhaps most significant of all, the question of nurturing small businesses (co-operatives or otherwise) in a relatively isolated region within Britain, over-reliant on shrinking coal and steel production and agriculture. One of the main points in the latter part of this paper is that the challenge to capitalist organization represented by co-operative development has obscured the *similarities* of many problems facing co-operatives to those experienced by other small business start-ups.

To evaluate this Welsh experience with co-operatives and the role of unions as support agencies, it is appropriate to begin with a brief outline of the economic and industrial context.

The Welsh Economic Context

Of the total working population of just under 1 million, the majority (over 600,000) are concentrated in industrial South Wales (the counties of Gwent, and South/Mid and West Glamorgan). Coal extraction and steel production, together with related shipping and engineering industries, have dominated this area since the mid-nineteenth century. The region has been in decline for a considerable period and in the last decade accelerated recession, and the resulting decline in production, has created a substantial unemployment problem, only partially offset by the growth in service industries and foreign-owned manufacturing plants. In mid 1988 the proportion of the labour force unemployed in Wales is just under 11 %, compared to an average in Britain as a whole of around 8½%. However, like certain black-spots in other "peripheral" areas (the North-East and North-West of England and parts of Scotland), the total Welsh unemployment figure masks a number of particularly severe problem areas where the proportion of those out of work is 30 % and above. In recent years there have also been indications of depopulation even in the most affluent counties. Standing on the margins of the British economy, "the economy in Wales has reflected very noticeably the ebb and flow of the wider economic tide" (Rees and Rees 1980: 28). As these authors also comment, "Wales's changing situation vis-à-vis other parts of Britain in respect of unemployment, average weekly earnings, net migration and so forth… (indicates an) unequivocal picture of Wales as a "problem region"" (ibid.: 29). Various explanations have been put forward for Wales's economic problems, including the "dependent" nature of much of the Welsh economy, whereby resources are controlled by externally based centres of capital, which thereby deny the local population the ability to create a balanced economic development (Williams 1980). Whilst not applicable in all respects, this portrait of Wales as having a semi-colonial relationship with England underlines the marginal nature of much of the former's economy and the unfavourability of the context for fostering co-operative ventures.

Co-operative Development in Wales

It is against this economic background that worker co-operatives have developed in Wales. Of the 95 co-operatives registered in 1987, 60 were located in industrial South Wales; one-third of the co-ops are engaged in manufacturing, particularly clothing, printing, and publishing, while the other two-thirds are in services, notably transport, distribution, catering arts, and entertainment (see Table 2). Most of these organizations are very small (the average size is 6 full-timers and just over 1 part timer), though the textile and transport co-operatives are somewhat larger being

Table 2: Industrial Distribution and Employment of Worker Co-operatives

Industry	No co-ops	% of total	full-time jobs	part-time jobs	total jobs	% of total jobs
Clothing	9	9	107	61	168	24
Printing & Publishing	8	8	23	1	24	3
Other Manufacturing	12	13	46	0	46	6
Other non-service*	9	9	22	6	28	4
Distribution	11	12	50	8	58	8
Transport	8	8	197	21	218	31
Catering	9	9	28	10	38	5
Arts/ Entertainment	13	14	70	12	82	12
Other Services	16	17	32	16	48	7
Total	95	100	575	135	710	100

* = includes fishing, quarrying and building and related trades.
Source: Wales Co-operative Centre, *Annual Report* (1986).

approximately double the average size of co-operatives in Wales as a whole.

A recent study of thirty of these co-operatives suggests that typically wages are low (often less than half the average wage for that industry), and in some hours are high, though overall, hours were fairly close to the national average (Bland 1984). Most of the co-operatives are non-unionized.

The various start-up and day to day problems which worker co-operatives face have been reasonably well documented (see for example Cornforth 1983, Thornley 1981). The indication is that like many other small businesses, co-operatives face considerable initial problems of creating an adequate business plan, obtaining finance, marketing their product, finding suitable premises, etc. Operational problems include maintaining an adequate cash flow, organizing production and meeting changes in customer demand. In Bland's study of the Welsh co-operatives this picture is reinforced; the biggest problems identified in the start-up period concerned raising capital, finding customers, and making business plans. Most severe day to day problems were meeting the costs of wages and equipment, finding customers, and setting aside time for meetings (Bland 1984: 63).

The difficulty of obtaining capital and the resulting under-capitalization of operations is apparent in many of the Welsh (and other) co-operatives, creating an acute vulnerability to market changes and a reliance on a low productivity, low wage system, and reflected in an over-dependence on second-hand machinery and inadequate premises. The capitalist banking sector is likely to show a greater suspicion towards a worker co-operative venture than an equivalent capitalist business enterprise (for various reasons, including a lack of knowledge of worker co-ops, a reluctance to deal with small organizations where financial responsibility is vested in several people rather than a single individual, and the lack of any proven financial track record among members of the co-op). As a result union support will be particularly important if it can ease these financial constraints on the development of co-operatives, either directly (by providing funds), or indirectly (by facilitating fund-raising through offering security, assisting co-operatives to make applications for funds, etc.). Given the contextual and financial problems facing the growth of co-operatives in Wales, what indications are there that trade unions can act as support agencies, in particular through organizations such as the Welsh CDTC?

Trade Unions as Support Agencies

Gregory points out that:

the basic ideology of the trade union movement, with very few exceptions, commits trade unions to seek and widen the social ownership of production. Hence the constitution of the majority of unions contain some reference which can be interpreted to imply at least support for worker co-operatives as one particular means towards this end.

Also from the same source,

the demand for democratic control over decisions affecting social, economic and production relations at the workplace again prefigures co-operatives as one way of approaching industrial democracy (Trade Union Research Unit 1983: 31).

Similarly, Cornforth (1982) has suggested various possible roles for trade unions in supporting co-operatives, and assisting both in their internal organization and in their external relations with the business and wider communities.

Yet despite the theoretical congruence of trade union and co-operative aims and their potential role as facilitating agent, historically trade unions in Britain have evidenced an equivocal approach to worker co-operatives, particularly so in comparison to certain trade union movements within Europe (see Thornley 1981). Partly, this union reaction in Britain can be seen to stem from the early period of labour organization when co-operativism was put forward as a possible *alternative* to trade unionism as the general vehicle for advancing the interests of the working class, and in particular, increasing the social ownership of the means of production. Also, the size of co-operatives (and the even smaller numbers of trade unionists involved) reflects their marginal position in relation to the major problems facing trade unionism (the loss of membership due to unemployment, decline in union bargaining power, erosion of union immunities, etc). More generally, while trade unions in Britain and elsewhere have continued to make some attempts to represent the interests of the unemployed and to take initiatives on their behalf (for example, in the establishment of around 180 unemployment centres in Britain), trade unions generally are geared far more to defending and advancing the interests of the *employed* workforce than they are for representing the needs of other groups (Barker et al. 1984, Blyton 1985).

Nevertheless, in the face of growing unemployment and as part of the search for alternatives following plant closures, unions have expressed a gradually increasing interest in worker co-operatives, partly as a result of the support given to three well publicised rescue co-ops in the 1970s (at Meriden, KME, and Scottish Daily News) which shifted the contemporary image of co-ops from being a predominantly middle class alternative life-style to a working class strategy for maintaining jobs and one supported by radical sections of the then Labour government. In Wales in recent years, the main explicit form of trade union support for co-operatives has been the establishment of the Wales Co-operative Development and Training Centre, which has come into existence as the result of initiatives taken by the Principality's trade union confederation (the Welsh TUC).

The Welsh CDTC's Structure in Brief

Initially the Centre was established for a three year period, its running costs funded by several agencies including the government (via the Welsh Office), local authorities, and the EEC. This three year period was subsequently extended through further grants, notably from the EEC Social Fund and the Welsh Development Agency. The Centre is overseen by a management committee made up of three unionists, representatives of the main funding bodies and a number of individuals including a lawyer, personnel manager, businessman, and academic. The staff of the Centre has grown to 30 including 16 "Enterprise Trainees" employed for two years and spread throughout the 8 Welsh counties. The permanent staff include 4 Regional Development Officers, a Marketing Officer, and a Finance Officer.

The stated objectives of the Centre include:

1. to provide individuals and groups who wish to form worker-owned enterprises with ready and continuing access to technical and consultancy resources in order that such enterprises can develop independent and robust operational forms;
2. to demonstrate and propagate the value of participative structures within worker-owned enterprises;
3. to transmit the necessary management skills to strengthen and educate worker-owned enterprises in the critical start-up and development stages;
4. to act as a focal point for the development of common services to co-operatives and worker-owned enterprises including: legal, auditing, cost and management accounting, financial control and cash-flow forecasting, buying and stock control, printing and advertising, sales and marketing;
5. to support the efforts of local agencies to develop and sustain worker-owned enterprises;
6. to broaden public and political awareness of the potential of worker-owned enterprises.

(drawn from Wales Co-operative Centre Annual Report 1983–84).

Evaluation

In its first years of operation, the Centre and its union backers can claim some successes, not least the ability to continue to raise funds to maintain its existence. Secondly, the Centre has increased the amount of publicity which the concept of worker co-operatives has received (though the impact of this publicity is hard to gauge, and difficult to differentiate from the attention which a number of the co-operatives themselves have attracted within Wales in recent years).

Yet these successes notwithstanding, the Centre can claim only part of the *direct* credit for the accelerated establishment of co-operatives within the Principality (for reasons discussed below), and appears to have made only limited headway in spreading an awareness of co-operatives within the trade union movement.

Three factors in particular may be seen to have limited the Centre's ability to directly facilitate the growth of co-operatives. Firstly, an initial emphasis on the short-term goal of job creation – characterized by the public statements emphasizing the objective of creating one co-operative per month and at least 1,000 jobs within 3 years – may be seen to have militated against development strategies which may have been more fruitful in the longer term. Support organizations rely heavily for their success on the quality of their contacts with relevant institutions and the gradual acquisition of trust and credibility. The pressures created by this initial announcement of targets became evident in various ways, not least the early turnover among senior staff and the apparent lack of early consultation with local bodies already working in the field of co-operative development.

The second and crucial factor shaping the Centre's early experiences was its failure to establish a fund to provide the risk capital upon which embryonic co-operatives could draw. Initial proposals to enlist the support of one of the existing national commercial banks, in order to establish an independent savings and investment fund were unsuccessful; subsequent attempts to find a mutually acceptable arrangement have not yet borne fruit. The difficulties experienced by co-operatives in raising necessary finance in the commercial banking sector continue to underline the need for an investment fund whose administrators are favourably disposed to co-operative ventures.

Thirdly, the resources in the Centre appear not to have been sufficient to prevent very long delays occurring between the original idea among a group to establish a co-operative and the actual commencement of the business. The identifying of new markets, creating an adequate business plan, and obtaining the necessary funding have been found in some instances to take more than a year, by which time enthusiasm may have dwindled, particularly where some of the original participants (and potentially those with skills most in demand) have obtained employment elsewhere.

Co-operatives as Small Businesses

In a number of ways co-operatives share similar problems to any other newly created small business – problems of raising capital and finding customers. In certain respects the development of co-operatives faces additional obstacles. Not only may commercial banks be less favourably disposed to co-operative ventures than their capitalist equivalents, but also co-operatives, particularly "rescue" co-operatives, may be seeking to establish a business with a much larger workforce than would be typical of non-co-operative ventures in their start-up period. The result is a much larger wage-bill in the former, whereas newly-created small enterprises generally seek to hold their overheads down to a minimum level (for example, often keeping the workforce to a single person until the business is established); co-operatives may well be seeking to establish with a higher number of workers. This compounds the difficulty in the latter of raising capital and maintaining an adequate cash flow.

Yet despite such differences, in many other ways the experiences and problems of co-operatives are identical to any other newly formed business – finding information about markets, available loans and grants, obtaining professional and technical assistance, finding suitable premises, etc. While the small business sector appears to be increasing in importance in industrial countries, it is only in recent years that it has begun to attract a significant research interest. Students of worker co-operatives would do well to venture more outside their normal hunting grounds to examine in greater detail how the growing literature on small business development can contribute to the understanding of the development – and obstacles to development – of worker co-operatives.

Conclusion

Worker co-operatives in Wales are a marginal activity in a marginalized region within Britain. The economic context appears generally unfavourable to the development of small businesses, whether or not of a co-operative form. Evaluation of the experience of Welsh co-operatives would appear to confirm and reinforce earlier studies which have highlighted the under-capitalized nature of many co-operatives, resulting in part from their difficulties in obtaining funds through commercial channels. In addition co-operatives may be adding to their problems by seeking to come into existence with too large an initial workforce, thereby creating considerable demands on achieving the necessary cash flow.

In theory trade union support agencies can be of considerable assistance to co-operative development, be this directly in the form of providing funds, markets, professional and technical assistance, or indirectly by acting as liaison bodies between co-operative and other agencies. However, as the early experience of the CDTC has shown, in unfavoured areas such as Wales, it is critical that this support is developed with care, building on what facilitating networks are already in existence, and using the resources and security of the large trade union organizations not for short-term impact but to create a long-term climate favourable to the fostering of co-operative ventures.

References

Barker, A., Lewis, P. and McCann, M. (1984): Trade Unions and the Organization of the Unemployed, *British Journal of Industrial Relations*, 22, 3: 391–404.

Bland, J. (1984): *Worker Co-operatives in Wales: A Study of the Development of Worker Coops as a Form of Alternative Employment*, Unpublished M. Sc. (Econ) project, University College, Cardiff, October.

Blyton, P. (1985): Workplace Democracy, Unemployment and the Reduction of Working Time, *Economic and Industrial Democracy*, 6, 1: 113–120.

Cornforth, C. (1982): Trade Unions and Producer Co-operatives, *Economic and Industrial Democracy*, 3: 17–30.

Cornforth, C. (1983): Some Factors Affecting the Success or Failure of Worker Co-operatives in the UK, *Economic and Industrial Democracy*, 4, 2: 163–190.

Cornforth, C., Thomas, A., Lewis, J. and Spear, R. (1988): *Developing Successful Worker Co-operatives*, London: Sage Pubs.

Gregory, D. and Logan, C. (1982): The Wales TUC: On Prospects for Workers' Co-operatives, *Economic and Industrial Democracy*, 3: 75–77.

Logan, C. and Gregory, D. (1981): *Co-operation and Job Creation in Wales: A Feasibility Study*, Cardiff: Wales TUC.

Rees, G. and Rees, T. L. (1980): Poverty and the Periphery: The Outline of a Perspective on Wales, In: G. Rees and T. L. Rees (eds.), *Poverty and Social Inequalities in Wales*, London: Croom Helm, pp. 17–32.

Thornley, J. (1981): *Workers' Co-operatives: Jobs and Dreams*, London: Heineman Educational Books.

Trade Union Research Unit (1983): *Developing Support Structures for Worker Co-operatives*, Study No. 82/0304, D. G. V of the EEC. October.

Wales Co-operative Development and Training Centre (1984): *Annual Report 1983–4*, Cardiff: WCDTC.

Wales Co-operative Centre (1986): *Annual Report*, Cardiff: Wales Co-operative Centre.

Williams, G. (1980): Industrialization, Inequality and Deprivation in Rural Wales, In: Rees, G. and Rees, T. L. (eds.), *Poverty and Social Inequality in Wales*, London: Croom Helm, pp. 168–184.

Chapter 9
The Possibilities and Limits of Self-Management in Cameroonian Enterprises:
The Case of an Artisanal Co-operative in the Building Trade

Emmanuel Kamdem

The Potential for Self-Management in Cameroonian Enterprises

In Cameroon there are two main types of enterprises:
– public enterprises and/or partly public enterprises
– private enterprises or co-operatives.
The chapter examines the potential for self-management in each type of enterprise.

Public enterprises

The state is the sole owner of this type of enterprise, and its influence is such that self-management has a very limited place. The state which is the sole provider of finance appoints the managers and controls the whole management. In Cameroon all the public enterprises are managed by civil servants or the state's agents in such a way that the other executives recruited by the enterprise, although highly competent, cannot hold a high position in the management staff; one of these positions is that of *Managing Director*. The group of workers, (a sort of small internal trade union) made up of the staff members who are directly recruited by the enterprise, has definitely no power in management and is excluded from all decision-making; its only role is limited to that of defending the workers' interests.

Partly-Public Enterprises

Here the capital is shared between the state and the private owner(s); the latter is generally a foreign partner, and nearly all the partly-public enterprises in Cameroon are joint ventures. In this case in addition to the civil servants appointed by the State, there are foreign executives who exert great influence over local workers. Once more there is an absence of identity between Capital and Labour, and this makes self-management difficult to achieve. These enterprises do not even practice co-determination, as is the case in West Germany where the workers' representatives are admitted as members of the superintendent board. To sum up we can state that in the public and partly-public enterprises neither self-management nor workers' participation exists. We think that the absence of self-management and workers' participation in management is mostly due to the retention of capital by the State or its partners, whereas the manpower is supplied by another group, the workers.

Private Enterprises

Here the whole capital belongs to the private persons or groups of private persons whose main objective is commercial, i.e. profit-making. The owners of these enterprises are either nationals or mostly foreigners who settled in the country. The main reason why these enterprises were set up in the colonial and independence periods is the exploitation of cheap manpower so as to repatriate the profits. Once more the notion of "identity" does not exist between those who own and those who work in the enterprise. The financial power of these foreigners helps them make friends with some corrupt leaders of the country against whom the President of the Republic of Cameroon fights to establish a society based on "rigour," "morality," and "democracy" in the framework of the Cameroonian policy of "New Deal."

As far as the workers' fate is concerned, the situation remains the same when the private owners are Cameroonian. In fact, experience shows that the workers prefer working with the foreigners who exploit them less than the nationals. There is a lack of training among workers, who are grouped in the national trade union, and must teach each other to defend themselves and their rights.

Co-operatives

In Cameroon, there are three categories of co-operative private enterprise according to their mode of management:
– State owned co-operatives with no self-management;
– "Free" co-operatives (without the influence of the state) managed by the members without the workers' real participation; and
– Workers' co-operatives where there is in theory an identity between capital and labour.

In theory, co-operatives are structures based on participation and democratic management and on the principles of self-help, self-management, and self-responsibility. But the close observation of the three categories of co-operatives we have just classified show that the State owned co-operatives are those created by the State to "promote the members" interests. They are found mainly in the agricultural field and produce for export products such as coffee and cocoa. In this category of co-operatives, even the members do not really participate in management because nearly all the highly ranked leaders are directly appointed by the Minister or indirectly (ordered to the administrative Board) by the Government. This shows that the members are not free as far as management is concerned; moreover, the workers recruited by the co-operatives are exclusively held as underdogs who bear the whole weight of the State's highly ranked leaders. Workers' self-management in such a structure is simply impossible; they should, first of all, have the possibility and the opportunity to become themselves members of the co-operatives, and the members themselves must become workers in the co-operative.

In the "free" co-operatives managed by the members, self-management does not exist just because one is a co-owner of capital. The free co-operatives managed by the members without the workers' participation are forms of co-operatives that are found mainly in the Moungo Division in Cameroon (Kampe 1984). They are all structures created by rich farmers who have associated a few country people in order to benefit from the advantages given to co-operatives in Cameroon and to meet their own needs, often to the prejudice of the small local farmers. Kampe (1984: 75) shows that in the coffee trading co-operatives in the Moungo Division as a whole, the *co-operators* take little or no part in decision-making. The power of decision belongs to a handful of co-operators. As a consequence, some members are outside the true life of the co-operatives and therefore become uninterested and consider the co-operative no longer their concern but rather that of a powerful person or group who uses the co-operative to influence and exploit others.

In these free co-operatives, not only are some members unable to take part in decision-making but so are the workers as well. As a result, we conclude that self-management means nothing to those members and workers. These "small" members are pushed to one side due mainly to their very small financial shares. As a matter of fact, the influential members of these co-operatives are the owners of the coffee husking factories. They have transformed their factory into co-operatives so as to get more customers because, in accordance with the co-operative law in Cameroon, a member of a given co-operative is bound to deliver all his produce to that co-operative. If one wishes to favour and boost self-management in an enterprise, it is necessary that the financial resources should be equally shared among the co-managers. This means that all of the members should be financially sound or that the assets brought into business should be valued in such a way that everybody has nearly the same share of participation in the running of the enterprise. Let us examine now the possibilities of self-management in the worker co-operatives where there exists at least in theory an *identity* between those who own and those who work in the enterprise.

The worker co-operatives are an association of persons who bring together their manpower to produce together. As such they ought to be a model self-managed enterprise, for the conflict that arises between the owners of capital and the workers no longer exists.

According to Dulfer (1984: 300), the question of sharing is the essential problem in co-operatives: "Ein zentrales Problem der Produktiv-genossenschaft – an dem sie in sehr vielen Fällen gescheitert ist, ist die Frage des Verteilungs-Schlüssels." Dulfer means by this that if a co-operative operates a policy of equal returns to members, then members who have proved themselves to be really efficient will lack motivation.

We share Dulfer's view point, but at the same time we suggest that the fact should be added that it is not abnormal to associate the equal sharing per head with another form of motivation. For instance if, for a given length of time, two co-operators have to set up a given production factory and if one of them builds up another one, there is no harm that the latter should benefit from this as well as receiving equal shares from the first factory. In addition, job motivation is not limited to the financial sharing of income; there are other sets of motivations which we cannot waste time to analyse. Nowadays in Austria you find worker co-operatives of which members play a double role according to the law: in fact, they are entrepreneurs on the one hand and workers on the other.

The case study described below will show us the results of an attempt to establish a self-managed enterprise in the south-Saharian part of Africa.

The Case of the Artisanal Co-operative in the Building Trade "Les Frères Camérounais" CONFRECAM

The Cameroonian economy, as well as that of many other countries in the Third World, is dominated by multi-national firms in the principal sectors of the economy. One of these important sectors in Cameroon is that of the building industry which is almost completely controlled by foreigners who overshadow the local craftsmen. Contrary to the agricultural sector, where the colonialists found great interest in regrouping the natives in the form of co-operatives, the building sector suffered during the whole colonial period from the lack of training for Cameroonians by the Authorities. Europeans were always invited to come and construct the buildings that the public and private sectors needed; the local craftsmen had to confine themselves to unimportant jobs in the indigenous quarters where nearly all the houses were huts. Cameroonians who were working in the building sites were nothing but manual workers with no right to claim and no way of self-management.

After the political independence of the country in 1960, the Government showed no interest in the promotion of the Cameroonian craftsmen. A vast programme of house buildings was launched but once more with the help of Europeans. The Cameroon Building Company – Société Immobilière du Caméroun (SIC) – was created in association with the State who completely ignored the existence of the local craftsmen. A policy of nation development should have consisted in launching a programme to train and promote building enterprises and local craftsmen.

It was an external promoter who in 1965 first thought of regrouping craftsmen so that they should form their own enterprise: he was a missionary priest called Jean-Marie Pouymirou. A group of 10 isolated craftsmen – all Christians – created a worker co-operative called "Co-opérative Artisanale de Bâtiment (Les Frères Camérounais)" CONFRECAM. Their members were made up of carpenters, bricklayers, plumbers, painters, electricians, and so on. The management of this co-operative was done exclusively by its members. In accordance with section 2 of CONFRECAM's internal regulations, the objective of the co-operative is to make its members:

1. join together in the same profession in order to undertake all forms of building work (carpentry, painting, concrete, and so on);
2. improve their working conditions and income; and

3. encourage in and among themselves the spirit of savings and brotherly self-help without any distinction of race or religion.

Section 4 of the same internal regulations stipulates that the co-operative reserves the exclusive right to work to co-operators, and that no co-operator can be unemployed because of the slowing down of the activities. According to section 5, the minimum number of shares is 12 of which at least one shall be paid up in full.

As far as salary is concerned (section 6), every co-operator is entitled to receive his own amount which is fixed by the Board of Directors after proposals from the Manager. In determining salaries, the following elements shall be taken into account:

- the collective conventions in force;
- professional reference of every member; and
- scales of salary.

The allowances vary from 20,000 FCFA for the Manager to CFA 2,500 for the storekeeper. Section 20, relating to new membership, stipulated that everybody who works in the co-operative has the right to apply for membership after a 24 months' period of uninterrupted work.

The analysis of some of these sections of the internal regulations brings us to make the following remarks: the objective of CONFRECAM was to favour the economic and social promotion of the members through self-management; but we notice that the number of shares a member can hold varies; this situation imbalances the members' financial power while creating the abuse of power in the holders of the majority of shares; even if management is democratic (one person one vote), it is known that the withdrawal of one financially important member would engender a decrease in capital for the co-operative as an association of persons and variable capital. The consequence of this is that the "big" members behave as capitalists in the trading companies. Given the fact that the maximum number of shares that one CONFRECAM member can have is not limited (contrary to the principles of the co-operatives), the rich members can increasingly gather shares and end up dominating the whole co-operative.

CONFRECAM has succeeded in solving the crucial salary problem faced by the co-operatives of workers. It has respected the scale of salary in force in Cameroon to fix the salary of its members; the same criteria have also been respected (professional skill, collective conventions, scales of salary, and so on). But the income gap keeps on increasing because the members receive returns of premium pro-rata according to the amount of their salary earned. Since salaries are "stratified," the return of premium is also "stratified."

It is also noted that in CONFRECAM the number of the members has not changed since its creation; only replacements have been made (in case of death). Although the employees have the possibility to apply for membership after a 24 months' period of uninterrupted work (section 20), they have never been admitted as co-operators, and for 20 years now CONFRECAM has been managed by only 10 members, 5 of which are administrators.

There is no doubt that CONFRECAM acts as a capitalistic company using the word co-operative to benefit from the enormous tax advantages given to co-operatives in Cameroon. Unfortunately the leaders of the country say that the state recognizes CONFRECAM juridically as a co-operative; but actually they recognize it as a capitalist company and therefore demand that it pays taxes accordingly. This has made CONFRECAM go through a period of crisis. But over the past 5 years its financial results have constantly improved. On the 30th of June 1984 its balance sheet showed a net surplus of 48,000 dollars. In addition, CONFRECAM's economic results are more and more permanent and solid due to its enormous achievements in the field of building in Cameroon. It is even competing seriously now with the foreign companies, it employs a large number of workers, but they are refused the opportunity of becoming members.

Concluding Point of View

Among the different forms of companies that exist in Cameroon, only the worker co-operatives could offer a real possibility of self-management insofar as the gap between the owners and the employees does not exist. The other forms which are financed by people other than the workers (the state or private individuals or firms) are first of all inappropriate for self-management because of the presence of conflicts of interest. Self-management has been a real failure in Cameroon. In CONFRECAM, which is a unique initiative in Cameroon, there is a clear-cut domination by "big" members who hold great quantities of shares and put big obstacles in the way of new workers' becoming members of the co-operative.

CONFRECAM lacks a co-operative and trade union training; both the employees and the leaders totally ignore the most elementary co-operative principles. As for trade unionism there is Trade Union of Cameroonian Workers (UNTC) in Cameroon; but few people know about it and it is not well armed to defend the workers of various sectors. Moreover, the trade union in the building sector recruits owner craftsmen and not workers – CONFRECAM reflects this situation. A real system of self-management cannot be properly achieved without the real participation of workers which requires the existence of a strong and powerful trade union of workers.

References

Dulfer, E. (1984): *Betriebswirtschaftslehre der Kooperative*, Göttingen:
Gernard, A. (1974): *L'autogestion, l'entreprise et l'économie*, Paris:
Kampe, (1984): *Les co-opératives du commerce du café dans le Départment du Moungo (Cameroon): Difficultés et possibilités d'amélioration*, unpublished thesis, ENSET, Douala University Centre.

Part III
Economic Change, Labour, and the Unions

Introduction

Paul Blyton

Workers' activity in pursuit of self-management systems of work organization can be traced, in one form or another, as far back as industrialization itself. During the twentieth century, this activity has taken place against a variety of economic and political backdrops, though frequently ones evidencing a high degree of change, fluidity, and uncertainty. As Ramsay (1977) has pointed out, advances in industrial democracy have tended to coincide with periods of increasing labour power, resulting either from economic conditions of growth and full employment or from political conditions, notably wartime emergency and the state's need to ensure maximum industrial production for the war machine.

In the past decade the central factor which has impacted upon industrial economies has been the recession in world trade in the early 1980s and the coincidence of this with other changes already taking place: the long-term transformation of labour-intensive manufacturing industries; the growing internationalization of production; the increased importance of computer-based technologies in both office and production operations; and the growing proportions of part-time, female, and non-manual workers in the overall workforce. The far-reaching nature of these changes, and the fundamental challenge they pose to traditional worker organizations, cannot be ignored by analysts of self-management systems and the conditions favouring the growth of industrial democracy. It is in this context that Drache's arguments are relevant to the themes of this book. In taking one example of a Western industrialized society (Canada), Drache identifies some of the major "de-industrialization" processes taking place, and their implications for trade unions and the development of democratic forms of work organization. One of the basic questions here is to what extent economic restructuring involves workers' losing positions in which they have gained a high level of competence, and either becoming unemployed or moving into jobs which are less stable, less unionized, and call for a different (and often lower level) set of competences.

By focusing on changes taking place in one industrial society, Drache points to some of the broader factors which need to be considered in any analysis of participatory competence and control in the late twentieth century. One conclusion from his analysis is that the group who must acquire sufficient competence for self-management is no longer a narrowly defined industrial workforce, but rather a broader "popular sector" which includes trade unions, women's groups, ecology movements, social agencies, and voluntary associations.

Yet while trade union influence may be under considerable threat as a result of the factors weakening the overall power of labour, unions remain a key actor in the articulation of worker interests and the development of industrial democracy. At the same time, union movements have shown themselves to be far from unified in their approach to self-management. Hancké and Wijgaerts illustrate this problem well in their examination of the evolution of the ideas of workers' control and self-management within the Belgian union movement. Again, current changes in technology are seen to pose fundamental questions for trade unions and their ability both to cope with the challenge to their power base and pursue strategies for achieving greater industrial democracy.

Several of these issues are also reflected in the way French trade unions are seeking to respond to changed economic, political, and technological conditions. In their analysis of three French union organizations, Jansen and Kissler consider the problems both of building up a successful relationship with left-wing governments and of contributing to the decisions and outcomes stemming from the modernization of both office and shop-floor technologies. At present, argue the authors, the unions are adopting a generally accepting position on technological change, but are achieving little in return in the form of negotiated control over the changes being introduced.

In the final contribution in this section, Heisig and Littek examine the issues of competence and control from the point of view of the actual levels of competence which exist among a work-group, and the level of involvement in decision-making that this produces. This involvement and the consent it engenders are seen as crucial aspects of the management of labour. In analysing this, the authors draw upon a study of white-collar work in three German manufacturing companies, all undergoing major technical change as a means to overcome market difficulties. In seeking to understand why the changes did not meet with resistance from groups apparently adversely affected, Heisig and Littek argue that this was in important part due to the participatory relationship which had developed between the white-collar staff and management, which in turn was built on the competence located in the workforce and management's dependence on that competence.

References

Ramsay, H. (1977): Cycles of Control: Worker Participation in Sociological and Historical Perspective, *Sociology*, 11, 3: 481–506.

Chapter 10
New Work Processes, Unregulated Capitalism and the Future of Labour

Daniel Drache

De-industrialization is almost singlehandedly changing the role of labour in Western societies. The current period of industrial upheaval is effectively dismantling the status quo of the last thirty years. Soon, a very large segment of the population will belong to a post-industrial proletariat that will have little job security and will be forced to work at contractual, casual, temporary and part-time employment (Gorz, 1980: 69). In addition to de-industrialization, new technology is creating a burgeoning unemployment economy.[1] The new technology is transforming the mass production industries that were once the bedrock of modern industrial society.

De-industrialization can be defined either as a process of relative job loss in industrial employment or the systematic erosion of investment in a country's industrial capacity. More important than the definition are its characteristics. These include: (1) a decline of industrial employment relative to total employment, (2) a rise in structural unemployment due to the slowing down of the economy, (3) the erosion of export-performance, (4) an increase in poorer quality jobs in services, clerical and sales and (5) significant import penetration of the domestic market. This kind of

---

[1] For a mainstream view of the inadequacy of the official concept of unemployment, see S. F. Kaliski, 'Why High Unemployment?', *Canadian Public Policy*, No. 10: 2, 1984; and The Economic Council of Canada, *Jobs in Short Supply*, Ottawa: Economic Council of Canada, 1983a. Leon Muszyniski, 'Unemploment in Toronto, Hidden and Real', Working Papers for Full Employment, Toronto: Social Planning Council of Metropolitan Toronto, 1980 has shown the inadequacy of relying on the shortcomings of relying on official figures. His calculations suggest that the real rate is anywhere between 4 and 6 percent higher than the government's figures.

wholesale economic restructuring has long been part of capitalist development.[2]

The current epidemic of plant shutdowns are the consequence of widespread systematic disinvestment in a nation's industrial capacity. Plants that close down have not necessarily been unprofitable. Indeed, a very large percentage of plant closures occur simply because the operation of the branch enterprise did not fit into the corporate strategy of the parent company. In theory, "disinvestment is supposed to free capital and labour from relatively unproductive uses in order to put them to work in more productive ones" (Bluestone and Harrison, 1982: 6). In fact, this is not happening. Corporations are milking older facilities as "cash cows", letting them deteriorate until they are no longer seen as profitable in light of the larger corporate strategy.

New competitive pressures are having an unprecedented impact on the global reach of multinational corporations. Coupled with portable industrial technologies these new competitive pressures are creating radically new conditions, especially for labour. Everywhere labour has seen its bargaining power weaken in a shrinking job market.[3] Since the slowdown in the world economy, all industrialized countries, be they big or small, strong or weak are experiencing a drop in both manufacturing output as a share of the GNP and in the size of their workforce, especially in the mass-production industries such as steel, auto, machine parts, office equipment and electronic equipment. In the United States, manufacturing employment is nearly 900 000 below the level of 1980. In an article in the New York Times, Janet Norwood, the United States Commissioner of Labour Statistics summarized the situation stating that only 58 percent of the jobs lost during the downturn have been recovered by American manufacturing industries as a group. "Many of these manufacturing industries face a troubled future. And many of the factory workers displaced from their jobs do not have the skills to move into other industries." (Norwood, 1985).

The situation in the U.S. is not atypical. At the same time, in all Western industrial countries, the number of jobs in the service-sector has risen dramatically. In the United States, for instance. 7 out of every 10

---

[2] Schumpter described the process as one of "creative destruction". For his views, see Joseph Schumpter, *Capitalism, Socialism and Democracy*, London: Allen & Unwin, 1943.
[3] For an analysis of the impact of de-industrialization on the third world, see Alain Lipietz, "Globalisation of the General Crisis of Fordism", SNID Occasional Paper No. 84–203, CEPREMAP/Paris, France 1984.

American workers are employed in the service-producing sector, while only 2 out of 10 work in the nations's factories. Despite the fact that ten million jobs have been created since 1982, many observers are predicting that perhaps as many as three million will disappear as soon as a recession hits. This is because many of the new jobs are not permanent. U.S. companies are using full-time temporary workers to lower job costs and drive down wages. (International Herald Tribune, March 17, 1988)

Given business' reliance on the proliferation of full-time temporary workers to maximize the firm's flexibility, many economic observers now believe that this phenomenon, along with the rise in longterm structural unemployment, accommodates capital's drive to cut costs and become "internationally competitive". The search for new methods to increase productivity means creating more competitive mechanisms in the labour market and requires altering the production system to permit the introduction of technology and other innovative procedures in the work place. These strategies on the part of state and capital, which Boyer (1984) has termed "la chasse des rigiditiés", entails having a system of production that acknowledges the employers' right to assign their employees to any work-position the employer wishes.[4]

The current search for "flexibility in the workplace" is a euphemism for dismantling existing entitlements. In particular, it means rejecting the policy understanding that in order to have a fast growing economy with high levels of effective demand, wage-earners had to share in productivity gains. The mechanism which made this possible was the legal recognition of unions and the negotiation of productivity agreements particularly in the core mass production industries in almost all industrial countries. These two institutional arrangements ensured a constant upward pressure on wages since the growth of mass consumption was premised on an increase in purchasing power. The effectiveness of such agreements can be seen in the fact that, in Western Europe, the increase in purchasing power of wage-earners paralleled the rise in productivity. (Lipietz, 1984: 11). Capital accepted this arrangement as the quid pro quo for labour stability so long as the economy was expanding. But given the economic slowdown in North America and Europe and the challenge in goods

---

[4] Robert Boyer, one of the founders of the Paris-based Régulation School of political economy has written prolifically on the question of economic restructuring. See his far-reaching article, "Les Transformations Du Rapport Salarial en Europe Depuis Une Décennie: Quelques Eléments de Synthèse, F.E.R.E. Paris: 1984. It also contains a comprehensive bibliography of Boyer's books and articles.

production from Japan, Korea and the newly industrializing countries of the third world, Western capital no longer finds these agreements useful. Under the guise of industrial reorganization, many firms have succeeded in overturning existing work norms by taking advantage of weak unions and a labour market flooded with the unemployed to alter the job and pay structure of the unionized work force.

Body Slimming: Rationalizing the Workforce

Japanese business calls this process of production rationalization 'body slimming' – a term that covers such 'initiatives' as dismissals, lay-offs, scrapping of entire factories, transfer of parent-firm workers to subcontractors, annexation of bankrupt firms and countless other corporate strategies for reorganizing production. (Muto Ichiyo, 1985: 53).

It is an innocuous, indeed, almost attractive-sounding strategy. But, under the guise of "coping" with de-industrialization, capital is toppling the "skill" hierarchy of the working class and creating new institutional arrangements to manage, deploy and discipline the ever increasingly "disposable" work force. The introduction of robots and other technological advances make it possible "to economize not just on human labour, but on labour and capital at the same time" (ibid: 129). It is estimated that the cost of an assembly line robot used 24 hours a day, seven days a week averages approximately \$ 5 – \$ 6 per hour, considerably less than the \$ 14 – \$ 16 per hour paid to an auto worker for a 40-hour week, excluding benefits. (Kaliski, 1984: 139).

One consequence of the changing position of labour has been that, in less than a decade wages have fallen so precipitously in the U.S. that it is becoming a medium to a low wage economy. In 1961, six out of 10 jobs in the U.S. were in the middle-wage occupations. By 1982, only five could be so classed. The number of production workers had fallen by seven per cent. Moreover, those who lost better-paying jobs and were able to find new employment took an average drop in pay of 30 percent. Bluestone and Harrison (1984) call this phenomenon "occupational skidding." This refers to workers who lose their jobs in the mass production industries and then are reabsorbed into the economy as part of a rapidly growing low-wage labour pool. Even though the U.S. still had close to 20 million factory workers in 1985, there has been *no increase in the number of factory jobs since 1970* (Norwood: 1985).

Canadian Labour: A Long Crisis of Adjustment

With its open, export-led economy the restructuring produced by de-industrialization poses no less a threat to the fabric of Canadian society. The state and business have responded to the pressures of unregulated competition with a view to reduce labour's standing both in the workplace and in the economy nation-wide. They have taken advantage of the harsh economic times and soaring unemployment levels to force wage and other concessions from Canada's industrial unions. Since 1982 Canadian labour has been losing much of the security and welfare that the postwar Keynesian compromise guaranteed. Indeed, Canadian workers are particularly vulnerable to the attempts of the state to transform the labour process and reorganize work to accommodate the flexible work arrangements proposed by employers. This is because the ability of Canadian workers to negotiate technological change with job security is very limited. At the enterprise level, their participation in planning for change is minimal The absence of the possibility to participate can be traced to the defects of the scheme of collective bargaining in Canada. The Canadian system of industrial relations is based on notions which presume a truly competitive market economy. The existing collective bargaining regime has kept employer-labour relations as closely wedded to the pure market model as it is possible to be and, therefore, is premised on the idea of a multitude of atomized employment settings even while allowing unionization something of a legitimate role. In practice, each group of workers has to negotiate at the factory gate with their employer. Sector and national bargaining of the kind that exists in Europe is the exception. This has handicapped Canadian workers and their trade unions who have finally become conscious of the fact that they are facing a major structural change in work and employment relations. Understandably, the workforce are suspicious of these new work relations. Moreover they have very little power with which to meet the new reality that the new computer-based technologies will cost them their jobs and reduce their control of the workplace rather than enhance their employment opportunities. (Drache and Glasbeek, 1988).

Faced with the restructuring of industries, Canada's workforce faces a long crisis of adjustment. For close to a decade almost all regions of the country have been affected by plant closures and massive lay-offs.[5] The

---

[5] The most dramatic instance of de-industrialization occurred in the Maritimes, which, at the turn of the century, was Ontario's economic rival. Since then the entire region has born

recession of the 1980s has caught the Canadian economy in a pincer-like vice, squeezed between capital's search for flexibility and an economy which has tied itself to the American business cycle.

With 40 percent of the manufacturing work force employed in the foreign-owned sector, Canada is highly vulnerable to shifts in American economic strategy. This is because of the dependent nature of the Canadian economy and the high foreign ownership levels.[6] Many of the troubled industries in the 80s are subsidiaries of American firms. With North American rationalization well advanced, the subsidiaries are prime candidates to be phased out. To make matters worse, many studies point to the fact that few Canadian corporations have developed any international expertise to cope with new global pressures. Therefore, Canadian industries are ill-equipped to compete in the new global economy. (Globe and Mail, September 16, 1988.) Add to this the increased competition from the newly industrializing countries and the exhaustion of the Keynesian growth model which guided the fortunes of the industrial economies since the end of WW II and it is not surprising that Canadian industrial development is in serious trouble.

With the state and employers deeply committed to an exported growth strategy, the economy has become more dependent on internationally-generated and -controlled supply and demand. This poses new risks and few benefits for workers in Canada's small industrial sector. Sectors in difficulty include: small Canadian family business that are forced to close down by a combination of rising interest rates, bad management and product shifts; firms in industries, such as textiles, that cannot compete with offshore imports; and mining and resource-based companies that are subject to dramatic turn-abouts in the international demand for exports and whose production methods are being rapidly automated. In addition to the well-publicized cases of the steel, auto and textile industries, many labour-intensive industries such as footwear, clothing and furniture are

the brunt of the effects of de-industrialization, meted out by the centrally-based banks and the state. Similarly, Canada's national developmental strategy was itself a response to both the lack of industry in Canada and the loss of industries that migrated to the U.S. See, R. T. Naylor, *The History of Canadian Business*, Toronto: James Lorimer, 1975.

6 For a discussion of the role of American capital in the Canadian economy, see Kari Levitt, *Silent Surrender: The Multinational Corporation in Canada*, Toronto: Macmillan, 1970; and Wallace Clement, *Continental Corporate Power: Elite Linkages Between Canada and the United States*. Recently, the question of foreign control of the manufacturing sector has also become a concern of the Ontario provincial government and its views are contained in the recent study, *Competing in the Global Economy*, Report of the Premier's Council vol. 1, Toronto: 1988.

under intense pressure and have been forced to reduce their work force. Other sectors affected are capital-intensive industries such as metals, metal products and transportation; and technologically-intensive industries such as chemicals, plastic products, machine and professional instruments. With a small, inefficient industrial base, Canada is in grave danger of losing the race to survive economically. A comparison with the U.S. shows that Canadian industries in an 'open' staples exporting economy have felt the effects of economic restructuring much more than their American counterparts.

Table 1: The Principle Differences in the Effects of De-Industrialization between Canada and the U.S.

A Comparison of Job growth in Canada and the U.S. (percent change 1980-87)		
	Canada	U.S.
Public & Social Services	+20.0	+14.3
Business & Fin. Services	+16.0	+28.3
Consumer & Personal Services	+18.3	+17.9
Goods Production	− 0.5	+ 0.2
Total	+11.8	+13.2

Source: adapted from Gower, 1988, p.99

With its weaker, dependent economy, the impact of the job loss on Canadian labour markets and entitlements has been especially damaging. Between 1980 und 1983, approximately one in five jobs disappeared from the manufacturing sector; unemployment rose by 68 %; and hundreds of long-established firms closed their doors forever. By 1988 aspects of Canada's unemployment had become alarming. Despite adding one million jobs since 1984, Canada's employment record was far from admirable. While unemployment in the U.S. had dropped by 3 percent between 1980 and 1987, Canada's level of unemployment had shot up by 37 percent for the same period. Longterm unemployment has remained high in Canada despite faster employment growth. Many of the new jobs were concentrated in the low-paying sales and service side of the economy which are largely non-unionized. (Grower, 1988) As well, most of the new jobs are concentrated largely in central Canada, thus increasing regional rates of unemployment. Workers in British Columbia and the smaller industrial centres in Western Canada have carried the brunt of job loss and plant shutdown.

American branchplants are a principal source of job loss in the capital intensive industries such as machinery, electrical equipment and autos. Laid-off workers are not finding new employment at comparable pay and skill levels. Many are forced to take paycuts or work in non-unionized plants and older workers frequently discover that they are considered unemployable. For many workers economic restructuring is the temple of doom as it means continuing job loss and economic uncertainty.

Some of the basic changes in the labour market predate the current wave of economic restructuring. The consequences for those who lose their job are devastating. This can be seen in the difficulty workers have in finding equivalent employment. The Ontario Ministry of Labour surveyed 2 500 workers who had been laid off between 1979 and 1981 from 19 plants covering a range of industries. (Ontario Ministry of Labour, 1984). This unpublished study merits special attention because it is one of the most thorough examinations of job loss and the existing state of labour markets ever attempted. Its most striking finding is that only one in five of workers who lost their job on account of a shutdown, found work in the same occupation. Of the men who had processing jobs in manufacturing, less than half found comparable work. Women had an even smaller chance of finding equivalent employment. Only 20 percent in the sample succeeded in working as an industrial assembler. Overall, women who were laid off were forced into clerical and service occupations or occupations requiring a 'lower skill level' than their previous job. (Ibid. p. 26. Also, Economic Council of Canada, 1983 b: 119–120, for similar findings) Of those who were lucky enough to find full time work, it took on average more than three months of searching to find a new job.

The study's most alarming finding was that 40 percent of the men and women who had been laid off were still unemployed two years later. This does not include the 20 percent of those who had found work but had subsequently been laid off and were unemployed for a second time. These "hard-core" unemployed were composed of older men and women with little job seniority, often low-skilled and in occupations already hard hit by unemployment. Of the workers surveyed, roughly 10 percent had given up looking for work and had left the work force or been forced to take alternative employment in part-time positions.

With occupational downgrading, pay levels also declined. Twenty-five percent of the men who found new employment earned less than they had previously and 42 percent of women took a paycut. Only a third of those who found work went to better paying jobs. Overall, the number of people working in an establishment covered by a collective bargaining agreement declined significantly. 68 % of workers were represented by unions at the time they lost their job. By contrast, only 39 % of those who found steady employment did so in a unionized establishment.

Table 2: Canadian Labour Productivity, Compensation Costs and Consumer Prices in Canada (% change)

Business Sector	compensation per hour	output per hour	consumer prices	real wages
1973-82	11.2	1.3	9.8	1.3
1982-87	4.3	2.3	4.5	−0.2
1987	4.0	1.4	4.4	−0.4

Source: Donner, 1988: 17

During a time of so-called recovery and expansion Canadian labour market conditions have worsened. Real incomes for most workers have fallen and labour's overall share of the country's domestic income has shrunk by nearly 5 percent over the past decade. The most telling sign of the crisis for labour is that real wages were actually lower in 1987 than they were in 1982 at the depth of the last recession. What these figures represent, according to Arthur Donner, "is a shift of market power towards management and away from labour because of the harsh competitive forces unleashed by the last recession" (Donner, 1988: 17). Since 1982 there is no doubt that the productivity-real wage link has become a thing of the past in Canada. The main beneficiaries of this drop in overall wages are first and foremost Canadian business and, in particular, finance capital whose share of the national financial pie has more than doubled over the same period.

These dramatic changes in market power have been accompanied by other consequences. Job shedding in the industrial side of the economy has continued down to the present. Despite all the new jobs created since 1983, Canada has failed to add new jobs to the goods-producing side of the economy. In fact, since 1980, on net, Canada lost another 25000 industrial jobs, jobs which were often better paying and more skilled than average jobs. Compared to the 1970s, Canadian employees have much less job security as a result of rapid technological change and continuing high levels of unemployment. Critically, long-term unemployment in Canada is on the rise and has come more prevalent than in the U.S. In the U.S., 14 percent of the unemployed had been out of work for six months or longer. In Canada the rate was almost double and for men forty-five and older, almost one in three had been out of work for more than six months. In the U.S. the proportion of older workers out of a job for more than six months dropped sharply from 33 percent in 1983 to 24 percent in 1985. All this is a further indication of just how different the two economies really have become as far as the picture of work and employment patterns are concerned.

Table 3: A Comparison of Canada-U.S. Long-term Unemployment Rates Both Sexes, All Ages, 1980 to 1987

	80	81	82	83	84	85	86	87
			(percent)					
Canada	15.3	15.9	20.0	28.2	26.3	25.9	23.4	23.8
U.S.	10.7	14.1	16.6	23.9	19.1	15.4	14.4	14.0

Source: Gower, 1988, p. 106

There are several possible reasons for the contrast in the respective national employment picture.

First, Canada has no equivalent to the American 'sun' belt region. In the U.S., industries that close down in the old industrial regions often relocate in the American south-west. When plants in Canada close their doors in one region, however, it is rarely to relocate elsewhere in Canada. Closures here tend to be permanent. When branch-plants close down, they return to the U.S or move elsewhere in the world such as Mexico and the Caribbean. Since the intensification of the crisis in the 80s, over 3000 U.S. manufacturers have set up assembly operations in Mexico near the Mexican-U.S. border (Grunwald and Flam, 1985). Leading Canadian companies in both textiles and auto parts among others have followed the immigration southwards of American multinational corporations to produce goods formerly made in Canada. In this period of experimentation with production re-organization, more and more Canadian firms can be expected to take advantage of the low wage levels and the anti-union atmosphere that results from the internationalization of production.

Secondly, in the race to create new jobs, Ontario with more than 70 percent of Canada's manufacturing capacity, is being out-performed by the Great Lakes Region of the American mid-west, its principal North American competitor. American companies based in Ontario have bowed to pressure from their head offices in Ohio, New York and Michigan to create new employment in the U.S. first. In New York State, over 500000 new jobs have been created over the last five years. (New York Times, August 29, 1985).

Thirdly, even if Canada's high-tech industries grow they cannot be expected to provide a sufficient number of new jobs for those who are displaced from the mass production industries. Canada's high-tech industries employ less than five percent of the workforce compared to more than 10 percent in the U.S. The other side of the coin is that import penetration into Canada of sophisticated end-parts such as computers and scientific equipment has risen dramatically. By the 1980s, 36% of all manufactured goods in Canada were imported; in the U.S. the comparable figure is a mere 10 percent. Canada's trade deficit in sophisticated end products topped $18 billion by 1984. With its open export-led economy Canada is losing the race to become technologically self-sufficient.

Fourth, the Canadian state has actually precipitated layoffs by reducing tariffs on all goods coming into Canada. In reducing tariffs too quickly, Ottawa has been responsible for job-loss in key industries which employ large numbers of women. This reduction has had a particularly adverse effect on employment in textiles and other labour-intensive industries, as well as in the more advanced sectors of plastics and chemicals. By 1987, 85 percent of all goods entering Canada will be free of any tariffs. By contrast, the American government has raised tariffs in an effort to save jobs. The percentage of U.S. manufactured goods protected by non-tariff barriers has risen from 20 percent on 1980 to 35 percent in 1983. (Thurow, 1984: 30).

All of these facts point to a single truth. As business restructures, Canadian capital is able to gain new control and leverage over its employees. The most important way this happens is that employers are able to demand pay concessions and other rollbacks. A survey of wage settlements in 1984, including cost-of-living adjustments, showed that despite a mild recovery, wage settlements continued to fall. Average wage settlements fell to 3.2 per cent in the first quarter of 1985, down from 3.6 percent in 1984 and 10.2 percent in 1982. (Globe and Mail, April 1 and June 13, 1985). In British Columbia and Alberta, two out of every three public sector settlements, and three out of every four in the private sector called for a wage freeze or cut wages in the first year of the contract. Nationally, in the private sector alone, a recent study done for the Department of Labour showed the number of contracts with wage concessions were "almost double 1983's total of 71." (ibid.).

In terms of the labour market, the consequences of industrial redeployment on job creation are far-reaching. Economic restructuring has accelerated the shift in demand from blue collar to white collar, from secure to insecure employment and from "men's industrial work" to the female job ghetto areas of the economy.

Job Creation in the 1980s

The problem for Canada's labour movement is that most of the new jobs that are being created demand less skills and pay less than traditional jobs and are often filled with part-time and casual labour. In the last decade, of the almost 2 million additional jobs created, nearly all were in service sector occupations. As the Twenty-First Annual Review of the Economic Council of Canada, shows "community, business, and personal service activities now employ more persons than all the manufacturing, construction, agriculture and other primary industries combined." (Economic Council of Canada, 1984: 67). Critically the Review neglected to note that many of the new jobs being created are in the public sector. Social and public services recorded the fastest expansion of any of the three components of the service industry. This underlies the fact that without the large and important role of the state in the economy, Canada would be facing an unprecedented job crisis. For instance, the private service sector job creation is much weaker in Canada than the U.S. There, business and financial services are without any question the fastest growing sector. (See table 1) In Canada, the job creation machine is centered on the public sector. But in a time of shrinking state expenditures this has not been enough to create enough new jobs in Canada's industries let alone recoup any of the estimated 450000 jobs that advances in technology cost Canada in the 1970s (ibid. p. 75). Greater reliance on robotics, the chip and other labour saving devices will intensify this trend. A recent government study estimated that over 1000000 more jobs are likely to disappear by 1990. (Bird, 1984). The fact that Canada's goods-producing sectors have failed to generate any jobs since 1980 combined with technology-induced job displacement underscores the seriousness of Canada's deep-seated economic problems.

What does the Future hold?

What are the prospects for the future? Job loss in Canada's industrial sector is long-term and likely to be permanent. Rapid technological change coupled with a slow-down in economic growth is in fact labour displacing. By 1987, several years after a strong recovery, there has been no employment growth in the industrial side of the economy. Secondly, and, most importantly, part-time work is overtaking full-time employment for both men and women. In 1985, during a period of recovery, for every full-time job for males, three part-time positions have been created. The figure is even more striking for women; there are two part-time openings for each full-time situation. The shift in labour market power gives management new control over its workforce. Finally, the rise of the service economy threatens to reinforce the female job ghetto areas of the economy such as services, sales, clerical and medical sectors. The key to job creation in the eighties relies exclusively on services to provide new employment opportunities for the growing labour force. The largest category within the service economy consists of jobs in "servant industries" such as the retail trade, amusement and recreation, personal services and the like. These are poverty jobs where the pay and quality of the job is poor, job security non-existent and they employ an ever-increasingly large number of women.

In this new regulatory environment of job slimming, the postwar compromise between capital, labour and the state is at an end. So also is the central premise of full employment capitalism. The idea was that the state was committed to a virtuous circle of economic growth based on price stability, a surplus on the current account, a rapidly expanding economy and a productivity/real wage link. This has all but been abandoned by the state and business in favour of a return to market-driven policies to support capital more directly.

Neo-Conservatism and the Mulroney Government

The Conservative government which was elected in September 1984 is much more prepared to support business than the former Liberal government. Indeed, in its first months in office, this new government devoted almost all its efforts to promoting private sector growth, laying out its strategies in a 115-page discussion paper, *A New Direction for Canada An Agenda for Economic Renewal*. This discussion paper called for a fundamental reordering of public policy which it claimed "will reach into every corner of economic and social policy." (See the Globe and Mail, November 17, 1984, B1 for a summary of the Report.) Its objectives are: smaller government; less regulation; more self-reliance by individuals and business; the encouragement of growth; and the building of a national consensus. In the Prime Minister's words, " re-energizing the economy" involves freeing capital as the key to growth and job creation. The government is "telling businessmen it's going to respond to their needs." The Final Report of the Macdonald Commission on Canada's Economic Future released in September 1985 goes even further than the Wilson budget. It recommends a fundamental change in the relationship between government and markets, free trade with the United States and a reduction of social welfare expenditures. Backed by the recommendations of the Macdonald Report, the Mulroney government has a powerful incentive to proceed with its neo-conservative policy agenda.

Since 1982, there have been more than twenty major legislative changes to the labour codes, employment standards acts and the unemployment statute, most to the detriment of labour. This flurry of legislative activity is a response to the massive transformation taking place in labour markets and work practices. The government's offensive has been instrumental in containing wage militancy in the public sector as well as making it more difficult for unions in the private sector to protect their existing level of entitlements. Many of the legislative changes have placed further restrictions on the right to strike, particularly in British Columbia, Alberta, and Quebec.

The centerpiece of the new system of economic regulation is the control of wages. As Tom Walkom, the Globe and Mail's specialist on economic policy explains, "wage rates must be kept low for the Government's low-cost export and small business strategy to work. This explains in part the Department of Labour's plan to hire up to 700 more investigators to scale down the unemployment roles. For nothing acts as a drag on wage rates than a pool of jobless people with no other means of support." (Globe and Mail, December 3, 1984).

Both the federal and provincial governments have led the offensive against workers by imposing wage controls on public sector workers. Since 1982, almost all levels of government have passed wage restraint legislation as the principal weapon to discipline the labour force. In addition, federal and provincial authorities have restricted the right to strike of their public sector workers as well as employing emergency back-to-work legislation against select groups of private sector workers. The magnitude of state intervention can be seen by a single fact. Between 1950 and 1965, there were only six instances of back-to-work legislation in Canada. Yet, in the period 1980–87, there were forty-three such measures that were used by governments to undermine labour's position. (Panitch and Swartz, 1988: 30)

This turn to the right has been reinforced at the provincial level by the provinces' labour boards, formally autonomous governmental institutions but, as John Deverell has recently shown, in reality are used by governments to put their stamp on labour policy (John Deverell, Toronto Star, July 9, 1985, A-13). The Ontario Labour Relations Board has taken the lead in encouraging a tough anti-labour stance on the part of business. In a recent decision it gave an Ontario employer the right to fire striking employees indiscriminately, once a union has lost a strike. (Globe and Mail, June 20, 1985). In another, it recognized management's right to operate during a 'lockout' and hire new personnel to replace those employees 'locked out' by management. The most brazen attack on labour was the Board's decision not to recognize an employer is bargaining in bad faith by refusing to put on the bargaining table customary bargaining issues such as working conditions, job classification and seniority.

A Blessing in Disguise

Despite the enormous pressure on labour, it is not a foregone conclusion that business' quest for flexibility will succeed nor that the government's economic policy, supporting capital's demand for reduced workplace costs, can be imposed on labour. Ironically, what business has not anticipated is labour's own ability to combat the demands placed on it.

Canadian unions fear being marginalized and have taken measures to combat new work methods that they rightly view with suspicion.

The current wave of economic reorganization is forcing Canadian labour to regroup both nationally and regionally though many problems remain. If labour is not going to become the arms and legs of the new computer-based technologies it needs to develop new forms of worker participation to limit management's prerogative in the workplace as well as give the state a new direction. The two most important changes it must make are to effect new organizational structures and to alter its bargaining strategy, to act less like a trade union and more like a trade union movement.

Despite a grim economic outlook, the labour movement has been able to regroup its forces somewhat. Union membership is on the upswing although gains in membership are very uneven. Significantly, these gains are located mostly in the public sector. The Canadian Union of Public Employees, Canada's largest union, saw its ranks grow by close to four percent. In fact, the three largest Canadian unions represent public sector workers.[7] It is not surprising that public sector unions are experiencing this growth given the fact that, as mentioned earlier, the state is, if not the principle job machine in Canada close to it. Even if the government's privatization programme has sliced the ranks of some public unions such as the Public Service Alliance of Canada, public sector unions occupy a key role in strengthening trade union rights. (Financial Post, August 20, 1988.) The most important step in this regard is the recent decision by Canada's three postal unions to merge as a 'super-union'. The Canadian Labour Relations Board ordered the unions to merge. This can hardly be said to be the unions' decision. Moreover, the application was initiated by Canada Post in an effort to curb labour militancy. Nonetheless, these unions have been among the most militant in Canada fighting for new rights for workers faced with rapid technological change.

In the industrial-side of the economy, there have been equally important developments. Recently, Canadian autoworkers decided to disaffiliate from the UAW in Detroit and create a Canadian auto workers' union. It is one of the most significant turns of events to happen to

---

[7] The ten biggest unions in Canada are in order of size: 1. Canadian Union of Public Employees, 2. National Union of Provincial Government Employees, 3. Public Service Alliance of Canada, 4. United Food & Commercial Workers International (U.S.), 5. United Steelworkers of America (U.S.), 6. Canadian Auto Workers, 7. Social Affairs Federation of Quebec, 8. International Brotherhood of Teamsters (U.S.), 9. Quebec School Board Teachers' Commission, 10. Service Employees International (U.S.)

Canadian labour in the last thirty years. The condition for the break was precipitated by the American leadership when it tried to force Canadian autoworkers at Chrysler to accept wholesale concession bargaining following the American example.

Canadian autoworkers rejected the American approach, struck Chrysler and won. This opened the way for more radical changes, the most important being that the Canadian members realized that it was no longer in their interest to be part of the American union which is far to the right of the social democratic traditions of the Canadian membership. This decision has set the stage for a possible fundamental re-orientation of the Canadian labour movement.

More generally, in the U.S. the rout of American unions by American capital raises many questions about the viability of the organizational links between Canadian affiliates and American unions. The presence of American unions in Canada once had a certain logic based on the premise of a North American labour market for the mass-production industries. Since this condition no longer exists, the more militant Canadian labour movement sees no reason to knuckle under and accept American-inspired 'flexible' work arrangements especially in manufacturing industries. Even though concession-bargaining has occurred, organized labour in Canada has potentially more clout on the factory floor than its American counterpart but whether it will use its power remains to be seen. Canadian labour needs a strategy that links workplace politics to larger macro-concerns. In today's global economy, what happens outside the factory is as important as what happens on the shop floor. Therefore, much depends on the ability of Canada's labour movement to oppose the government's pro-business free trade strategy of continental integration which, if implemented, will place workers at the mercy of employers and the state who are committed to the tenets of free enterprise in an atomised labour market.

The comprehensive free trade agreement which the Mulroney government has just signed with Washington is much more than a trade deal. Canada's unions are opposed to it because it would lead to greater regional inequalities, serious job loss for many workers, and a reduction in social entitlements. Given the disparity in power between Canada and the U.S., Canada would be forced to make most of the adjustments leaving industries such as textiles, food-processing, automobile highly vulnerable to American competition. It is estimated by labour researchers that possibly as many as one million Canadian workers would have to seek new employment. Since Canada has a much more extensive system of social security, including a universal health plan and a unemployment insurance programme with special provisions for workers in the disadvantaged regions of Canada, the economic process of adjustment would be particularly brutal for Canada. Canadian employers can be expected to argue that the Canadian social wage must fall to the lower American level if they are to compete dollar for dollar with their American counterparts. For this reason the entire labour movement is completely opposed to the free trade deal, which it sees as bringing more competition, lower wages and more unemployment for Canadian workers (Drache and Cameron, 1985).

Even if the political future of the trade deal remains uncertain, there is no doubt that Canadian labour is under enormous pressure to make further concessions, as labour is doing everywhere. With its weak industrial sector, Canada is something of a bellwether for the thrust of new productivity-driven techniques. As work and employment relations are being reshaped, the state is prepared to help employers to compete in the North American market on the crudest terms possible. Canadian business remains wedded to the classic notion that increased competitiveness comes principally through lower wage costs. This shows again how little managers understand the full range of options open to them. Direct labour costs are no more than 10 to 15 percent of most industrial products. Yet, management continues to press for more wage concessions as the principal way to subjugate the workforce to market forces. In this situation, workers can expect greater and increasing inequality; continued long-term unemployment; lack of job security for the employed as well as new oppressive work processes together with a reduction in social entitlements as the state responds to employers' needs. On balance, the search for new flexibility in the workplace is likely to reinforce the institutionally embedded fragmentation of Canadian labour.

The Search for Flexibility

There can be little doubt that the current anti-labour mood in Canada shares much in common with the attacks on labour in the other industrial economies. Across a broad front, the wage/salary relationship is being reshaped.

At one extreme, this search for new institutional and economic flexibility takes the form of incorporating existing practices and entitlements into new production relations such as in Germany and Japan. "The changes are compatible with existing arrangements because individual salary is not tied to the individual occupation or job but to personal mobilitiy compatible with maintaining the existing salary structure" (Boyer, 1984: 29). These policies have well-established precedents. During the 1970s, for example, almost all European countries followed a policy of 'mastering' salary costs. At the other extreme, when the search for flexibility is defined principally as a defensive cost-cutting strategy – wage cuts, a reduction of social spending and a weakening of existing legal rights – it results in a fundamental reassessment of the principle that the working class is both socially and economically entitled to share in productivity gains. Adopting this line, business and the state are committed to a new model of industrial and economic relations based on a resegmented labour market, a low-wage economy, minimal job security and a 'minimalist' state. Boyer adds that this strategy entails not only the high risk of living with permanent economic instability but progressive social anomie and stagnation as well. The Mulroney government, which speaks openly of the need for an ideological and political cleansing, is obviously in agreement with Reagan's view of the new industrial order and is willing to turn to a 'leaner and meaner' economic strategy in order to build for tomorrow. Certainly Canadian labour can expect no new deal from the state or business. It has to rely on itself to protect it from the uncertainty of the new global economy.

A Final Word

The attack on existing work and employment practices everywhere involves such massive change for the existing institutional arrangements of industrial societies that new theoretical perspectives are needed to make sense of what is happening. As the industrial societies move from a high wage to a low wage economy, a fundamental regrouping of forces is taking place. As production in the industrial economy has become "uncoupled" from employment manufacturing employment will continue to decline further. Clearly, if this trend continues the prospects for a return to full employment capitalism are indeed poor. Labour has not only seen job-slimming cut into its industrial ranks but, in a more fundamental sense, labour's role as an indispensable factor of production is being questioned. This is because new production technologies undermine the dominant role of human labour in most productive processes. As the physical and mental functions involved in the production of goods and services can be performed without the participation of human labour, labour faces an unprecedented crisis as its bargaining power over the sale of its labour power can only be affected negatively. It seems that the displacement of labour by increasingly efficient machines has no identifiable limits. If this it true, technological employment will increasingly devastate the ranks of the industrial working class (Leontieff, 1983).

With the indispensability of industrial labour in question, both Bahro and Gorz are right in suggesting that the traditional forces of socialism are not identical with the forces that will press for a resolution of the present crisis. The left's preconceived notion of waging everything on the class struggle stands in the way of perceiving who the new forces for change are (Bahro, 1982: 64). On the right, "the dominant orthodoxy tries to push people back into the patterns prescribed by the old theoretical paradigm that must be dialectically superceded" (ibid. p. 57). The fact is that there are far more forces ready for social change than the traditional left, the trade union movement or the general public imagines.

In Canada, there is a large, important, broadly-based popular sector comprised of churches, trade unions, woman's groups, social agencies and voluntary associations which reject the tyranny of market economics as the best method of determining Canada's economic future. In their totality, they constitute a deuxième gauche of an un-conventional sort. They are an alternative to both party politics and a simple two-class model of society. This fundamental regrouping of forces represents an alternative to the rigidities of Canada's two-and-a half party system and a simple two-class model of society. The proof of the popular sector's existence are the coalitions that have been built regionally and nationally with critical support of both the public sector and industrial unions. This was the case in the Solidarity movement against government cutbacks in British Columbia, the court challenge to the cruise missile testing, the defence of abortion rights, and the Social Policy Reform Group to monitor federal government cutbacks.

The groups active in these coalitions constitute Canada's counter-institutions, and they draw on a counter-discourse of political economy. The popular sector calls for a fundamental break with the conventional value system of policy-making and economics that is based on having people adjust, accommodate and lower their expectations to the short-term profit considerations of business. With the massive upheaval in work practices and the elimination of hundreds of thousands of jobs, it is necessary to create alternative economic models that address the contradictory messages that the new work and employment practices present for labour as well as the new social movements.

The need for new flexibility has been made to appear inevitable and is often sold to the labour movement as a way to broaden the scope of individual freedom on the job. On the face of it, better placed workers can, and do, benefit from increased worker participation. But many of these schemes have little to do with extending worker control over the workplace. Overall economic restructuring resulting from the introduction of the microchip, robots and the like are the means by which capital, harshly and often brutally, seeks to maintain and, indeed, expand its control of the workplace. If unions are to be effective instruments of workplace control, these institutions need to learn to make demands for increased worker participation in the planning of the workplace as well as with respect to investment decisions. In addition, organized labour needs to find ways to hobble capital while simultaneously pushing the state to act in more independent ways. Understandably, labour needs to promote a strong industrial strategy to support the reindustrialization of the economy.

There is no single model that has all the answers to combat the pressures of international competition. But, given the continuous importance of productive activity as a central and vital goal for all societies, the maintenance of employment and a renewed commitment to job creation remains both in the short and longterm the principal concern of workers everywhere. Today's alternative economic model will be, more likely than not, a mix of socialist ideas, eco-socialist values and eco-socialist-feminist principles. The key is to begin to think of quite new combinations of social groupings as the "solution to the crisis at the general level" (Bahro, 1982: 64) This means finding those cultural, regional and economic forces which seek to create a new, ethical and more equitable society free of the tyranny of markets and a world dominated by the interests of the powerful. Il y a plein de choses qui clochent: tant mieux.

References

Bahro, Rudolph (1982). *Socialism and Survival*, London: Heretic Books

Bird, Richard (1984): 'Is Increasing Employment in "High Tech" Industry a Sensible Policy Goal For Ontario?' Institute for Policy Analysis, U. of T., No. 84-4

Bluestone, Barry and Harrison, Bennett (1982): *The De-industrialization of America*, New York: Basic Books

Boyer, Robert (1984): *Les Transformations du Rapport Salarial en Europe Depuis une Décennie: Quelques Eléments de Synthèse*, Paris: F.E.R.E.

Clement, Wallace (1977): *Continental Corporate Power: Elite Linkages Between Canada and the United States*, Toronto: McClelland and Stewart

Donner, Arthur (1988): 'Labour's Shrinking Share', *The Facts* 10: 3, fall

Doherty, Midland (1985): *Monthly Update and Perspective*, July, 8

Drache, Daniel and Cameron, Duncan (eds.) (1985): *The Other Macdonald Report. The Consensus on Canada's Future that the Macdonald Commission Left Out*, Toronto: James Lorimer

Drache, Daniel and Glasbeek, H.J. (1988): 'New Fordism in Canada: Capital's Offensive, Labour's Opportunity?, *Osgoode Hall Law Review*, December

Gorz, André (1980): *Farewell to the Working Class*, London: Pluto Press

Gower, David (1988): 'The Labour Market in the 80s: Canada and the United States', *Labour Force*, Ottawa: StatsCan, July

Grunwald, Joseph and Flamm, Kenneth (1985): *The Global Factory Foreign Assembly in International Trade*, Washington D.C.: The Brookings Institution

Ichiyo, Muto (1985): 'State Politics and Labour in the 1980s', *Canadian Journal of Social and Political Theory* 8: 3 January/February

Kaliski, S.F. (1984): 'Why High Unemployment?', *Canadian Public Policy*, No. 10: 2

Leontief, Wassily (1983): 'Technological' Advance, Economic Growth, and the Distribution of Income', *Population and Development Review* 9: 3 Sept. pp. 403–410

Levitt, Kari (1970): *Silent Surrender: The Multinational Corporation in Canada*, Toronto: Macmillan

Lipietz, Alain (1984): 'Globalisation of the General Crisis of Fordism' SNID Occasional Paper No. 84–203, CEPREMAP, Paris, France

Muszyniski, Leon (1980): 'Unemployment in Toronto, Hidden and Real', Working Papers for Full Employment, Toronto: Social Planning Council of Metropolitan Toronto

Naylor, R.T. (1975): *The History of Canadian Business*, Toronto: James Lorimer

Norwood, Janet, L. (1985): 'The Growth in Service Jobs', New York Times, Aug. 8

Ontario Ministry of Labour (1984): *Labour Market Experiences of Workers in Plant Closures. A Survey of 21 cases*, Toronto: Ontario Ministry of Labour

Panitch Leo and Swartz, Donald (1988): *The Assault on Trade Union Freedoms*, 2nd. ed. Toronto: Garamond Press

Report of the Premier's Council (1988): *Competing in the Global Economy*, Toronto: Province of Ontario, vol. 1

Royal Commission on the Economic Union and Development Prospects for Canada (1985): *Final Report*, Ottawa: Ministry of Supply and Services

The Economic Council of Canada (1983a): *Jobs in Short Supply*, Ottawa: Economic Council of Canada

The Economic Council of Canada (1983b): *The Bottom Line: Technology, Trade and Income Growth*, Ottawa: The Economic Council of Canada

The Economic Council of Canada (1984): *Steering the Course,*, Twenty-First Annual Review, Economic Council of Canada

Thurow, Lester (1984): 'Losing the Economic Race', New York Review of Books, Sept. 27

Chapter 11
Belgian Unionism and Self-Management[1]

Bob Hancké and Dany Wijgaerts

Introduction

This article presents a short overview of the evolution of the concepts of workers' control and self-management in Belgian unionism. Our impression is that Belgium occupies a particular position in this respect as compared to other countries. It appears that a whole spectrum of relations between self-management and the unions can be established. On one end of the spectrum, there is almost no relation between the two phenomena. The American and Dutch cases seem to typify this position. Next, situations can be found where the relation is slightly stronger: a certain (institutional) relation can be identified. The German and French cases might be regarded as examples of this. Finally, as in Britain, Italy, and Belgium, we find cases where the relation is highly institutionalised with self-management and workers' control constituting a fundamental part of trade union ideology.

Within this general comparative view, we shall attempt to study the evolution of these ideas in Belgian unionism. A short introduction, pertaining to some essential components of the Belgian unions, will be followed by a more detailed account of the way the concepts of self-management and workers' control became essential features of Belgian labour movement ideology. A concluding section sketches some hypotheses with respect to these questions and considers their relevance for a union counterstrategy to economic recession.

---

[1] We would like to thank Jan Geluck, Gilbert Eggermont, Jacques Vilrokx and Frank Winter for their critical remarks and help with this paper. Wherever possible, we will refer to English texts on the Belgian situation. We have also translated quotations from Dutch and French texts.

Belgian Unionism

The level of unionisation in Belgium may be considered high (for a brief outline of Belgian industrial relations, see Rombouts 1975). In the European context, Belgium clearly holds second position, with a union density of about 65 percent (Beeckmans 1983: 50). With a total workforce of approx. 3.8 million, this means that more than 2.5 million workers are unionised. There are, however, important differences between levels of unionisation among manual workers (about 90 %) and clerical workers (about 40 %) and between industrial branches. In the Belgian structure of industrial relations three separate union confederations exist. This separation is a consequence of the high degree of "pillarisation" ("verzuiling") in Belgium. In addition, each union confederation has two wings: a Flemish and a Walloon wing, reflecting the Belgian language structure (Dutch-French). These two additional cleavages (a philosophical-ideological and a cultural-ethic) have a high impact on class solidarity, because of crosscutting. The Christian union confederation ACV-CSC and the socialist union confederation ABVV-FGTB are the largest, as can be seen in Table 1. The liberal ACLVB-CGSLB is relatively small (the acronyms used in the text stand for (in alphabetical order): ABVV-FGTB (Algemeen Belgisch Vakverbond – Fédération Général du Travail Belge – General Union Federation); ACV-CSC (Algemeen Christelijk Vakverbond – Confédération des Syndicats Chrétiens – General Christian Union Confederation); ACLVB-CGSLB (Algemene Centrale van Liberale Vakbonden van Belgie – Centrale Générale des Syndicats Libéraux de Belgique – General Federation of Liberal Unions in Belgium); KWB (Katholieke Werkersbond – Catholic Workers Union).

Table 1: Evolution of Union Membership in Belgium 1950–1980

	ABVV FGTB	ACV CSC	ACLVB CGSLB	Total
1950	631,075	567,587	75,681	1,274,343
1960	706,087	761,705	111,407	1,579,199
1970	818,399	961,655	123,210	1,903,264
1980	1,126,814	1,318,845	200,000	2,645,659

Source: Martens 1985.

The two largest union confederations are both vertically structured per industrial branch, while the ACLVB-CGSLB is organised on a local basis, which means that workers are intercategorially organised per region. Officially, each vertical sub-union branch within the ABVV-FGTB is completely autonomous. It is obvious that this rather decentralised union structure has important implications for collective bargaining and union strategy. The ACV-CSC is more centralised; more decision-making power is concentrated at the top level and decisions taken can more easily be introduced into the union structure. This is very important for achieving results in collective bargaining. Moreover, this has important implications for the political links of the Christian union, its financial capacities, and the individual services they can offer their members and might thus help to explain the "attraction" of the Christian union to workers. This short sketch of the Belgian unions suffices to characterise some of their structural elements.

With respect to the ideological positions held by the different unions, a short overview of the programmes and doctrines is presented below (see Stroobant 1982: 54–67 and Van Outrive 1974 for a more detailed discussion).

ACV-CSC

The ideological position of the Christian union is characterised by a structural ambiguity. On the one hand, the union is part of the Christian "pillar," which is described by Belgian sociologists as a social system, concentrically constructed around some essential Christian values. These values in turn are echoed in the union programme. On the other hand, the union could also be considered as being an offshoot, rather than a part of the political ideology of the Christian-democratic party, CVP. (Two more remarks on the Christian union, to clear up its position in the Belgian structure of labour relations. First of all, the political party to which the ACV-CSC is linked by pillarisation (CVP-PSC) has been in office almost constantly in the post-war era. Since the institutional and personal links between the union and the party are strong, this had a considerable impact on the positions taken by the ACV-CSC. Secondly, the difference between the socialist and the Christian union is often made in terms of their orientation towards the formalised structure of industrial relations. The socialist union is considered to have a more militant attitude towards the industrial relations system, whereas the Christian union sticks more to the consensus model of collective bargaining.) In this respect, the ACV-CSC claims to be a genuine union, with a social project geared towards a self-managed economy. (As will be discussed below, the shift away from purely Christian personalist values has occured only recently. In no way, however, are these principles equally such strong guidelines for action as in the socialist union's case.)

ABVV-FGTB

The socialist union holds a clearer ideological position. In line with an extensive socialist tradition, its aims can be summarised schematically as the abolition of capitalism to make way for a socialised (socialist) economy in which the workers decide what will be produced in what way and how the produced goods will be distributed. The doctrine thus consists of a socialist programme with strong Marxist influences. Because of the institutionalised links with the socialist party, these programmatic principles are of course somewhat loosened, but they still provide important ideological points of reference.

ACLVB-CGSLB

The ideas of the French Enlightenment are the most important roots of the ACLVB-CGSLB, whose programme is characterised by liberal-democratic principles. Free enterprise and other fundamental elements of capitalism constitute the normative backbone of the liberal union. Essentially, it aims at a slightly modified status quo. This means an acceptance of capitalism and an abolition of the "unacceptable" aspects of it, without fundamentally changing the socio-economic structure. Class collaboration is therefore seen as the most adequate strategy for the workers.

From this sketchy outline of the ideological positions, we can already draw some conclusions. First of all, it is important to recognise the political-ideological backbone of Belgian unionism. Partly this is due to the pillarisation process Belgium has been going through. The three main contemporary ideological and philosophical currents (Christianity, liberalism, and socialism) are thus reflected in the Belgian labour movement. As a result of this and their political affiliation, the unions became highly institutionalised (Lorwin 1978), while maintaining a certain degree of "originality" and "mutual distinction."

Secondly, it is obvious that the liberal union, ACLVB-CGSLB, will be omitted from the following analysis, because of the fundamental acceptance of capitalism, which does not provide a basis for strategies towards self-management. Thirdly, with respect to the ideological basis of the Christian union, it is remarkable that here, too, a strategy towards (a kind of) socialism has been adopted, although its strategy towards self-management is more restricted than in the ABVV-FGTB's case. Basically, the ACV-CSC aims at establishing self-managed "islands," while the socialist union denies this possibility of working within capitalism and, instead, focuses on the whole economic structure. Moreover, the ideological cleavages between the Christian and the socialist union that exist at top levels seem to disappear at the level of the rank and file, whose ideological framework is rather homogeneous. Finally, within this context of highly politicised union programmes, the relevance of the analysis of workers' control and self-management as elements of the union ideologies and strategies is clear.

Workers' Control, Self-Management, and Belgian Unionism

As pointed out above, two union confederations will be analysed: the ABVV-FGTB and the ACV-CSC. The attitude of each union towards three problems will be analysed: workers' participation, workers' control, and self-management. These could be regarded as positions on a continuum of control, workers' participation being the most moderate and self-management the most extensive and radical pole. Workers' control (workers have all the information on the economic processes within the enterprises, but do not share management responsibility) could then be seen as an intermediate alternative. As a question of definition: the concept of control can be used in two senses. It either refers to the control executed over (the means of) production, the organisation of production, etc. as an intrinsic characteristic of the actor's position, or to the act of checking a finished job, economic and financial records of companies, etc. as, for example, in "quality control." In the case of "workers' control" in the Belgian context, it means that workers check the (economic) activities of the enterprise, without taking part in management etc. To us it seems that self-management is a more appropriate term for the more extended concept of workers' control, where workers actually plan and execute production according to their own standards. However, as we pointed out above, the self-management notions adopted by the two unions are to an important extent different. The ABVV-FGTB aims at a planned economy, within which enterprises are conducted on a self-managed basis, while the ACV-CSC plans self-managed enterprises, without really taking notice of the whole political-economic structure.

Before commencing this analysis, we have to solve a theoretical problem pertaining to the positions on the continuum. Are they really "continuous" or can we establish qualitative differences between them? In other words, is there a gradual and continuous line of involvement, ranging from participation to self-management, or are the three concepts situated at distinct levels? Some of the implications of the latter are obvious: for example, a strategy aiming at a socialist economy could then only succeed if unions aim at self-management through workers' control, without paying attention to the possible (temporary) advantages of workers' participation.

We consider this latter position correct, because it appears to us that the sanctioning and incorporation mechanisms in the case of participation ("Mitbestimmung") would make a socialist strategy impossible (see also Sallon 1976 and Mandel 1973: 355). One more remark has to be made before turning to the analysis. In the text, we sometimes refer to "the socialist" and "the Christian labour movement." Unions are only one component of this (though a very important one) and the development of union strategies can only be analysed adequately when taking into account the interactions with the other components of the labour movement (e. g. mutual insurance societies, cooperatives, etc. and, more particularly, in the case of the ABVV-FGTB, the Socialist Party.)

The Christian Union Confederation

The contemporary Christian union movement was unified, and changed its name to ACV-CSC in 1923. The original Christian union, however, was founded at the end of the nineteenth century, following the papal encyclical "Rerum Novarum," as a means to counter the emerging socialist union movement. This anti-socialist attitude has always been very important within the Christian union. So it is hardly surprising that the first socio-economic doctrine developed within the Christian labour movement was firmly corporatist: employers and workers were to be organised in one professional organisation on an industrial branch basis. This was mainly due to the ambiguous character of Christian unionism already mentioned. The Catholic Party of that time and the present Christian Party CVP are the "preferred partners" of the ACV-CSC, combining and organising all socio-professional groups in society (employers, workers, farmers, etc.). Within this general structural and ideological constellation, experiments on self-management are not very likely. The few catholic cooperatives that existed were either founded by bourgeois and paternalist welfare organisations, or regarded as being essentially socialist instruments. In fact, until 1930, the Christian doctrine was characterised by these anti-socialist, conciliatory features.

During the economic recession of the 1930's, the corporatist ideology re-emerged, partly under the influence of the German occupiers' nazi-ideology. The union's programme until the Second World War with respect to workers' participation, self-management, and workers' control is easily summarised: the position of workers within the economic structure was "God-given," so workers had no rights to claim, except basic working conditions. In the post-war period, however, some differences appeared. Alongside the evolution of the socialist union's ideology on workers' participation, self-management, and workers' control (which will be discussed below), some (small) changes were noticeable within the Christian union. The welfare-economic model established in this period provided some guarantees for recognition of the workers' position within the economic structure. Within the bargaining economy workers were allowed some rights at enterprise level. As a result, conciliation and workers claiming economic and social rights became the two strategies simultaneously promoted by official union ideology, thus starting an era which turned out to be of crucial significance for the evolution of the ACV-CSC's position on workers' participation, self-management, and workers' control.

In the evolution of the modern Christian union three stages can be identified in connection with the three problems. A first one (from approximately 1945 to 1960) when participation (in the German sense of "Mitbestimmung") was the most important strategy; a second stage, during the sixties, when some essential elements of capitalism were analysed critically; and a third one, starting in the early seventies, when self-management was adopted as the most important long-term goal.

1945–1960: Workers' Participation or Collective Bargaining?

The 1944 "Social Pact" between employers' and workers' representatives is considered to be of crucial importance in any adequate analysis of Belgian unionism, because it outlined the bargaining model of the economy. Socialist and Christian union representatives, on the one hand, and employers' representatives, on the other, both assessed their mutual dependence. Workers were given some social benefits if the unions were willing to leave the capitalist enterprise structure and its economic decision-making alone. A kind of "peaceful co-existence" was the result. In the conceptual phase of the pact, some ideas on workers' participation were formulated, finally resulting in the setting up of factory councils (see Dambre 1985 for a historical account).

This conception of workers' participation was firmly supported by the Christian union, precisely because it was perfectly compatible with the principles of "Mitbestimmung." Around this participation model based on factory councils, the ACV-CSC action programme was centered. The (few) critical remarks coming from the socialist union (see below) were not considered to be important. In the period between 1945 and 1960, therefore, the original ideas on workers' participation were primarily based on the "Mitbestimmung" concept. No serious attempts were made to adopt a radical long-term strategy towards self-management or workers' control, because the idea of self-management was regarded as ultimately anti-Christian in origin.

1960–1970: Workers' Participation within Capitalism?

The renewed thinking on workers' participation and on the extension of economic democracy was rooted in the KWB conference of 1964, where some doubts on the position held by workers within the capitalist enterprise system were expressed. At this conference the KWB, an important faction of the Christian labour movement, adopted a text on economic democracy, demanding its extension (KWB 1964). It is, however, important to mention the ideological basis for the document. Instead of taking a fundamental conflict of interests between capital and labour as an ideological framework, a number of personalist, Christian-humanitarian values provided the legitimation for the text. The worker as "a human being" had to be revalued within the economic system and an extension of the available participation channels was regarded as one of the most advantageous options. An action programme to "humanise" work and especially the (heavily criticised) capitalist enterprise structure was adopted.[2]

This critical attitude towards capitalism on the one hand, and the demands for "real" workers' participation, on the other, became very important elements of the thinking on unionist strategies throughout the sixties. For instance, at the 1968 conference under the theme "Verant-woooordelijk voor de toekomst" (Responsible for the future) the principles of workers' participation, integration, and collective bargaining were to some extent abandoned by the ACV-CSC (Van de Kerckhove 1979: 201) and the need for alternatives to the original workers' participation concept became very acute. At the beginning of the seventies, the Christian union fundamentally re-thought its strategy, stating workers' control and self-management as central elements.

1971: Self-Management or Ambiguity Revisited?

In 1971, the Council of the ACV-CSC adopted a document that completely changed its position towards workers' participation and self-management. The original concept of workers' participation, drawing on the German model, was considered inefficient, and a restructuring of the enterprise was suggested. When the most important elements of this doctrinal change are considered, self-management became the ultimate goal for the ACV-CSC. The union also tried to work out a general strategy in a practical way, defining four intermediate goals. The topic of workers' control made its entrance into the union programme: workers must have access to all necessary information. Alongside this, two new collective bargaining channels were suggested: work consultation and works councils. The latter's functions were strictly circumscribed: they would be an advisory body on financial and economic problems and would have decision-making power in social issues. This meant that the

---

[2] It is important to mention here the position of the KWB within the structure of the Christian labour movement. Officially, the KWB organises catholic workers and is therefore part of the Christian labour movement. In practice, however, it exists and functions alongside the ACV-CSC, which formally and factually is the representative of workers within the labour movement. The ideological impact of the KWB should therefore not be overestimated. In a certain sense, there has always been some kind of competition or rivalry between the ACV-CSC and the KWB, and in some respects the KWB might be regarded as "the other face" of the Christian labour movement, sometimes adopting more radical points of view, without really sharing the power basis of the ACV-CSC.

works councils would be a kind of factory council consisting only of workers (ACV 1975: 43). Finally, a restructuring of the investors' and shareholders' council was proposed, allowing workers some power in the technical and economic spheres. During the 1980 conference, these principles were reaffirmed (Slomp and Van Mierlo 1984: 101).

The ambiguous character of the latter proposals is clear: on the one hand, the ACV-CSC is aiming ultimately at self-management while, on the other hand, the intermediate goals set out are such that they could reinforce the integration of unions in the existing economic order. Moreover, as Lewin and Joye, two students of the Christian labour movement, point out (1980: 443), the self-management strategy is "merely" a conference text and not a genuine point of reference for the Christian union and its leaders. This is of course very important in an evaluation of the evolution of the ACV-CSC. If the conference texts are not ideological guidelines for both analysis and action, but "just papers," their impact must be considered very small. In the final analysis, the attitudes of the militant unionists towards this ideology will be fundamental.

The three stages outlined above, from "convicted" workers' participation to "conditional" self-management, are therefore more or less clear. It is important to stress that the shift towards self-management in the union's ideology has occurred only recently (i. e. in the 1970's). Until then, the ACV-CSC ideology was derived directly from papal encyclicals and other socio-religious texts. Partly as a reaction to the development of the socialist union, the ACV-CSC changed its attitude. This reactive attitude towards the ABVV-FGTB has, since its foundation, been a crucial feature of the Christian labour movement. The institutionalised connections with the Christian-democratic party most probably provide a very important explanatory basis, because this has partly conditioned the perspectives of the union with regard to independent action (Kritak 1977: 114–115).

The Socialist Union Confederation

The ABVV-FGTB in its current form was founded in 1945 through the integration of several craft unions and several communist unions. Its predecessor, the BVV, was completely dominated by the Belgian Workers Party. The ABVV-FGTB, on the other hand, is, according to its founding platform, formally totally independent of the current socialist party. This independence was a necessity, precisely because some of the founding union organisations were strongly communist-orientated. In practice, however, there are very close institutional and personal connections between the Socialist Party and the union.

In the "older" socialist movement, between 1890 and 1940, the idea of self-management was mainly established through setting up production and distribution cooperatives, in order to create a so-called parallel "socialised" economic structure. The case of Vooruit in Ghent is well-known in this field. Equally important in this respect is the "Bank van de Arbeid" (the Bank of Labour), founded in 1913 by the leaders of the socialist labour movement. The experiences of the bank were dramatic. Set up as a countervailing power to the capitalist financial system and banks, workers started saving their money at the bank. Because of the hostility of the other banks and internal problems, the "Bank van de Arbeid" was unable to survive, and millions of Belgian francs were lost. After some years, most of the cooperatives disappeared, thus ending the only experiments of real and worker-founded self-management systems (for a more detailed account of the socialist cooperatives, see Van Haegendoren and Vandenhove 1983: 669–675). The idea of self-management, however, has been important in the strategy of the socialist labour movement ever since, but it shifted away from the somewhat utopian ideals of cooperatives set up by workers. Instead, it became a fundamental element in the union strategy towards a take-over of the economy (Vandenbroucke 1981: 94).

As mentioned above, the ABVV-FGTB was founded in 1945. In its founding platform (ABVV 1945) the aims of the union are given with a remarkable clarity: a socialist economy through the abolition of wage labour and the installation of self-managed production units within a planned economy. However, there has always been the problem of the correspondence between goals and principles on the one hand, and actual strategy on the other hand. The union has constantly faced this problem and has tried to solve it. Conferences, study group sessions, etc. were dedicated to it. The rather traumatic experiences with the cooperatives in the previous years restrained a lot of the original enthusiasm with which some groups within the union had started, and the result was an orientation towards the existing macro-economic structure. In the end, a gradual take-over of the enterprises and a socialisation of the capitalist economy became the final goal.

This orientation towards industry can be outlined in phases: a first one (from around 1945 to 1955), when self-management was to be attained through workers' participation, a second stage (ca. 1956–1970), when the issue of workers' participation was discussed and questioned, and finally, starting in 1971, a stage when the strategy based on workers' participation was abandoned and the issue of workers' control became a fundamental feature of the socio-political union strategy. A detailed analysis of the most important texts will help to clarify this evolutionary scheme.

1945–1956: Self-Management Through Workers' Participation

In the founding platform of the ABVV-FGTB the strategy towards self-management is essential. A dominant tendency inside the union thought self-management had to be attained through workers' participation:

Workers' participation is playing a constructive role in this period – in a socialist perspective – as a link between control over the enterprise and over social and economic life at societal level (Dambre 1985: 93).

It is stated very clearly that workers' participation, workers' control, and self-management are seen as positions on a continuous line of involvement and control. Particularly when the collective bargaining model of the economy was first conceived, an important current within the trade union adopted this strategy. A first attempt to fill the gaps between principles and action was made in 1954, when a conference on economic democracy and structural reforms was called (ABVV 1954). The main line of reasoning consisted of the idea that economic expansion had to go hand in hand with an extension of existing economic democracy and social welfare.

In 1956 a second report, prepared by a study group of left wing intellectuals and unionists, was published by the union (ABVV 1956). Here, the strategic problems posed by the options derived from the 1954 conference were studied. More particularly, the question of the socio-political strategy of workers' participation, workers' control, and self-management was raised. One of the conclusions of the report was that workers' participation had to be attained under very strict conditions: the integration of workers' representatives in factory councils (the legal framework in which workers' participation has to be situated) must be very limited (see ABVV 1956: 34–38). In fact, the original goal (i.e. unconditional workers' participation in factories) was replaced by a very conditional type of workers' participation, stressing the *representation* (and not merely the integration) of workers within the economic structure of the company. Nevertheless, the gradual strategy from workers' participation to self-management was retained.

1957–1970: Workers' Participation Questioned

In the period immediately following the 1956 conference, the strategy of self-management through workers' participation was questioned thoroughly within the union. One of the most important advocates of this strategy, André Renard, rethought the concept, drawing on German experiences with the "Mitbestimmung" model. His disappointment with the experiences in the Ruhr led him to very different conclusions on the strategy to be adopted by the unions. He made the point that workers' participation would lead to the integration of workers in the capitalist system. To avoid this, another union instrument had to be developed:

Workers controlling the administration and management of large enterprises ... Workers' control within the capitalist economy, workers' participation within the socialist economy. This is the most advantageous formula for the labour movement (Renard, quoted in Vandenbroucke 1981).

The shift heralded the union's critical and sceptical attitude towards participation. A rejection of the old strategy of self-management through workers' participation would inevitably follow. At the 1965 conference, the decision was taken to set up a committee that would study the problem of workers' control, in preparation for the 1971 Ideological Congress. The radicalisation of workers at the end of the sixties, the renewal of Marxist thought (in universities) and its impact upon the labour movement, the legitimation problems the unions were facing, liberating movements that emerged everywhere, and the severe criticism of "consumer capitalism", together led the union to rethink its strategy. By the beginning of the seventies a conference was called that would handle the problems of a strategy towards self-management, starting from the existing socio-economic structure.

1971: Self-Management Through Workers' Control

The 1971 conference on the ideological position taken by the socialist union is the most obvious indication of the fundamental changes the ABVV-FGTB had gone through. We have already described the emergence of the idea of workers' control within some union circles, but now the issue would become a fundamental feature of the ABVV-FGTB programme. By doing this, the union also renewed its opposition towards capitalism. The 1971 Congress led to three conclusions. First of all, the assessment that full "economic democracy" was not achieved; second, the obvious danger of an institutional integration of the unions within the capitalist economy; and finally, the assessment that society still "had to be transformed" (FGTB 1971).

Taken together, these conclusions posed serious problems for the union's strategy. By which means was the ABVV-FGTB able to resolve them, facing both the dangers of remaining completely incapable of changing anything at all, on the one hand, and a (partial or complete) integration into the system on the other hand? The Congress thought a solution could be provided by the concept of workers' control: workers would have access to all necessary information on the enterprise and could thus impose a check on management, while taking no responsibility at all in management decisions and thus staying out of the political-economic structure of the enterprise. The same line of reasoning led to the definition of the role of the shop stewards. The union wanted to establish a strong demarcation between the formalised collective bargaining institutions and the bodies of union representation on the shop floor. In this context the "syndicale delgatie – delegation syndicale" (SD) at company level, a body that resembles the shop steward committee, was rediscovered, whose function was to represent both union and workers in the enterprise. In this way, the SD would be the most appropriate way of preparing workers' control, precisely because it is not incorporated into the economic structure (ABVV, no date: 28–30). The main argument was that only within a socialised economy would (and could!) workers play a serious role in the organisation of production. Within the capitalist system, however, workers' control was the only solution for the long-term strategic problems imposed upon unions. At the 1978 and 1981 conferences, the ideas on workers' control developed at the 1971 conference and on the functions of the SD in this process were reaffirmed (see ABVV 1978: 22–24 and ABVV 1981: 48–50).

Looking back on the post-war period, an evolutionary line can easily be traced back, following the stages pointed out above. Until 1956 workers' participation was seen as an advantageous strategy for the socialist labour movement. In the 1960's a number of questions were raised on the "class collaboration" nature of workers' participation. From 1971 on, workers' participation as a means towards self-management was abandoned and workers' control became the most important ideological point of reference.

One additional remark has to be made on the relation between the union and the Socialist Party. As we have pointed out above, there have always been very close links between the party and the union movement. One of the most serious problems the union has always faced with respect to the evolution of its ideology and strategies has pertained to the (basically social-democratic) party that never used these strategies and analyses as guiding threads for its own analysis of capitalism. The concept of self-management, very important in the socialist union, has never been an important item in the political party. Apart from initiatives of some (younger) left wing intellectuals, no serious attempt has ever been made to introduce general strategies on self-management into the party's programme. This has of course considerably limited the union's potential to work out a practical strategy: the political wing of the socialist labour movement has never seriously attempted to use self-management as a socio-political option, while the concept and the strategy, on the other hand, was of great importance in the development of the union's programme (see Vandenbroucke 1985).

Self-Management In Belgian Unionism

From this sketch it has become obvious that there indeed exists a highly institutionalised relationship between Belgian unionism and the concepts of self-management and workers' control. In both the Christian and the socialist unions, self-management is the main goal, and workers' control is the main instrument to achieve this. The differences between the evolution of the socialist and the Christian conception of self-management and workers' control have been explored in this chapter. The Christian union's strong links with the Christian-democratic party were crucial in this connection.

The process of pillarisation, a well-known characteristic of the Belgian political system, is very important and appears to influence in a fundamental way the union ideologies. On the other hand, it could also be held responsible for the highly politicised union structure (both in terms of the organisational structure and in terms of ideology). Indeed, a very remarkable feature of Belgian unionism is its manifestly ideological and political approach to social and economic problems. As such, the strategies of workers' control and self-management are political issues, going beyond the problems of who is running the economy and questioning the total social, economic, and political structure. This is especially prominent in the case of the socialist union, which has always held a more radical position than the socialist party, thus attracting more politically conscious militants who are able to introduce political alternatives into the ABVV-FGTB. But also in the case of the ACV-CSC this ideological profile has become more important. In fact, recent developments show that some groups within the union are calling for a more "fundamentalist" attitude towards the Belgian political system, rejecting the "preferred partnership" of the CVP. The way this can influence union ideologies is far from obvious, but it appears to us that the cleavage emerging between some parts of the Christian labour movement and the Christian party is very important for the future evolution of Belgian unionism and might result in an even more ideologically oriented approach adopted by the unions.

However, our (descriptive) analysis of the phenomena is far from complete. We wish to point to some questions that have occurred to us while preparing this chapter. First of all, contrary to many current appreciations of union behaviour and ideology (e. g. Von Beyme 1981), which explicitly take into account environmental changes, we have primarily accentuated the internal factors that were, in our view, responsible for the changes mentioned. This is due partly to the lack of research data on Belgian unionism and Belgian industrial relations. We are well aware of this problem and are trying to solve it by doing more research on the relation between the union's environment and its internal functioning (e. g. Hancke 1985 and 1986). Secondly, we have to point out that we have only analysed *ideological* positions. Action as such was beyond the scope of this chapter. However important this may be, here, too, we have to admit that Belgian data on the subject are almost non-existent. Finally, we oriented our approach almost exclusively towards contemporary unionism in Belgium. The new cooperatives, emerging in Belgium as well as in other countries, were not part of our study. Our impression on this subject (but it is merely an impression) is that they are not yet an important part of new union strategies and that any relations between unions and new cooperatives that might exist are mostly of an ad hoc nature.

More important than these questions, however, are a number of other issues. The way in which the general concepts of workers' control and self-management can provide a basis for a unionist counterstrategy towards recession seems to be a fundamental issue. We will turn to this problem in the next and concluding sections.

Workers' Control and Self-Management in the Light of the 1980s Recession

Western industrial relations are passing through an important crisis that could change most of the outlook of Western Europe (Blanpain 1985). This general statement is also true of Belgium: as a consequence of the recent (and in some respects continuing) recession, Belgian unions have been facing problems of organisation, mobilisation, and, more generally, of legitimation and functioning. Moreover, the challenges imposed upon unions through changes in work organisation, employers' actions, the composition of the labour force, technological equipment, etc. are of a crucial nature. In this final section, we would like to raise some issues on the importance of self-management, workers' control, and democratisation of the workplace in the context of economic recession. For we believe that certain "new" elements that might be regarded as "disadvantages" could also be used as a basis for change in favour of unions and workers.

The Belgian Industrial Relations Crisis

To examine this general proposition, it is necessary to sketch the recent evolution of industrial relations in Belgium in a little more detail. One of the most important consequences of the changes now occurring is that the positions defined by the 1944 "Social Pact" between employers and workers' representatives are *de facto* questioned. To a large extent, this may be regarded as a by-product of the economic recession.

Three features were crucial in the Pact. First of all, a tacit agreement between unions and employers defining negotiable issues. The so-called social issues were supposed to be the subject of collective bargaining, while the "economic" issues were considered to be an exclusive part of the employers' decision rights. Secondly, a trade-off between "economic" benefits for employers and "social" benefits for workers was part of the 1944 Pact. In practice, this meant that unions would not aim at changes in the property and control structure of the enterprise, while employers would share some of the economic gains with workers. The above-mentioned factory councils were the most appropriate instrument to achieve this. These factory councils and the extended network of collective bargaining institutions point to the third crucial characteristic of industrial relations in Belgium: in the post-war era, the institutionalis-ation of conflict was firmly promoted by unions, employers, and governments.

The 1980s recession has had important consequences for the function-ing and structure of collective bargaining. One of the most important aspects of the new developments are the problems arising in making the trade-off mechanism work. "Social" problems seem to be less easily substituted by material and/or technical problems. The sharpening contradictory relationship between workers and employers and the defensive positions of unions and rather offensive positions of employers (both consequences of the recession) are commonly regarded as the main factors in this process (see Bundervoet 1983: 323 and Vilrokx 1981: 49–78).

With respect to union strategies, then, it is becoming clear that the so-called economic sphere in the "Basic Compromise" (i.e. the 1944 Social Pact and its aftermath), and in particular the institutionalised collective bargaining system (see Bundervoet 1974), is becoming more and more important in the strategic options now taken by unions. Without supposing that a voluntaristic strategy exists, some changes are, however, noticeable in the unions' strategy. Both as a result of structural forces, i.e. the economic recession and its impact upon collective bargaining, employers' positions, and union organisation, and of analyses made within the unions (see Beaupain 1985), Belgian trade unions seem to be reconsidering their activities in industrial relations in order to cope with the challenges they are facing.

However, this rather positive line-up of union reactions has to take into account some other (institutional) elements. In general, it appears that Belgian unions are "fighting a war using arms appropriate to fight the previous one." Very important structural, ideological, and traditional obstacles are limiting an elaboration of a critical union strategy. Without pretending to present an exhaustive list of conditioning factors, the following items seem to be important. Unions have always sought a growing influence and decision-making power in the Belgian socio-political system. A critical rethinking of strategies, leading to a questioning of both socio-economic policies and the collective bargaining system, will of course at the same time question the unions' own positions in society. Belgian unions and their "think tanks" thus seem to have constructed their own structural barriers. Besides, in the development of the Belgian labour movement (both the Christian and the socialist), a strong diffusion of the (often more moderate) party programmes of the

Christian democrats and socialists has taken place. The main effect of these diffusion processes is evident at the level of the actual construction of union programmes that have always been compromises between strictly unionist points of view and strategic political options. Moreover, due to the "pillarised" structure of Belgium, the unions have almost constantly played a subordinate role in the respective labour movements they are part of or the political organisations they are affiliated to, despite their quantitative input into the power basis of the political party.

Finally, some internal elements of a traditional nature are limiting the unions' potential for a critical rethinking of their strategies. The problems unions are facing, the challenge of new technologies, flexibility, unemployment, etc., seem to be of such a complex nature that a thorough analysis of these issues should be made in close collaboration with, for example, physicians, computer designers, economists, sociologists, and engineers. But one crucial feature of the Belgian labour movement, especially of the socialist union, has been a refusal of solid cooperation with scientists and a firmly anti-intellectualist attitude. Apart from some experiments, the unions have, until only very recently, not seen scientists as valuable helpers in their efforts to cope with the problems arising. In the last few years, however, things seem to be changing. The Christian union is now playing an important role in social scientific research by means of the HIVA (Higher Institute for Labour), affiliated to the Catholic University of Louvain (KUL). The ABVV-FGTB, on the other hand, has recently set up a research institute (RIAT) to help unionists with the elaboration of strategies, by means of scientific research.

New Technologies and Workers' Control

As Briefs (1985) has pointed out, relying on the German experience, the introduction of new technologies has had very important consequences for industrial action by both workers and employers. He also clearly demonstrates that the demands for a reduction of working time, one of the most important trade union issues, could take (and is taking) two forms: a quantitative reduction (e. g. a 30-hours working week) to solve immediate unemployment problems and a qualitative change in the use of time. According to this last line of reasoning, time could then be used "for a democratic control of production by the workers themselves" (Briefs 1985: 5). This point of view is the basis for our appreciation of the necessity to use workers' control and self-management as strategic options for the labour movement. We justify our attention to new technologies by the importance unions themselves attach to it (see also Eggermont 1983 and 1985 on the Belgian case). Especially in this field, concerning the introduction of new technologies, the concepts of self-management and workers' control could be seen as valuable and necessary counterbalances to the technological-deterministic thinking most prominent in trade unions. Several research study results from other European countries (e. g. Ehn 1985, Kyng 1985) indicate that there exists what may be called a "design space" (TURU 1984), i. e. a phase in the introduction of new technologies where strategic and socio-political options are taken by those concerned with the introduction (mostly management). While negotiating technological change, ideological starting points and guidelines such as workers' control and self-management are very often put aside and quantitative aspects and consequences constitute the major discussion basis. It is possible, however, that through self-management and workers' control, democracy at the workplace could be introduced into the discussion. In our view, this is possible in two ways. Firstly, the evaluation of new technologies should not only be made in terms of unemployment, changes in the wage structure, etc., however important these issues may be. Attention should also be directed towards changes in control mechanisms, loss (and gain) of autonomy at work, job requirements, etc. In this way, unions could avoid a determinist attitude towards new technologies and be a creative agent in this process (the Swedish experiences referred to above show that this is not merely "utopian" thinking). Because workers themselves choose (parts of) the machinery to handle and (can) transform elements of the organisational structure of the enterprise, this approach is likely to make a real contribution to "humanising work" and "democratising the workplace." In this way, classic concepts such as workers' control and self-management could be updated.

A second point pertains to the use of working time referred to by Briefs (1985). New technologies reduce the absolute amount of "socially necessary time" (i. e. the time needed for production). This surplus of time could indeed be used to develop alternative structures and organisation of work within the company. If unions and workers could use this time to expand democracy at workplace level (self-management and workers' control being the basic concepts for this), the line of reasoning pointed out above can be extended and self-management and workers' control could be basic and fundamental elements of union strategies for the nineties. Very important in both cases, however, is the need for expertise within the unions. Neither the evaluation of the so-called "design space," nor the qualitative use of a possible surplus of working time for democratising the enterprise are, in our view, possible without firm support, both at the level of social organisation and of technical requirements. In practice, this means that, for instance, computer experts, sociologists, and other social scientists need to continually work together with trade unionists in order to develop "case-specific" strategies. This does not mean that the union structure should be "technocratised." On the contrary, we are convinced that the perpetual confrontation of scientists with unionists may be a condition for a more democratic and critical adaptation of union strategies. Moreover, we think that this kind of co-operation between scientists and workers can only be achieved through the integration of science within the unions' institutions, where every problem could be studied scientifically from a unionist perspective, keeping in mind scientific criteria and necessary scientific autonomy. Several international examples could be cited here. In Germany, for instance, the Bremen Institute is well-known, and the English examples (TURU Oxford and Sheffield) are also important. And, to take a less institutionalised example, the Dutch union confederation FNV has set up a specialist group for the introduction of new technologies.

Conclusion

The concepts of self-management and workers' control have been important ideological guidelines in unionist thought in Belgium. The Christian Union as well as the ABVV-FGTB adopted these ideas, and they became in both cases fundamental strategic options for the unions, despite the obvious difficulties to put this ambitious programme into practice. But since the beginning of the current recession, these ideas have moved into the background. We think, however, that both ideas can provide a suitable basis for a union strategy towards the recession. The complexity of the new problems unions now face means that a positive collaboration with scientists seems to be a precondition for this strategy. In this chapter, we have only dealt with new technologies, but the same applies to the problems posed by, for example, flexibility and quality circles. The ultimate success or failure seems to depend, to a large extent at least, on the willingness of unions to initiate a discussion with scientists and of scientists to adopt a non-elitist, non-technocratic attitude vis-à-vis union problems. The "defensive" use of workers' control and self-management (as for example in factory occupations) could then be replaced by a more offensive starting point for analysis and action (e. g. in relation to new technologies). The changes in industrial relations occurring now seem to force unions towards this shift in attitude in order to avoid becoming an anachronism, limited to either antique strategies or mere "business" unionism.

References

ABVV (1945): *Beginselverklaring*, (Platform text), Brussels: ABVV.

ABVV (1954): *Naar sociale vooruitgang door economische expansie*, (Towards social progress through economic expansion), Brussels: ABVV.

ABVV (1956): *Holdings en economische democratie*, (Holdings and economic democracy), Brussels: ABVV.

ABVV (1978): *Congresresolutie, Luik 24–25 november 1978*, (Congress resolutions), Brussels: ABVV.

ABVV (1981): *Ontwerpresoluties Statutair Congres 19–21 november 1981*, (Congress resolutions), Brussels: ABVV.

ABVV (No date): *Arbeiderscontrole en syndikale afvaardiging*, (Workers' control and shop stewards), Brussels: ABVV.

ACV (1971): *Democratisering van de onderneming*, (Democratising the enterprise), Rapport goedgekeurs op de raad van het ACV van 19 januari 1971, Brussels: ACV.

ACV (1975): *De bedrijvigheid van het ACV: 1972–1975*, (The activities of the ACV: 1972–1975), Brussels: ACV.

Beaupain, T. (1985): Evolution des fonctions des syndicats en Belgique, Paper presented at the ECWS conference on "The Role of the Trade Unions in the Coming Decade," Maastricht, November.

Beeckmans, J. (1983): Sociale kaart van de arbeidsverhoudingen in Belgie, (Social map of industrial relations in Belgium), In: Huyse, L. and Berting, J. (eds.), Als in een spiegel? (As in a mirror?), Leuven: KRITAK, pp. 39–53.

Blanpain, R. (1985): The Present Stage of Industrial Relations in Europe: An Era of Change, speech given at the ECSW conference on "The Role of the Trade Unions in the Coming Decade," Maastricht, November.

Brepoels, J., Huyse, L., Schaevers, J., and Vandenbroucke, F. (eds.) (1985): *Eeuwige honderd jaar socialistische partij*, (Eternal dilemmas: the socialist party one hundred years old), Leuven: KRITAK.

Briefs, U. (1985): New Technologies – New Conflicts: New Kinds of Union Demands and of Defense Strategies?, Paper presented at FAST, The Press and New Technologies, Brussels, 7–9 November.

Bundervoet, J. (1974): Vakbeweging in herorientering, (Unions in re-orientation), *Gids op maatschappelijk gebied*, 4: 303–320.

Bundervoet, J. (1983): Vakbond en politiek in crisistijd, (Unions and politics in an era of recession), *Res Publica*, no. 7: 219–236.

Dambre, W. (1985): Onstaansgeschiedenis van de ondernemingsraden in Belgie, (Emergence of the works councils in Belgium), *Res Publica*, no. 1: 87–124.
Eggermont, G. (1983): Visie van de werknemers, (The workers' point of view), Speech held at the T-Day "samenleving en technologie", (Society and technology), *Gerv-berichten*, 41: 41–55.
Eggermont, G. (1985): De nieuwe informatietechnologieën: een uitdaging voor de vakbondsstrategie (Information technology: a challenge to the union strategy) (in) *Links*, January.
Ehn, P. (with the collaboration of M. Kyng) (1985): A Utopian Experience, paper presented at FAST: The Press and New Technologies, Brussels, 7–9 November.
FGTB (1971): *Congrès extraordinaire*, Bruxelles: FGTB.
Garson, D. G. (1973): The Politics of Worker's Control: A Review Essay, In: Hunnius et al., *op. cit.*, pp. 469–488.
Hancké, B. (1985): Vakbondsleden in hun organisatie: ACOD-Antwerpen, (Union members in their organisation: ACOD-Antwerpen), Brussels: TESA-rapport, Centrum voor Sociologie VUB.
Hancké, B. (1986): Vakbondsleden en vakbondsdemocratie, (Union members and union democracy), *Tijdschrift voor arbeidsvraagstukken*, no. 4, pp. 30–43.
Hunnius, G., Garson, D. G., and Case, J. (1973): *Worker's Control: A Reader on Labour and Social Change*, New York: Vintage.
Huyse, L. and Berting, J. (eds.) (1983): *Als in een spiegel?* (As in a mirror?), Leuven: KRITAK.
Kritak (1977): *Wat zoudt ge zonder 't werkvolk zijn?* (What would you be without the working class?), Vol. 1, Leuven: KRITAK.
KWB (1964): Activiteitenverslag, (Activities report), In: *Gids op maatschappelijk gebied*, no. 6, pp. 535–556.
Kyng, M. (with the collaboration of P. Ehn) (1985): Trade Unions and Computer Users, paper presented at FAST: The Press and New Technologies, Brussels, 7–9 November.
Lewin, R. and Joye, P. (1980): *Voor's werkmans recht*, (For worker's rights), Leuven: KRITAK.
Lorwin, V. (1978): Labour Unions and Political Parties in Belgium, *Industrial Relations*, 2: 243–263.
Mandel, E. (1973): The Debate on Workers' Control, In: Hunnius et al., pp. 344–373.
Martens, A. (1985): Vakbondsgroei en vakbondsmacht, (Union growth and union power), *Tijdschrift voor Arbeidsvraagstukken*, 2: 31–41.
Politisering & Professionalisering (1979): *Proceedings of the Dutch-Flemish Sociologists' Conference*, Wilrijk: UIA.
Rombouts, J. L. (1975): The Belgium Industrial Relations System, In: *Sociological Contributions from Flanders*, Deurne: Kluwer, pp. 7–22.
Sallon, M. (1976): *L'autogestion*, Paris: PUF.
Sibille, H. (1981): Perspectives from Belgium, In: *Ten Cooperative de counseils*, Vol. 3, Paris: B1–B3.
Slomp, H. and Van Mierlo, T. (1984): *Arbeidsverhoudingen in Belgie*, (Industrial relations in Belguim), Vol. 2, Utrecht/Antwerpen: AULA.
Stroobant, M. (1982): *Arbeidsrecht*, (Labour Law), Lecture notes VUB, Brussels.
TURU (1984): *The Control of Frontiers*, Oxford: Ruskin College.

Van de Kerckhove, J. (1979): De opstelling van de vakbeweging op de achtergrond van de industriele ontwikkeling van Belgie, (The position of the union movement against the background of industrial development in Belgium), In: Politisering en Professionalisering, *op. cit.*, pp. 179–209.

Vandenbroucke, F. (1981): *Van crisis tot crisis*, (From recession to recession), Leuven: KRITAK.

Vandenbroucke, F. (1985): De moeizame weg der structuurhervormingen, (The hard way of structural reforms), In: Brepoels et al., *op. cit.*, pp. 159–202.

Van Haegendoren, M. and Vandehove, L. (1983): Morfologie van de socialistische zuil, (Morphology of the socialist pillar), *De Nieuwe Maand*, 10: 640–675.

Van Outrive, L. (1974): Les syndicats chrétiens et socialistes en Belgique, *Recherche Sociologiques*, 1: 3–38.

Vilrokx, J. (1981): *Werknemers in onzekerheid*, (Workers in uncertain work situations), Gent: Masereelfonds.

Von Beyme, K. (1981): *Challenge to Power*, London: Sage.

Young, M. and Rigge, M. (1981): *Prospect for Workers Co-operatives in Europe*, Vol. 1, London: Mutual Aid Center.

Chapter 12
Trade Unions and the Challenge of Modernisation and Computerisation in France

Peter Jansen and Leo Kissler

Introduction

French trade unionism is at present going through a crisis of adjustment caused by a combination of two factors. The first is political – the trade unions find it difficult to get used to cohabiting with the government. They are trying to substitute a constructive policy for an oppositional policy, and this implies acceptance of the policy of modernisation. The second factor is economic – the third industrial revolution is getting under way in the context of a world-wide recession. While in the short term the repercussions of modernisation may be harmful, French trade unions are not systematically opposed to it, since it is seen as the only way out of recession. Acceptance of technical progress does not yet go hand in hand with negotiated control of the advantages and drawbacks of that progress.

The analysis we present here may at first appear to be replete with pessimism. Our conclusion that French trade unions are powerless against modernisation ought not, however, to conceal the gravity of a question which we are unable to answer; in other words, is modernisation necessary or not?

If modernisation is deemed to be necessary, then the attitude of French trade unions appears as "rational." If, however, it is looked upon as an "industrial revolution" with unfortunate side-effects, the same trade union attitude will have to be considered as a sign of weakness, even as a betrayal of the collective interests of the working class. It appears to us that the reality of the situation ought to be looked for somewhere in between these two extremes.

We intend to proceed as follows: to begin with, we shall define the general political context of modernisation, including an explanation of the technological myth as it was transmitted by the left. Secondly, we shall prove that a "Holy Alliance" of modernisation actually exists. We shall be referring to the political language used by the working-class unions who see their role as defenders of technical progress.

We will also show that despite their general approval of new technology, the trade unions pursue policies designed to put a brake on technical progress and accept such progress only in circumstances where it at least involves gains for wage-earners. Fourthly and lastly, we shall summarise the outcome of negotiations. In this way, it will be possible to show that the shape taken by technical innovation remains in large part outside the ambit of negotiations and collective bargaining which may give a new lease of life to the institutions that defend workers' interests on the shop floor.

It is a question, therefore, of a reformation of French trade unionism.

The Political Context of Modernisation (1981–1986)

The policies pursued by the left-wing government since 1981 have been "reformist," in other words, they are based essentially on legislative reform.

The machinery of state, now operated by the left, is therefore seen as an instrument designed to implement the economic and social transformation that was set out as objectives in the electoral platform. The paradox of the situation is that, on the one hand, the left is calling for decentralisation, which on the other hand can only be operated by the intervention of the central power: this power has to introduce the legislation on the form and content of decentralisation.

Decentralisation extends far beyond the framework of administrative structures (the legal status of regions, communes, etc.). Its aim is the society of the social contract as defined by Rousseau. It aims to replace the unilateral decisions of the central power structure with negotiated solutions. The legislation on decentralisation thus forms the contours of a process of democratisation which will also deeply affect the entire system of industrial relations, including working conditions.

The origins of this political determination lie in the tradition of *socialist humanism*, which includes the emancipation of the workers and employees. This emancipation has always been attached to the notion of expropriation, which, since the Liberation has taken the form of nationalisations, looked upon as a series of stepping-stones towards a truly planned economy. The State thus becomes directly responsible for investment and can therefore steer the economy in the desired direction, the central power structure being reinforced by the process. In this way, the *tradition of interventionism* acts as a counterbalance to the noble ideals of humanism.

The analysis of the recession undertaken by the left has acquired a decisive importance in this context and has brought about change within the very process of change itself. After "Year 1," characterised by increased purchasing power, came the U-turn, dubbed "une politique de rigueur" ("a policy of economic austerity") in June 1982. The failure of reflation gives credence to another view of the recession – henceforth it is going to be necessary to acknowledge the international scale of the depression. The result is that official policy pronouncements stress the importance of the international competitiveness of the French industry. Having refused the protectionist option, the only remaining choice is to improve competitiveness and productivity. The restoration of the French economy depends on it.

The lack of productivity is due – according to the left-wing government – to technological backwardness. (We are referring here only to the French industry; the situation in the tertiary sector would seem to be less catastrophic.) Mitterrand's predecessors and the governments that they had appointed are held responsible for the dilapidated state of the economy. Emphasis is laid on ill-conceived and inadequate investment policies. Modernisation of the industrial fabric has foundered on account of the so-called market gap policy which, according to later governments, has abandoned whole sectors of the French industry. Accordingly, the left will try to correct the imbalance by proposing a vertically integrated stream strategy. French industrial policy thus advocates modernisation based on

– industrial restructuration (the strengthening of advanced technology sectors); and
– modernisation of the industrial infrastructure.

At the nub of the modernisation drive is the electronics sector. The massive introduction of electronics, in other words of *computerisation*, is reflected in a new vocabulary – alongside informatique (informatics) and robotique (robotics) one now may read of productique and monétique (productics and monetics) – in a word, nouveautique (newrotics).[1] (Why

---

[1] *Le Monde*, 25 June, 1985: Tics, and G. Métayer: *Futurs en tiques (bureautique, informatique, robomatique, télématique...)*, Paris, 1982.

not use a term like modernisatique (modernics) to signify modernisation through electronics?)

As set out in the 9th Plan, industrial policy is intended to pursue an economic objective, its primary aims being to eliminate the balance of payments deficit and to recapture lost domestic markets. It is expected that reflation will eventually solve the unemployment problem and, since priority is being given to economics, social preoccupations take a back seat, or to be more precise, the social becomes an instrument of the economic. Modernisation of labour relations is to be achieved by giving more responsibility to the workers, within an institutional framework of democratic, albeit partial, reform of labour law.

The recognition of the value of manual labour (to borrow a notion put forward by Lionel Stoléru) is a prerequisite for "social dialogue" which, in the eyes of the government, will lay the foundations for a new social consensus. As the Auroux report put it, the workers are to be the "protagonists of change" which means that they are to play the central role in the programme of modernisation. The "emancipation" of the workers is only a secondary aim of direct participation (groups of expression); the primary aim is to unfetter the competence and know-how of workers. At the same time, direct participation offers opportunities for training. This provides the opportunity to broadcast the virtues of modernisation and to explain that, in any event, people are going to have to learn to live with it, since there is no other way. The ground is thus prepared for modernisation, the use of new technology and computeris-ation by these new democratic procedures in the workplace. At a time of "economic war," they have become a means of enrolling the workers in the "holy alliance" of modernisation.

The "Holy Alliance" of Modernisation: New Technology plus Growth: A Way out of Recession?

To a large extent, the policy of modernisation is determined by government and captains of industry, both of whom control the conditions of international competition. French trade unions have accepted the equation proclaimed by the advocates of modernisation, namely, that new technology plus growth equals a cure for recession. Such a recipe, if only on account of the simplicity of its formulation, can scarcely be expected to resolve the complex problems involved.

The spectrum of possible rank-and-file reactions of a Luddite variety range from the extremes of total acceptance to total rejection of modernisation. However, by rejecting the Luddite option, French trade unions are now obliged to participate in the special social dialogue organised by the government through the reform of labour law. This may be an opportunity to put a constructive trade union policy to the test. But whether the trade unions play an active role from now on in the process of innovation (participation in planning prior to the introduction of new technology on the shop floor) or whether they opt for a strategy of social compensation, *the only course of action open to them is one of reaction.* Their role in the process of modernisation is a passive one.

In view of a massive drop in membership and of the workers' attitude of resignation, it is doubtful whether the trade unions are politically strong enough to play the sort of role that might redress the balance. The drop in membership[2] is a reflection of the crisis of organisation and legitimacy within left-wing French trade unions[3] which, as a result, have come under pressure from a politically and employer-inspired strategy of modernisation. They are in no position to develop any truly combative strategy of their own.

The present strategy (the offensive strategy of constructive proposals) of French trade unions as described below may be understood if two essential factors are borne in mind: *the resigned attitude of French workers* in relation to modernisation and *the optimistic assessment of the trade unions* regarding technological progress. The findings of a number of opinion polls[4] reveal attitudes among wage-earners that would have been unimaginable at the beginning of the 80s. Workers in the private sector (open to competition), for example, feel that employers' demands over the question of "flexibility" are justified, although such an admission involves a loss of existing benefits.

Workers' attitudes have changed as a result of high unemployment; the lives of almost 40% of French families are affected by unemployment (this includes unemployment, unsuccessful jobhunting, and insecure employment). When faced with such lack of security, workers cling to even the frailest of hopes, and the employers' proposal to create new jobs

---

[2] M. Noblecourt: Le syndicalisme dans le monde, *Le Monde*, 6 June 1985.
[3] On the subject of the slump in trade union membership see G. Groux and C. Levy, Gewerkschaftskrise und Unternehmeroffensive, *Prokla*, 54, 1984: 106–130; and P. Jansen, L. Kissler, P. Kühne, C. Leggewie, and O. Seul: *Gewerkschaften in Frankreich. Geschichte, Organisation, Programmatik*, Frankfurt a.M./New York, 1986.
[4] According to *L'Expansion*, 259, 5/18 April, 1985: 54 ff.

on condition that flexible working practises are accepted is one such hope. Yet 70 % of wage-earners and 64 % of employers feel that the government's modernisation policy will involve fresh redundancies. The attenuation of the social side-effects of the innovation process is of utmost significance in view of the fact that modernisation is now considered to be inevitable. The notion that unemployment ought to be treated as a welfare problem adumbrated by the government (early retirement, retraining leave, reduced working hours, the youth opportunities programme (known as "TUC," in its French acronym)) depends upon approval by workers and employers. The TUC involves the creation of low-paid, short-term jobs that go beyond the employers' desiderata (as expressed by the French Employers' Federation, the CNPF) in the matter of flexible working practises (fixed-term contracts, interim employment). The policy of "flexible" recruitment, involving for the worker even greater lack of job security, goes hand in hand with flexible working hours as advocated by the employers. The objective is to obtain increased availability for the employer. And yet 53 % of workers are in favour of the proposal that hours of work be calculated on an annual basis; 47 % are in favour of greater use of temporary labour and fixed-term contracts.

According to the same survey, 55 % of workers would agree that their salaries be linked to the economic circumstances of "their company." It is not the level of the individual employee's income that is seen as of greatest importance but the economic well-being of the enterprise.

At the same time, there has been a drop in the frequency of labour disputes since 1981. The number of work-days lost due to strikes in 1985 fell to the "all-time" low of 1965.[5] It would appear that the threshold beyond which workers decide to take strike action has been rising, and the strike has become an instrument that is used almost exclusively to defend jobs. The "silent majority" of French workers tolerate the consensus that has formed around the notion of modernisation promoted by the government. But it is passively accepted and receives no active support. This is one of the features of the attitude of resignation referred to earlier, and it is precisely because of this attitude that it is still impossible to speak of a lasting change in workers' attitudes.

In the present situation, even if the trade unions wished to, they could scarcely dictate conditions concerning the implementation of new technology. But do they really want to? French trade union organisations

---

[5] See *Liaisons Sociales*, 1247, 7 June, 1984, and C. A. Wurm: Die Gewerkschaften unter Mittérrand, *Dokumente*, 1/41, March, 1985: 54 ff.

insist, with unusual unanimity, on the necessity of modernisation. Their attitude is determined by the hope that the introduction of new technology within the framework of a massive process of restructuration will have positive repercussions in the long term. Perspectives for the future would seem to be a function of actual experiences of the introduction of new technology, some of which have been positive and others negative.

Before outlining the positions of the four trade unions, it would seem timely to make the following remarks:
– Trade union activities within the workplace are substantially affected by the practical problems of the company (economic circumstances, strength of the trade unions, attitude of the staff, type of management structure). It is not possible to follow directives from central office literally. The implementation of a coherent strategy is thus impeded by the recurrence of sectional interests. In other words, pragmatism has not just replaced ideology but has caused hitherto monolithic trade union policy-making procedures to disintegrate. The basic principles of the trade union programme generally set out the main lines of policy pursued by each trade union, the implementation of which depends on particular circumstances.
– The introduction of computerisation in the 60s concerned the services sector and the administrative departments of industrial concerns more than any other. This means that the employees and representatives of the "technical intelligence" sector were among the first to be affected by the "industrial" revolution. During the same period, theories about a new working class[6] began to appear while the functions of trade union organisations and professional groupings were being reassessed. This may be explained by the expansion of the tertiary sector and by an increase in the number of white-collar workers among the active population. It was in these circumstances that the executive trade unions left their mark on the content of discussions organised by each of the trade unions on technology. The origins of a propositional form of trade unionism may be found in these discussions.[7]

While the structural change in industry is put forward as one cause of the crisis affecting present employment policies, new technology appears

[6] S. Mallet: *La nouvelle classe ouvrière*, Paris, 1963.
[7] See G. Groux: *Les cadres*, Paris, 1983, and P. Jansen: Auf der Suche nach einer neuen Identität? Die französischen "cadres" und ihre Gewerkschaften, *Die Mitbestimmung*, 10 + 11, 1984: 465–467.

to trade unions as a way out of recession. As a contribution to the process of modernisation, the trade unions give as much support to investment in high technology sectors as to applied research programmes. Attributing no particular dynamism to technical progress as such, they see the application of new technology as a way of resolving new economic and social problems. It is not just possible but desirable to come to terms with new technology.

That trade unions are in favour of the development and application of new technology at a time of economic crisis is justified by an approach that lays emphasis on the national economy. It is deemed possible to preserve a certain independence of the national economy and of general well-being in the country thanks to the increased competitiveness of the French economy. But the protectionist trap has been avoided and seems acceptable only as a temporary expedient. Protectionist measures (if necessary, at the European level) may be applied only as long as necessary to develop high-tech industries capable of playing a leading role in international markets.

Trade union understanding of new technology and the reasons that are put forward to explain their attitude may be found in the representative declarations of the CGT, the CFDT, and the FO.

The CGT: An Age-old Faith in the Virtues of Technology and in the Ideology of Growth

The CGT's point of view may be expressed as follows: "The introduction of new technology can and must make it possible to produce more and better goods so as to contribute to full employment and the creation of new and better jobs."[8]

For the CGT, technological development is a decisive asset in extending the activities of French industry, enabling companies to improve their competitiveness and the quality of their products which, in turn, makes it possible to diversify production and to use machinery more cheaply. It also permits the production of staple commodities and thus contributes to the growth of the Gross National Product which has a knock-on beneficial effect on job creation.

The overlap between the ideology of growth and technical progress (to be found in government circles, in the opposition, and also among

---

[8] *Le Peuple*, 1182, 15 November, 1984: 10.

employers) attributes three essential virtues to new technology, irrespective of labour relations in the workplace:
- an improvement of working and living conditions;
- greater satisfaction of social needs; and
- higher efficiency.

The logical consequence is that an attitude of technological fatalism is now totally out of place. "There is no such thing as technological fatalism." It is not technical progress but the financial strategy of the major industrial conglomerates that have a deadly effect, concludes the General Secretary of the UGICT-CGT.[9]

He quotes two examples in support of his argument:

a) France has a modern steel industry (Ugine-Aciers, Fos, Gadrange). The decision not to continue modernising these high-productivity industries is tantamount to abandoning them altogether. The reasons are probably connected with European Community quota regulations.

b) Creusot-Loire is one of the leaders in the nuclear energy business. The potential markets are in the USSR and in China.

The withdrawal of the main shareholders (Schneider, Empain) and the refusal of the government to assist in putting the company back on an even keel are seen as the reason behind the decision to opt for a judicial settlement.

The CFDT: From a Criticism of the Ideology of Global Growth to Selective Growth in High Technology Sectors

Up to the beginning of the 80s, the CFDT severely criticised the ideology of growth and rejected the model of productive development. The debate on technology within the CFDT in the aftermath of the events of 1968 remained heated throughout the 70s. The profound uncertainty about the value of labour that has come about as a result of recession and the general change of social values as a whole led to the appearance, in 1981, of the slogan "Produire autrement" ("There is another way to produce") reflecting a rejection of alienating types of work that had emerged in the course of the labour disputes of the 70s.

The crisis in industrial society, initially interpreted as a crisis of values, will have to be overcome by the introduction of new technology. These will be used to promote *better working conditions* and to develop post-

---

[9] *Le Peuple*, n° 1182.

Taylorist forms of the organisation of work. The reference here is to the debate over "autonomous work groups" along "Volvo model" lines. The new forms of organisation of work were discussed as part of company democracy.[10]

From the CFDT's later statements it emerges that the *variations on the content of the discussion on new technology depend largely on the economic climate*. The emphasis placed on the idea that the delay in applying a coherent policy of modernisation was responsible for recession in France amounted to *de facto* acceptance of the notion that the only way out of recession was increased productivity and economic growth.

The CFDT's new-found realism, although it has caused internal division, has resulted in the formulation of a constructive trade union policy. The CFDT's statements on industrial policy imply approval of temporary redundancies. The CFDT is ready to make concessions in return for selective growth through the introduction of new technology.

The CFDT's most recent analysis (criticism of the ideology of growth seems to have ceased when economic expansion ended) suggests minimal and superficial consensus in this area between representative trade union organisation in France. This may be verified from a comparison with the attitudes adopted by the so-called reformist unions, the CFTC and the FO.

FO: "The Reform of Capitalism" Through the Introduction of New Technology?

There have been very few forthright statements of policy on this matter by the FO, whose earliest published writings on the subject[11] at the beginning of the 80s are not yet familiar to competing unions. Each organisation seems to formulate its own policies on technology without informing itself of its competitors' views. The coincidence between declarations on the subject of new technology is therefore accidental and may not be considered as the expression of a collective analysis.

In the FO's view, the introduction of computerisation marks a new stage in the application of technical progress. While the union is aware of the value of technical progress inherent in certain of its positive aspects,

---

[10] See *CFDT Aujourd'hui*, n° 49, May–June, 1981: Une nouvelle ère industrielle.
[11] FO: *Demain, dans l'usine, la robotique!*, Paris, 1983; *La bureautique*, Paris, 1984; *Le syndicalisme dans la civilisation de la télématique*, Livre blanc, Paris, 1985.

the FO remains vigilant as to the possible negative aspects; there can therefore be no question of opposing or rejecting progress. However, the social features of technical progress require particular attention, and this demands that information be made readily available. Its short- and medium-term negative effects need to be explained since it does not, *per se*, automatically bring about potential improvements. Its use is closely linked to a political and economic strategy which is not necessarily compatible with the common good.

The computerisation of society may have certain harmful effects in the short- and medium-term:
– the pursuit of profit to the exclusion of all other aims;
– redundancies;
– the dehumanisation of work;
– restriction of freedom;
On the other hand, if properly managed, it may lead to a global improvement of employment, of working conditions and of society in general.[12]

Like its competitors, the FO in its working document notes the discrepancy between the desirable and the real, thus emphasising that the introduction of computerisation leads to new forms of working practises which in fact reproduce the phenomenon of the segmentation of labour. The monotony, the repetitiveness, and the shifting of workloads (as in the case of VDU work) are obvious results of these new practises. It is feared that the negative consequences on the labour market will result in a geographical division of labour in which the traditional industrial countries will be in charge of the expertise, while production is transferred to developing countries.

What are the FO's chances of exercising social control over technical progress?

Force Ouvrière does not feel that it is the business of the trade unions to decide on overall industrial strategy. However, it absolutely must be informed and consulted prior to all decisions so as to be able to study their impact on working conditions and thus be in a position, as speedily as possible, to take all necessary measures to preserve workers' interests through the channel of collective agreements.[13]

---

12 FO, *Livre blanc*, p. 3.
13 FO, *Livre blanc*, p. 12.

Trade Union Strategy on Modernisation: Defensive or Offensive?

To Oversee Policy or to Shape it: The Problem of a Preventive Trade Union Policy

Verdier's typological analysis of trade union policies towards technical progress[14] establishes a conventional distinction between "defensive" and "offensive" strategies. He considers British trade unions to be the typical representative of a defensive strategy. The three characteristic features of such a strategy are the preservation of existing benefits, compensation, and, possibly, prevention.

The criteria that Verdier uses to differentiate between defensive and offensive strategies go as far as investment decisions. An offensive strategy (judged to be that of the CFDT) is characterised by the fact that, prior to the introduction of new technology, the trade union includes itself in the decision process. He looks upon early intervention in this area as more important than the social supervision of decisions that have already been taken. Verdier sees the CFDT as a champion of the offensive strategy since, in his view, the feature of investment surveillance is to be found in no other French trade union, including – he says – the CGT.

This (artificial) polarisation of offensive and defensive strategies is a reflection of a sectional vision of the French trade union movement which traditionally establishes a distinction between "revolutionary" and "reformist" unions. In view of the present crisis in the movement, the distinction may appear rather "platonic." In present circumstances, no French trade union is in a position to apply a truly offensive strategy, and the differentiation between offensive and defensive remains arbitrary, reflecting the brand image that this or that union seeks to present of itself (see Table 1 below).

This overview of the orientation of the policies of the major trade union organisations towards technology remains, of necessity, concise. It nonetheless demonstrates that all that is perceptible at the level of strategic orientations are differences of degree. For while the FO may refuse to take an active part in the investment decision process, it actively pursues the objectives of a preventive technological policy aimed at triumphing over competing organisations in the matter of supervision of investment.

---

[14] E. Verdier: *La bureautique*, Paris, 1983, p. 108 ff.

Table 1: The Strategies of French Trade Unions Faced with the Challenge of New Technology

Organisation	Orientation and strong points of policy
CGT	offensive. Objective: global supervision of the process of technological innovation; priority given to the preservation of existing rights.
CFDT	offensive. Objectives: global supervision of the process of technological innovation; democratisation by the right of expression concerning decision-making processes whereby new technologies are installed and developed.
FO	defensive. Objective: social supervision of the consequences of technical progress by means of an active policy of collective negotiation.
CFTC	an offensive strategy of cooperation. Objectives: preparation for a policy of negotiation on the introduction of new technology; prevention and supervision of social repercussions.
CGC	an offensive, sectoral strategy. Objectives: assessment of competence and provision of a certain flexibility for executives, identifies with a policy of social management.

Since it would be illusory at the present time to imagine that such a demand could be accepted, the FO's pragmatic negotiating stance is being imitated by all of the other unions.

We now turn to investigate the objectives that trade unions set themselves in the matter of negotiating policy to see whether any practical results have been achieved. To conclude, we shall look at the institutional spread of trade union representation within French enterprise.

How Is Modernisation Presented as a Subject of Negotiation?

The following outline of the objectives of trade union negotiations is based mainly on the CGT's "catalogue of negotiations," although it is true, as Sellier[15] rightly points out, that the CFDT's positions were far more entrenched. The CGT's demand for negotiations on the three planks of its "pact for modernisation" loses some of its point insofar as the main thrust of the union's demand for negotiations was security of employment.

---

[15] F. Sellier: *L'impact des nouvelles technologies sur l'action syndical et le système français de relations industrielles*, CNRS (L. E. S. T.), Aix-en-Provence, 1984, p. 18 f.

The CGT felt that this issue gave it a free hand, after the withdrawal of the Communists from the government, to adopt a hard line – approved by the rank and file – on security of employment. Opposed to the CGT was the CFDT which, linked to the Socialist Party, remained far more attached to a policy centred on democracy in the workplace, that had been defined before the change of government. It therefore tried to sponsor the corresponding legislative reforms that, with its unofficial assistance, had been adopted with some difficulty in 1982.

In order to refurbish its policies, it had to prove that the new rights granted to workers and to the organisations that represent them had a real influence on the implementation of modernisation. The emphasis placed on other CFDT strong points (the organisation of work, working conditions) were derivatives of the so-called "qualitative" demands that had come to the fore in the 70s.

The FO experiences even less difficulty in formulating the objectives of its negotiating policy and can directly relate them to the policy of collective bargaining pursued since the 60s which had remained unchanged when the new government came to power. Traditional trade union objectives (security of employment, preservation of purchasing power) are to be pursued as part of general collective bargaining. What was already true of the assessment of the various strategies is also true of the objectives to be attained in the actual negotiations themselves. In other words, all the unions broach the same subjects. The CGT's presentation of its negotiations (within the limits mentioned above) is exemplary in this connection.

At the end of 1984, the CGT proposed that interprofessional negotiations centred around three main themes. Three modules of modernisation as put forward by the CGT[16] were defined in the terminology of the interprofessional agreements:

  I: Employment – modernisation – restructuration,
 II: Employment – modernisation – qualification,
III: Employment – modernisation – working conditions.

The aim of the *"employment – modernisation – restructuration"* theme is a form of supervision of investment. Contractual agreement has to be reached over objectives concerning the social and economic repercussions linked to modernisation. The extent of restructuration automatically caused by investment has to be quantified prior to the installation of any

---

[16] *Le Peuple*, n° 1179, 13 September, 1984.

new technology. It is therefore necessary to determine the number and kind of jobs, qualifications and training arrangements, working conditions, etc. Here, then, was a detailed enumeration of the foreseeable consequences of restructuration for the workers concerned. The problem was to negotiate a breathing space until such time as the social repercussions of the new industrial structures and the applications of new technology had come to be accepted by all.

The *"employment – modernisation – qualification"* theme seeks to draw up new rules for the widening of qualifications that have become necessary in the wake of technical innovation. Participation in training programmes designed to adapt existing qualifications to new requirements must be linked to a guaranteed position provided for in a contract of employment for each worker. The CGT demands that workers be allowed to choose their retraining programme freely and to get advice from the trade union official of their choice.

What the CGT is aiming at is a multi-purpose type of retraining to enable workers to manipulate "transfunctional" techniques (the utilization of different electronic operations at various stages of production). The end objective is one of qualification, the adaptation of qualifications being seen as a lever to increase the level of qualification which logically leads to a better job rating and, in the final analysis, a higher salary.

Finally, through the *"employment – modernisation – working conditions"* theme the CGT seeks to regulate working conditions, which include working hours, the content of work, and health in the workplace. The introduction of new technology must lead to reduced workloads. Segmentation of work and repetitive manipulations must be avoided.

These "modernisation" themes form a whole of which the common denominator is the *"employment – modernisation"* tandem. It is obvious that the preservation of employment is even less easy to negotiate than training schemes or restructuration. Yet the CGT anticipated problems by proposing solutions that moved down from a maximalist to a minimalist standpoint. Priority (ideological) is given to the maximalist attitude: modernisation and new technology must be introduced in such a way as to create new jobs. If this should prove impossible, then at least the present level of employment must be guaranteed. The CGT goes on to admit that even their defence of the status quo may fail. In which case they maintain their minimalist demand, in other words, that redundancies are out of the question. The reduction of the workforce must be brought about by "natural" (retirement) or by "voluntary" means (the return of immigrant workers to their native countries).

These three modernisation themes (they might also be called employment themes) were to be integrated into a system of interconnected negotiations. The CGT acknowledges – as do the other trade union organisations – that the outline agreements, signed at the interprofessional national level, are not directly applicable at branch level and on the shop floor. Consequently, outline agreements serve as a reference for negotiations at branch level and on the shop floor where general guidelines are adapted to suit local negotiating conditions.

The importance that the CGT attaches to collective bargaining may be seen in the proposal to set up "supervision committees"[17] which, within the company, will have the task of overseeing the application of rules and agreements.

Although it pursued the same objectives, the FO does not set minimal demands.[18] While it is considered as the trade union that most favours collective bargaining, it does not simply demand that existing negotiating rights be guaranteed.[19] At the same time, it advocates the creation of a national body composed of representatives of all the economic and social partners concerned by the general consequences of computerisation and automation. Representatives from ministries with even peripheral responsibility for modernisation would also have seats on this body. Discussions at the national level are seen to be necessary in order to lay down guidelines in the following areas: regional development, the establishment of new sectors of activity (to answer socio-collective needs), and the application of ergonomic measures.

Along the spectrum of interconnected negotiation, in-house discussion remains the pre-eminent form of negotiation for the CFDT. Generally speaking, it pursues the same objectives as the CGT and the FO, although it tends to place particular emphasis on the right of the labour-management committee to make its views known.[20] What is striking is that all of the trade unions seem to want to take part in social dialogue. They apparently want to take advantage of the economic climate to force

---

[17] *Le Peuple*, n° 1179.

[18] FO, *Livre blanc*, p. 12 ff.

[19] The interaction between interventionism and the "autonomy" of contractual policies is illustrated by P. Jansen, In: L. Kissler (ed.): *Industrielle Demokratie in Frankreich*, Frankfurt a. M./New York, 1985, p. 42–51.

[20] See the 9 propositions des cadres CFDT permettant le contrôle des investissements informatiques par les travailleus, (9 Proposals by CFDT Executives for the Control of Computer Investment by the Workers), September, 1979, In: *Cadres et Technologies*, 6th UCC-CFDT Congress, Strasbourg, 18–20 October, 1984, p. 7.

the employers to engage in such a dialogue. But do employers need to negotiate over modernisation?

If one looks at the outcome of negotiations, one gets the impression that they have got bogged down. The employers are free to negotiate as they see fit and may terminate the discussion once they feel that their proposals have not met with approval. In other words, the employers do not systematically oppose the negotiated introduction of new technology. The economic climate enables them, however, to wrest negotiated concessions from the trade unions and this facilitates the process of innovation.

The Practical Outcome of Negotiations on Technical Progress

Sellier[21] has analysed a series of successful negotiations. He notes that the first collective agreements relating to the introduction and application of new technology were signed in the tertiary sector, which is hardly surprising in view of the fact that in France this is the sector that has been most affected by the introduction of new technology.[22]

No branch agreements (national or regional) had been signed up to the end of the 70s. The trade unions won their case only in a number of major companies (banks, insurance companies, the civil service). Company agreements hardly went beyond regulation of VDU work. The results of trade union negotiations are not, however, insignificant: the maximum duration of VDU work was set at 5 hours per day, with no more than 2 hours without a break. Another important trade union demand has been satisfied (in the Crédit du Nord Bank) on advance testing for planned changes. Certain branches are set up as experimental laboratories, as "pilot stations" so to speak, to put new changes to the test. The entire staff of the pilot stations will be closely associated with the adoption and development of the new methods.[23]

The agreements signed at this time in the banks and insurance companies reflect the CFDT's priorities to a certain extent. On the other hand, the CGT, with its monopoly in the printing industry, was in a position to put forward a different set of demands. It was able, for

---

[21] F. Sellier, 1984, p. 38 ff; and: A. R. E. T. E.: *Négocier l'ordinateur? La concertation sur les nouvelles technologies dans l'entreprise*, Paris, 1983, p. 15–104.

[22] See, for example, Y. Lasfargue: Qui utilise l'informatique, *Futuribles*, n° 80, September 1984: 72–75.

[23] F. Sellier, 1984, p. 44.

example, to negotiate guaranteed employment through re-training and transfer programmes in a number of publishing houses.

While VDU work is the chief concern in administrative areas, the modernisation of basic industries and of manufacturing have brought other problems to the surface. Negotiations were above all concerned with job reductions, with the union demanding that heavy and tedious jobs be abolished, while at the same time limitation of work pollutants like dust and noise were negotiated. In view of the fact that the introduction of new techniques in this sector, unlike the tertiary sector, require substantial and costly investment, the problem of shift work quickly came to the fore. From the various collective agreements emerged a multitude of models for shift work, linking "flexibility" to working hours.

The examples referred to by Sellier are perplexing: although some of the results here and there would seem to be substantial, it has to be admitted that a coherent negotiating strategy is lacking. While at the ideological level the unions see themselves as adopting an "offensive" strategy, in practise the opposite is the case. All of the collective agreements in question were signed after the introduction of the new technology, which proves that the underlying strategy was defensive and reactive. With the exception of two branch negotiations[24] (the banks and insurance companies), the unions were unable to implement a preventive strategy.

Is Modernisation the First Step on a Return to the Past?

This overview of collective negotiations highlights the weakness of negotiated defence. The failure of branch negotiations is even more flagrant than that of subsequent negotiations at company level.

Although the Auroux laws[25] introduced the obligation to hold annual talks (law of November 13, 1982), the results of the negotiations are meagre indeed where new technology is concerned. The overwhelming

---

[24] The situation has scarcely changed in the meantime. The only new agreement has been "the agreement on the introduction of new technologies" signed in the steel industry on 21 January, 1987. See: Liaisons Sociales, *Législation sociale*, n° 5906, 4 February, 1987, C$_2$ 306.

[25] See J.C. Javillier: *Les réformes du droit du travail depuis le 10 mai 1981*, Paris, 1984.

number of wage settlements[26] put one in mind of the discussions that were organised on the topic of the so-called qualitative demands. These were given pride of place, but the structure of properly negotiated demands remained relatively stable. This time round, everybody is talking about modernisation, computerisation, and the need for collective negotiation covering the social problems raised by the introduction of new technology. This unanimous approach does not prevent negotiations held at national level from failing (see the negotiations on the subjects of "flexibilisation" and the relation between training contracts and job hunting).

Successive failures have not just blocked negotiations at company level. The wait-and-see attitude that has become the salient feature of collective bargaining (the rhythm of elections play a role in this respect) does not indicate stability. The collapse of traditional trade unionism is clear when one sees the employers going on the offensive over deregulation.[27] However, the threat to the collective protection of workers is not frontal but modulated; the employers want to soften the rigidities that exist at national and branch level. The extra latitude thus obtained will be used to strengthen the social dialogue within the workplace, thus making it possible to introduce a powerful "company rationale." This will give the employers the opportunity to use blackmail tactics of the variety – "If you don't give in, we'll close the place down!"

This sort of company patriotism gives a new lease of life to in-house trade unionism. The revalorisation of labor-management committees (Comités d'entreprise) which, for a section of employers, have become *bona fide* interlocutors (despite the illegality of the practise) clearly suggests an intention to abandon the notion of trade union pluralism.

The employers know how to manipulate the Auroux Laws to their advantage. The social dialogue introduced in conformity with the law of August 4, 1982 is merely symbolic, since this revival of dialogue has wrongfooted unions more used to advocating class struggle. In retrospect, it seems legitimate to suspect that it was no accident that supervision of the consequences of the introduction of new technologies should have been entrusted to the labour-management committees and to the institutions emanating from them (the Committees on Hygiene, Security,

---

[26] As an indication: *Le Monde* of 28 June, 1985 for the outcome of collective negociations in 1984: for 1983, see Liaisons Sociales, *Législation Sociale*, n° 5633 of 15 April, 1985, C_2 274; more recently, Liaisons Sociales, *Documents*, of 17 June, 1987, n° 61/87.

[27] See: P. Morville, *Les nouvelles politiques sociales du patronat*, Paris, 1985.

and Working Conditions, the CHS-CT whose area of competence is regulated by the law of 23 December, 1982). The labour-management committees traditionally represent one type of institution whose predominant feature is cooperation. Given that composition of the committees remains unchanged (the employer acts as Chairman!) it is not possible to claim that the new legislation has completely broken with tradition. Besides, the mixed membership of the committees explains why it is undesirable that they be given rights of negotiation.

The implication of this state of affairs is that meetings of the labour-management committees give elected representatives and trade union representatives (they have consultative status on the committees) an opportunity to be consulted and to receive information. The committee may express its opinion, but that opinion is in no way binding. The committee is no more than a forum for social dialogue endowed with no right of decision. Control of technical progress can be exercised by the committee on one condition – that the employer agrees.

The UCC-CFDT table (see Table 2 below) outlines the possibilities of "trade union involvement in new technology." The labour-management committees really only come into play in the fourth and fifth phases.

The legal framework of joint negotiations on new technology in the workplace is "ill adapted" to the choices to be made in the area of computerisation; "the problem of technology and more specifically of computerisation does not feature explicitly in the Labour Code as a fully-fledged area of information and consultation." This was true of the situation prior to 1982.[28]

The new legislation introduces a series of measures intended to give more weight to the trade union voice in this area:
– information and consultation prior to any major plan concerning the introduction of new technology (Labour Code, article L. 432-2);
– appeal to an outside expert (article L. 432-4).
But the old problems remain: the length of time allowed for reflection within the framework of prior consultation is short. And the law does not stipulate at what point consultation becomes obligatory – from the very beginning? at the planning stage? when new machinery is actually being installed?

The new rights remain ambiguous. They strengthen the power of the labour-management committees and at the same time introduce a

---

[28] A.R.E.T.E. *Négocier l'ordinateur?*; p. 25.

"rationalisation" of union policy. The committees are urged to fall in line with the positions adopted by the experts.

In conclusion, we find that the central contradiction of the situation is characteristic of French trade unionism. On the one hand, the unions accept social dialogue and are anxious to act "responsibly." On the other hand, this increased commitment has not led to equal rights of decision. Allegiance to the ideology of the Charter of Amiens militates against this. French trade unionism runs the risk of finding itself burdened with responsibility for unpopular decisions without being able to exert any real influence on the actual decision-making process. Given that the plurality of trade unions rules out any progression towards the "German model" (which is also going through a period of crisis) of "joint management" and that "disputatious" trade unionism is now superseded, the outcome of the modernisation movement within French trade unionism remains uncertain. For, confronted with the problems posed by computerisation in France, trade unionists (and the sociologists) are in a quandary.

Table 2: Trade Union Involvement in New Technology – Procedures and Areas of Involvement in the Introduction of Computer Technology

Phases of trade union involvement	Possible areas of trade union involvement	Level 1 National interprofessional	Level 2 Regional interprofessional	Level 3 Industrial branches and sectors of activity	Level 4 Company or establishment	Level 5 Workshop and office
Phase 1 Overall plan of data processing and computer hardware		• Participation in the activities of the ADI (Agency for the development of data processing) and of the CNIL (National commission on data processing and human freedom) *Examples*: Modification of the computerised national identity card – Application for rules governing VDU work – Contributions to research policy	• Contributions to the activities of the regional delegations of the ADI and Préfectures *Examples*: The telematics experiments in Saint-Malo	• Contributions to the design of materials at both production and consumer level *Example*: Telecommunications and computers	• Study groups within union branches with assistance from researchers and executives in charge of planning. This sort of activity is even more necessary in "advanced" industries that function as "pilot" experiment stations for the others	
Phase 2 Definition of the industrial policy		• Participation in the work of the Ministry of Industry • Contribution during the preparation of the 8th and 9th Plans *Example*: The development of the electronics industry	• Contributions to regional development • Contributions to high-employment zones			

Phase					
Phase 3 Construction of the data processing project	The need for a national agreement or regulatory provisions: • so that the labour-management committee might play its full role in the control of investments data processing • to organise, officially, the complete analysis of pilot experiments • to organise training (this is what the 9 proposals by the CFDT on computerisation signify)	• Involvement at the regional level to get a certain number of large-scale data processing systems decentralised and regionalised Example: The supplementary benefits data processing system is highly decentralised (hardware and software). On the other hand, the data processing system for hospitals and social insurance systems are spread out over the country as a whole but the programs remain centralised	It may occasionally by worthwhile envisaging the possibility of "branch agreements" on the design and repercussions of technological mutations Example: the use of robots in the motor industry and of data processing in the insurance industry	At the labour-management committee level. Development of information: • Analysis of the main lines of data processing policies (employment, human rights, etc.) • Trade union counter-proposals on data processing proposals and systems of organization	• Proposal on collective training prior to planning • Contribution to discussion on job organization and the machine/organization of work tandem
Phase 4 Installation of the equipment				At the labour-management and hygiene and security committee level • Involvement in discussion on conditions of installation • Analysis of pilot schemes	• Request for collective training prior to planning • Analysis of pilot experiments
Phase 5 The system comes on stream				At the labour-management committee, hygiene and security committee, and staff delegate levels • Use of new indicators in analysing the consequences of computerisation in the social report	• Contribution to analysis of consequences • Discussion of consequences and of counter-proposals at workshop level within the framework of employees' right of expression (1 % of hours worked is the CFDT demand)

Source: Cadres et technologies: UCC-CFDT, 6th Congress, Strasbourg, 18–20 October, 1984, p. 14.

Chapter 13
Technical Change and Informal Participation: The Role of Competence and Control in Administrative Work

Ulrich Heisig and Wolfgang Littek

Introduction

The thesis we want to develop in this chapter is that a high degree of participation of employees is to be found in the work processes and the restructuring of work within companies. Without a certain amount of participation the work processes would actually not function, at least in sensitive areas, because it is impossible to elicit performance by coercion and hierarchical control alone. This sort of informal but vital participation is often overlooked in discussion, which tends to concentrate on institutionalised forms of participation only. A thorough analysis of the actual work processes within a company will reveal a network of social interaction beyond the limits of formal institutionalisation and structurally defined class positions. Such participation is especially apparent for the skilled administrative work in industry which we have studied. The material basis for such participation is the *competence* of skilled white-collar workers which is founded in their experience and expert knowledge of functionally necessary work tasks. Management depends on the qualified co-operation of competent administrative workers in successfully organising and restructuring a company's labour process. Management is never fully independent of workers' knowledge and skills even in keeping up the work-flow of everyday activities, and this is the more true in keeping up the potential for constant technological and organisational restructuring, which has to be preserved for a company to survive under the pressure of competition which is a vital feature in the capitalist mode of production (see e.g. Briefs 1984: 86, Littler 1982: 32).

In order to gain the "use value of labour power," that is, the knowledge and skills accorded voluntarily, procedures in everyday "effort bargain-ing"[1] at the work place and in processes of technological and organis-ational change are often found to be constructed as processes of action and reaction between management and employees. Taken this way, "consent" is produced at the point of production between the structurally antagonistic interests of labour and capital, which is a necessary feature for organisational performance that will not be attained by mere class struggle and hierarchical enforcement. The preconditions for this to happen are recognition by management of the vital interests of workers, matched by compliance or even participation in work (re-)organisation on the part of the workers. The occurrence of such conditions is, however, heavily dependent on the degree of workers' competence, as research findings show.

Our arguments are drawn from an empirical study on the effects of technical and organisational changes on white-collar work, and em-ployees' reactions to changes in their working and employment con-ditions. The fieldwork was carried out between 1980 and 1982 in three large manufacturing companies in Northern Germany in the sectors of office machinery, television and hi-fi equipment, and steel. All three companies were affected by the economic recession. The first aim of the study was to evaluate the companies' economic situation, personnel policies, and measures of technical and organisational restructuring, and the response of the trades unions to innovation. This was pursued through "expert"interviews with top and middle managers, members of works councils, and union officials. The main aim of the study was to examine the experiences and reactions of skilled male employees to these changes. This was done through open-ended interviews with skilled male commercial and technical employees. The topics covered in the course of these interviews were technical and organisational changes in work; the effects on working conditions (e. g. skill requirements, autonomy and control, stress and strain, etc.); the effects on effort and income, career prospects, employment security, and chances in the external labour

---

[1] *Effort bargaining* is due to the fact "that the production process is overlain by the market process – that the labour contract is in practice being renegotiated every second of the working day" (Lee 1981: 60). Labour contracts that are bargained out between employers and the union on the level of a certain industry are the institutionalised framework of the effort bargaining that goes on in the labour process. As the total amount of wages is fixed in collective bargaining procedures, the topic of effort bargaining is the ratio between fixed wages and the amount of effort the wage-labourer has to deliver in the labour process to get his wage. The subjects of the bargaining procedures at the workplace are the validity of contracts inside the labour process.

market; the possible forms of reaction open to employees (individually and collectively); and finally an evaluation of white-collar employees' social status in the firm and in society.

At the centre of our study were, on the one hand, the effects which the introduction of new information technologies and consequent work restructuring had "objectively" on office work, and on the other hand, the employees' subjective experiences and their reactions to these change processes. With the fieldwork completed, the necessity arose to explain why conflicts on the office floor and workers' resistance were minimal though the work environment and work requirements had changed drastically with the implementation of the new information technologies. Obviously, there must have been something which mitigated these technically induced alterations in working conditions and employment opportunities.

Changes in the Labour Process of White-Collar Workers

In all three companies the management engaged in a restructuring of the working processes of blue- and white-collar workers alike, due to slackening sales and necessary changes in product lines. The white-collar sections experienced a rapid introduction of electronic data processing, connected with work reorganisation. In many departments this led to extensive personnel reductions which were performed through relocations, "natural wastage," or redundancies. Aside from the quantitative effects, which posed a severe threat to employment security, the changes in the quality of working conditions were considerable, so that marked reactions of employees were to be expected.

However, in order to fully comprehend the effects of the change process brought about by the new office technologies and work reorganisation, it is not sufficient to consider only the apparent "objective" changes in working and employment conditions, but also the employees' role in the processes of change must be examined. This latter aspect depends very much on individuals' "subjective" interpretations and is related to their standing as actors in the system of social relations rather than to features of the technical system of the work process.

As far as apparent objective changes in work content and organisation were concerned, our findings are largely in accordance with those of other recent German studies of administrative work in industry (cf. Baethge and Oberbeck 1986, Hartmann 1984, Koch 1984):

(1) More than half of the employees working with electronic data processing reported pressure to increase productivity, in the form of extended or additional tasks, and being given less time to do those already allocated. Increased physical and psychological stress as a result of prolonged work on VDUs were frequently reported. Where decentralised electronic data-processing terminals had become the main means of integrating work processes, direct co-operation between workers was reduced and feelings of isolation and alienation were reported.

(2) Development of autonomy in the individual's control of the work process showed no unilinear tendency. On the positive side, personal supervision had been reduced and the heat taken out of personal relations in the hierarchy as an outcome of the new machine-mediated co-operation. On the other hand, the potential provided by the new technologies for technological monitoring of work performance was definitely recognised and widely resented. Since all circumstances of completion and efficiency are automatically recorded in computing work, it was feared that this information could be used by management to monitor and control workers. However, no cases were reported where this technical potential of monitoring was actually used for tighter control of employees' performance.

(3) The development of skills was a major concern for employees. They clearly distinguished between skill as the requirement of a job and skill as the attribute of a person, and the social dimension of skills was particularly emphasised, as compared to their technical dimension. On the development of skills in a technical sense, evidence of both de-skilling and re-skilling was observed, cautioning against oversimplification in delineating one general trend. Highly subdivided and routinised jobs with narrow task ranges were characteristic in systems where centralised computers were used indirectly in batch processing, but this tendency was reversed with the introduction of decentralised on-line computer-linked work stations. In the new decentralised system the clerk is required to interact directly with the computer in order to fulfil his task. Whereas formerly tasks had been further fragmented in order to enhance data preparation throughput, they were now often more complex in their functional range. Skilled knowledge here remains an essential prerequisite, even though data processing becomes "automatised" by programs.

(4) Most importantly perhaps, we found a very specific notion of skill applied to work practice by the employees interviewed. This notion

stressed the *social and political dimension* in evaluating the performance of particular work roles. Skill was often mentioned in connection with the personal capacity to stand one's ground, to survive, and even to take advantage of the fluidity of the change process. This was an individualistic competitive skill characterised by always having an eye for the main chance. It was stressed as more important for gaining a good position in the firm than the skill demanded by the job in a *technical* sense, or skill as a *formal* requirement. This reflects very well the awareness of the importance of the subjective factor in the labour process (cf. Manwaring and Wood 1985: 171), upon which management depends and which employees can utilise strategically in pursuit of their individual interests, measured by success in income and career. Competence, in other words, was clearly seen as being decisive in one's standing against management.

(5) Our study showed no evidence for growth in unionisation or in collective forms of resistance including activation of the works councils. Employees strongly advocated the necessity of unions and the right to strike. Actual action, however, was reserved for the (hypothetical) extreme case: the closure of one's department or plant. Thus, active resistance was reserved for those cases in which employees' immediate security was directly and unambiguously jeopardised.

Taken all in all, the minimal occurrence of overt conflict and the lack of resistance in such major processes were surprising and unexpected in terms of industrial sociology and industrial relations theorising, which always sets out from the structurally given antagonism of interests between capital and labour in the labour process. The negotiation of interests in reality seems to take more differentiated avenues, especially given such conditions as those which govern the area of skilled administrative work. Competence and evaluations inherent in human labour power play an important role here.

Reactions to Change: The Lack of Conflict and Resistance

On the basis of the research findings, we hold the lack of active resistance to be attributable to the distinct work restructuring experiences of the employees. It shows the process of work rationalisation as being a process of largely "informal" interaction. Workers' competence here is the basis for their "participation," and while management cannot win over skillful co-operation merely by threat or coercion, it has to do so by concessions and by establishing mutual "trust" relations (cf. Fox 1974: 66). Thus the social standing of employees finds a certain recognition, and their subjective evaluations are important for understanding what is happening in a work process. In this way, the most noticeable findings on subjective evaluations of changing working conditions in our study were:

(1) The introduction of the tangibly new technologies was seen not as a dramatically new feature but as a part of the normal process of change and a prevailing feature of work in capitalist society. Employees thus personally experience, and regard as an intrinsic aspect of their work, what Marx had analysed as a characteristic of the capitalist mode of production: the constant revolution of the productive process.

(2) Work mechanisation and automation were not seen as the only and ultimate reason for threats to employment security. Technical change did not serve as a general scapegoat for complaints. Employees also appeared to take it as axiomatic that management's reasons for work rationalisation (including personnel reductions) had to be accepted in the recession under the pressures of competition, though rationalisation was unanimously seen as being undertaken exclusively in the company's interest, not in the workers' interest.

(3) Management's methods of introducing new technologies into work processes tended to be characterised by caution. Typical examples of the attempt to introduce change gradually were pilot projects in selected departments and preferential application of new technologies to areas where a previous reduction of workers and/or expansion of work volume had led to work overload. Change never occurred in one big step at a distinct moment, which could have triggered a unified, collective reaction among employees. The management policies obviously also avoided immediate reduction in income and status for employees and often provided for a higher income or status, or at least expectations in that direction.

(4) Management's policies of technology implementation were backed by workcontent-related interests of certain groups of employees. These were more quantitatively oriented in cases where an employee's workload had increased to being almost unbearable, so that the installation of the new technical devices was regarded as a relief. They were more qualitatively oriented in cases where particular employees were interested in enhancing the information available to them so

they could react to fast changing external situations and internal demands more appropriately. In general, those employees who began to work with the new technologies saw themselves as being in a more favourable position with regard to job security as compared with others, since they had managed to "survive" the period of uncertainty when the new technologies and work structures were introduced. In some cases we found competition between employees to work with the new technologies in order to show management their willingness and effectiveness. Ambitious employees especially saw it as a specific skill to stay ahead rather than to fall back under conditions of change.

(5) On the whole, there was a high amount of compliance with work restructuring by employees, which was shown in the actual behaviour. Compliance here was not just acceptance of enforced changes but included *participation* in the implementation of change. Skilled white-collar employees, who were affected by work restructuring in connection with the new information technologies, actively took part in the rationalisation process because they expected to advance if they used the new technologies successfully and easily fulfilled the increased achievement requirements of the company. Employees let it be understood that by actively supporting the process of change, they intended to influence the outcomes of change and expected to partake in the positive results of change. Such participation applied less to the active design of the technical or material working conditions than to the recognition of economic and social interests in work design. By such positive participation employees expected to secure their employment and to improve or at least hold on to their organisational position. Managers, on the other hand, let it be understood that they knew that they should put a limit on change in order to gain its positive results. If managers consciously or unconsciously paid attention to the existing fabric of social relations and the work-related interests of employees, which nearly always seemed to be the case, the technological and organisational change could take the form of management-initiated self-rationalisation of work and working conditions. In the case of a reduction in the number of employees in a department, for example, the remaining employees had to organise their work performance themselves to cope with the new work load. They did this voluntarily and were proud of it.

(6) Employees evaluate the effects of technical and organisational change on their personal and group situation in a considered way. On the one hand, employees stress the negative effects that changes in the labour

process have for their occupational group. On the other hand, the recognition of these problems did not necessarily have an effect on the employees' perceptions of their own work situation. A common pattern in the interview responses was for employees to draw a generally pessimistic picture of future prospects but to emphasise that personally they were perfectly secure and would continue to be so in the future. It seems that only the immediate threat to their own jobs is seen as being of practical concern to employees as individuals, whereas posts eliminated in general may make them pessimistic about prospects but do not elicit actual resistant action (cf. similarly Hartmann 1984: 282, also Kadritzke 1982: 238).

The Functional Basis of Trust Relations, Consent, and Informal Participation

The empirical findings reveal that the effects of the economic recession and organisational restructuring on working conditions have been significant since the mid-seventies, in West Germany as in other Western countries. In particular, the new microelectronic information technologies have proved to be powerful instruments for the rationalisation of work. In the face of such drastic restructuring of the labour process, the widespread acquiescence and minimal resistance by employees is surprising. In terms of a *macro-level* analysis, which focusses on the structural features of society, the question arises why do large groups of wage workers apparently not act according to their class interests? However, if we leave the abstract level of class interest definition and focus our analysis on the processes of technical and organisational change and employee reactions on the *micro-level* of group behaviour and individual action within the firm, the lack of overt resistance and the acceptance of change is no longer astonishing. From an action approach it can be learned that all labour processes depend on mutual interaction and, therefore, are organised to some degree on the basis of mutual "trust" (Fox 1974) and "consent" (Burawoy 1979). The very complex processes of technical and organisational change can be detected as being constructed by management in a way which anticipates worker resistance. This means that the vital economic and social interests of those groups of manual and administrative wage workers, who are important for the functioning of the firm's labour and valorisation processes and the success of technical and organisational changes, are recognised and very carefully secured by management.

The co-operation of workers is reinforced by another factor. All forms of technical and organisational change strengthen the competitive power of the individual firm; innovation is the core of capitalist development. Therefore management is primarily engaged in the *permanent* transformation of the technological and organisational basis of the labour process, and it aims at all transformation processes being fast and successful. To achieve this, it is advantageous to organise the transformation in the forces of production not in the form of class struggle, because this could (and probably would) cause worker resistance, work stoppages, strikes, interruptions, and delays. Rather, to avoid such "negative" effects, capitalists must to some degree seek a co-operative relationship with labour (Littler 1982: 32). Management, therefore, tends to be open to compromise in order to obtain the active co-operation of workers.

To some degree management is practically conscious of the distinction between labour and labour power: by fulfilling the work contract the wage-worker is forced only to do his prescribed job ("coming to work" – Burawoy), but not to bring in all the subjective forces of his labour power, i. e. competence, knowledge, know-how, and skill in doing his job (which means "working" – Burawoy). As management is dependent on the workers' capacities to run the labour process and successfully transform working conditions and implement new technologies, "it cannot just exploit the capacities that can be brought into play by bribery and coercion" (Littler 1982: 32). Rather, by recognising the economic and social interests of employees and by organising the labour process and the processes of change in such a way that workers can "subjectively" participate, management tries to get the (skilled) workers to bring more of their competencies to their work.

The Importance of Workers' Competence and Knowledge for the Construction of the Labour Process and Processes of Change

The extent to which management is dependent on the consent and active co-operation of labour in order to run a work process effectively differs for groups of workers of distinct function and skill. In almost all enterprises it is possible to differentiate between groups of marginal workers who perform highly prescribed, low discretion jobs of a

Taylorian type, and groups of central workers who execute the firm's key technical or economic functions in jobs which are little prescribed, and have high discretion (Friedman 1977: 53). Whereas the skill basis of the peripheral work is small, the performance of central jobs requires a high degree of skill, knowledge, and know-how.

Because their fragmented jobs need little skill, peripheral workers are interchangeable and are easily recruited on the external labour market. For management there is little functional reason to be aware of the co-operation of those groups of workers in everyday activities and processes of change. Management may therefore treat unskilled labour as a mere commodity.[2] In contrast, the core functions of the firm's technical and economic processes are executed on the basis of skill and expert knowledge, and core workers must be loyal to the firm's general goals. Among these groups "working" is not identical with the performance of prescribed tasks; to be effective and successful in the evaluation and analysis of information and data, in solving technical or economic problems, or adapting "routine" solutions to uncertain and changing internal organisational or external market conditions, skilled workers have to bring in their abilities and knowledge and have to engage personally in the performance of their jobs. Whether a skilled job is done well or badly depends to a great extent on the experience of the individual

---

[2] The distinction between the exchange value and the use value aspect of wage work and its importance for the relationship between capital and labour and the organisation of work is explained by Cressey and MacInnes (1980: 12–15). In going back to "Marx's own comments about the *dual* nature of the labour process," Cressey and MacInnes develop a critique of the "inadequate theorisation of the capital-labour relation at the point of production" in the Theory of Real Subordination of Labour. To prove the degradation of work theoretically, Real Subordination of Labour theorists like Braverman (1974) concentrate their analysis on the exchange value aspect of the capital-labour relation in which wage labour is reduced to a pure commodity. In doing so they over-estimate the tendency of capital to divorce the workers "from the means of production in order to maximise the alienation of surplus value and to abolish all dependency on the workers' own skill and initiative." To develop the relations *in* production in this one single way would mean that capital is going to destroy the use value of labour, the subjective potentials that make labour different from any other commodity. As these subjective forces are the basis of capital's productivity and innovative capabilities, the complete degradation of work would destroy capital's changeability. "Thus contrary to the implications of the R. S. L. (Real Subordination of Labour) argument capital has an active interest in suppressing its own dominance in the workplace to the extent that finance flows purely from the social forms of the relations of production and not from the requirements of production itself. To develop the forces of production capital must seek to develop labour as a subjective force to unleash labour's power of social productivity rather than abolish these powers. Thus in the use-value aspect of its relation with labour capital will seek a purely co-operative relationship in order to abolish the antagonism between the worker and the means of production that its capitalist form throws up."

workers and their voluntary engagement. Management therefore cannot treat skilled labour as a pure commodity, but has to care for the individual worker as a person. The functional implications for work-organisation are apparent in "expert" service work, leading to what Berger and Offe (1981) and Berger (1984) call the "rationalisation dilemma of administrative service work."

Even though the distinction between peripheral and central workers is not identical with that between blue-collar manual work and white-collar technical and administrative work – as there are relatively central or peripheral groups in each sector[3] –, there is some relationship because the proportion of central functions is much higher in technical and administrative sectors. The groups which generally stand much nearer to top management are white-collared, as Friedman (1977: 109) argues:

The progressive separation of conception from execution (via the manufacturing division of labour, mechanisation and Taylorian-type scientific management) has encouraged a hierarchy of workers in terms of their importance as individuals to top managers. The increasing complexity and integration of operations implied by these developments has meant that as skills have become concentrated into a smaller group of people, generally of white-collar technical staff, those skills themselves have become increasingly specialised within the technical staff group.

A similar development occurred in the commercial sectors as the complexity of the economic functions in- and outside the enterprise grew. Here as well the economic skill of the administrative staff were concentrated and specialised.

Skill and knowledge are functional prerequisites for labour processes based on responsible autonomy where piecemeal control is impossible and management is forced to organise the relations *in* production in the form of consent and trust. These forms of social labour relations in skilled white-collar sectors widely include specific *bargaining* relations. The securing of interests in everyday activities and in processes of change is mostly done *individually* and in "informal" ways. Even if the skill basis that underlies such co-operative relations and individualistic strategies is weak in peripheral sections of administrative and technical staff, individualistic and co-operative behaviour tends to be an overall

---

[3] As Kern and Schumann (1984) show, there are new central groups of blue-collar workers whose working conditions, relations to management, and individual behaviour are very similar to those in white-collar sectors. Membership of a central or peripheral group inside the firm's labour market is one of the main characteristics for group behaviour. On the other hand, we can see that in white-collar work even groups that are peripheral to the actual labour still behave as if they were members of the central workforce and belonged to the "high-discretion," "high-trust fraternity" (Fox 1974).

dominant and obligatory pattern among white-collar workers. Under such conditions there is little room for general solidarity and collective behaviour.

For blue-collar workers, stability of employment and relatively high earnings are much less connected with individual skills and the existence of trust relations. They also do not depend as much on influencing management decisions through the control of "areas of uncertainty" (Crozier and Friedberg 1979) to personally demonstrate one's functional relevance. In blue-collar sectors, bargaining power depends highly on collective forms of resistance, the strength of the works council inside the firm and the degree of unionisation among groups of workers. The securing of interests is generally done collectively. In everyday activities and processes of technical and organisational change in a company, blue-collar workers act contrary to management by collective procedures which are institutionalised in work council/management relations. Union policies concerning technological and organisational influence on working in the Federal Republic of Germany are staged on a level above the single company or workplace because of the principle of industrial and central organisation (cf. Müller-Jentsch 1983: 374). If few conflicts are to be found in everyday work activities and processes of change among blue-collar workers, this is mainly because conflict is institutionalised as bargaining between management and works councils: everyday consensus is reached by compromises between labour and capital within the firms' legal participatory institutions.

Among white-collar workers the strength and bargaining power of individuals and groups is much more dependent on the skill content of an individual's or group's work and the individual's or group's social standing. Here therefore the organisation of work, the recognition of skills, and the establishment of production relations on the level of the concrete work process are an important issue between workers and their superiors and are negotiated again and again in everyday activities. The stability of mutual trust relations and "informal" effort bargaining are relevant here for the effectiveness and efficiency of the labour process. As *both* management and employees benefit from this form of social labour relations, they are in most situations "consciously" aware of this relationship and avoid destroying it. Therefore even in processes of extensive technical and organisational change no automatic changes occur in the behaviour of white-collar workers. In general, no replacement of individual forms of behaviour through collective forms has been observed in central white-collar work sectors.

Informal Participation and Collective Bargaining: Some Notes on the Relations between White-Collar Workers and Works Councils

As we have already seen management, because it does not possess the competence to run and change the labour process by itself, depends heavily on the support of skilled workers. In order to gain their active co-operation in work processes and in processes of change, it makes concessions in work content and discretion and allows the members of skilled groups to at least partially partake in the profits of technical and organisational change. Through their "participation" skilled white-collar workers feel that their material interests are appropriately recognized. They very much identify with their work and voluntarily join in its restructuring. If they feel in a strong position, they try to advance up the hierarchy and to secure their future employment conditions or, if they recognize that they are in a weak position, they mobilize their resources to try to at least avoid the fate of the unsuccessful ones who are made redundant.

Skilled white-collar employees, who are usually very aware of managements' dependence on their "active" support, use their personal competence and readiness to co-operate as a strategic means to try to make the best possible bargain. Intending to preserve or even enlarge their social benefits and individual privileges, they collaborate with management in order to influence decisions in their favour. Because of the close connection between active co-operation, influence on management decisions, and individual success the mutual relations between management and white-collar employees are usually close and harmonious, while, at the same time, the lateral social relations between different white-collar functional groups and individuals are highly competitive. The largely unrestricted and unchecked competition which is enacted inside the labour process between white-collar groups and individuals for relative advancement in the internal labour market, however, causes a process of selection. The highly skilled, strong, and established groups and individuals are nearly always successful in their endeavour to ascend, while the weaker, usually less skilled groups and the elderly, mostly less efficient employees loose ground, become marginalized, and at last are made redundant.

In white-collar sectors of employment individual strength and social success are closely connected with the personal ability to secure one's interests on an *individual* basis. This is a central part of white-collar *reality* and *identity*. If someone is successful, he proves to himself and his

companions that he is one of the *intimate members* of the "privileged"
high-discretion, high-trust fraternity; if he is unsuccessful, he shows that
he no longer legitimately belongs to the privileged high-trust fraternity.
To remain successful, according to the understanding of skilled employees, is a personal affair. Therefore to reach a privileged position and
stay there, each and every white-collar employee averagely furnishes a lot
of effort towards personal advancement without any direct gratification
and shows very little active solidarity with those colleagues who – because
of the competitive behaviour of their "stronger" colleagues – are
negatively affected by unfavourable relocation or redundancy. On the
part of the "winners," the bad luck of the "victims" is associated with
weakness and personal incapacity.

Because of the *competitive* social *construction of reality* the privileged
position of established groups and individuals is always in danger of being
conquered and taken by advancing younger employees of better skilled
groups. White-collar workers who want to stay at the top are permanently
forced to fight back attacks by constantly proving their expertise and high
productivity inside the material work processes. Therefore in white-collar
sectors individuals or groups are never in a stable social position; they are
either on the advance or on the retreat. Because it would be a confession of
weakness, skilled members of white-collar groups never, or at least very
exceptionally, mainly if their social position is definitely threatened, call
for help from the collective of workers or ask for the protection of
institutions like works councils. White-collar workers will stick, as long as
possible, to individualistic forms of behaviour and bargaining using their
competence to fight to retain, or rather expand, the discretionary content
of their work and hence their influence, even in situations when collective
forms of resistance or pursuit of interests would undoubtedly be more
effective.

As long as the processes of technical and organisational change do not
massively affect their economic and social positions, white-collar employees usually seek to secure their interests on an individual basis. They
recognize little need to react collectively and see little reason to change
their behaviour towards collective interest orientations.[4] Therefore the

---

[4] Contracts and income-levels are mostly negotiated in the Federal Republic of Germany in
collective bargaining above the level of the single company and for all occupational
groups within one industry. Negotiated between the union and employers' association of a
certain industry, contracts actually apply to non-union members as well (except for the
fraction which has a contract as "außertarifliche Angestellte" in leading positions). What

well-established works councils in the Federal Republic of Germany are passed over by most administrative workers as a means of representing their interests or as a means of participating in structuring working and employment condititons. This has two obvious consequences:

(1) Since the results of informal effort bargaining are concessions on an individual or group level and are not officially recognised, they must be refought continually by every person or group. Therefore the benefits and privileges which were won by groups or individuals in the past can be withdrawn by management immediately without negotiation if new technologies change the skill requirements and undermine traditional power relations inside the firm, or if the economic situation of the enterprise or conditions in the external labour market deteriorate.

(2) Since the good working conditions and economic privileges of individuals and skilled groups are seen by unprivileged or competitive working groups as improper, or even as being at their expense, the withdrawal of the economic and social privileges of the, up till then, core groups and the deterioration of their working conditions is often applauded by others. This is another reason why there is little solidarity among the total work force of the firm. The informal bargaining practice by skilled groups is therefore an important cause of the separation of administrative workers into various competitive groups and individuals.

Even if in the short run some groups secure their interests in the internal labour market better than others on an individual basis and increase their job security at the costs of others, it is likely by the same processes that new technologies and work structures will make their skills obsolete, so their position will eventually be weakened. Therefore individualistic forms of bargaining, although successful at a certain time, very often turn out to be short-sighted in the long run.

In past years the works councils in the productive industries in West Germany were hardly informed about or even engaged in technical and organisational change or economic and social bargaining in the white-collar sectors. They were seldom used or informed by administrative workers, and therefore they did not know very much about the specific problems of processes of rationalisation in white-collar work. This had

---

we are talking about here in the text is individualistic versus collective behaviour in the immediate work process, behaviour which is then displayed as well vis-à-vis the works council or the union.

the effect that works councils – especially those which are heavily involved in blue-collar conflict solving – were not interested very much in white-collar problems and possessed little competence to deal with them. To act in a sector where conditions are unknown and relations are complicated seemed to be frustrating for most members of works councils. They preferred to concentrate on the blue-collar sectors where conditions are more favourable for them and where success was more easily attained.

This situation led to a vicious circle. On the one hand, works councils were recognised by most administrative workers as part of the firms' legal institutions which mainly looked after the interests and well-being of blue-collar workers. On the other hand, as long as works councils did not engage actively in white-collar problems, there was no change in white-collar/works council relations: they remained of minimal importance. White-collar employees largely felt that their interests were respected by management individually and that they could successfully look after themselves; because of this a fabric of mutual trust relations prevailed in this sector.

As long as works councils and unions showed no real interest in white-collar situations, white-collar employees could truly believe that works councils and trade unions were neither competent to deal with nor efficient in solving their problems. This state of affairs which was common until recently has now partially changed. Works councils' and trade unions' traditional "hope" that white-collar workers would become "proletarianised," and consequently become class-conscious and active union members, has been undermined by the facts. In order not to loose ground inside the firm, works councils and unions have altered their opinions and begun to recognise the growing importance of the strongly expanding white-collar sector. In order to attract the positive attention and support of white-collar employees, trade unions recently initiated a publicity campaign and encouraged works councils to seriously engage in white-collar activities.

In the changed political context it is of great importance that trade unions and works councils realise and learn to understand the specific features and modalities which structure white-collar sectors. As we sketched and partially analysed in this chapter, skilled white-collar employees "act in the way that is characteristic of members of privileged strata: that is, that they will seek to use the superior resources they possess in order to *preserve* their positions of relative social power and advantage, for themselves and for the intimate members of their groups" (Gold-thorpe 1982: 180). This intrinsic feature of white-collar behaviour, however, conflicts quite strongly with the "traditional" attempts of unions to reduce and at last to abolish privileges and to create more egalitarian relations in production. Certainly skilled white-collar groups will only actively support and personally engage in works council and trade union activities, if these activities coincide with and at least partially push ahead their particular interests. Works councils and unions which recognise skilled white-collar workers as clientele and buttress their existence on the support of these groups will, therefore, quickly be confronted with the claim that they have given up the egalitarian content of their traditional policies and become an exclusive instrument for securing and consolidating the economic advantages and social privileges of "elitist" groups. Whatever their existing position and whatever the temporary answer to this "problem" may be, works councils and trade unions inevitably have to move inside this challenging field of contrary interests and intentions, because otherwise they – inasmuch as the proportion and importance of skilled white-collar employees will surely grow – will loose their influence inside firms and consequently their political importance inside society as well. Because of this pressure works councils and trade unions, whether they like it or not, have to learn to move inside a political field which is not structured on principles of solidarity; the new political arena is competitively structured and bears a lot of risks for all engaged in the game.

References

Baethge, M., Gertenberger, F., Oberbeck, H., Schlösser, M., and Seltz, R. (1983): Bildungsexpansion und Beschäftigungslage von Angestellten; (Forschungs-bericht), Soziologisches Forschungsinstitut Göttingen

Baethge, M. and Oberbeck, H. (1986): *Zukunft der Angestellten. Neue Tech-nologien und berufliche Perspektiven in Büro und Verwaltung*, Frankfurt/New York: Campus

Berger, U. (1984): *Wachstum und Rationalisierung der industriellen Dienst-leistungsarbeit*, Frankfurt/New York: Campus.

Berger, U. and Offe, C. (1981): Das Rationalisierungsdilemma der Angestellten-arbeit; In Jürgen Kocka (ed.), Angestellte im Europäischen Vergleich, Geschichte und Gesellschaft, *Sonderheft* 7, 39–58.

Braverman, H. (1974): *Labour and Monopoly Capital*, New York and London: Monthly Review Press.

Briefs, U. (1984): *Informationstechnologien und Zukunft der Arbeit*, Köln: Pahl-Rugenstein.

Burawoy, M. (1979): *Manufacturing Consent*, Chicago and London: Univ. of Chicago Press.

Cressey, P. and Mac Innes, J. (1980): Voting for Ford: Industrial Democracy and the Control of Labour, *Capital and Class*, 11: 5–53.

Crozier, M., Friedberg, E. (1979): *Macht und Organisation. Die Zwänge kollektiven Handelns. Zur Politologie organisierter Systeme*, Königstein/Ts.: Athenäum.

Fox, A. (1974): *Beyond Contract: Work, Power and Trust Relations*, London: Faber.

Friedman, A. (1977): *Industry and Labour*, London and Basingstoke: Macmillan.

Giddens, A. (1979): *Central Problems of Social Theory*, London and Basingstoke: Macmillan.

Goldthorpe, j. (1982): On the Service Class, its Formation and Future, In: A. Giddens, and G. MacKenzie (eds.), *Social Class and the Division of Labour. Essays in Honour of Ilya Neustadt*, Cambridge and London: Cambridge Univ. Press.

Hartmann, M. (1984): *Rationalisierung im Widerspruch. Ursachen und Folgen der EDV-Modernisierung in Industrieverwaltungen*, Frankfurt/New York: Campus.

Kadritzke, U. (1982): Angestellte als Lohnarbeiter. Kritischer Nachruf auf die deutsche Kragenlinie, *Kölner Zeitschrift für Soziologie und Sozialpsychologie: Materialien zur Industriesoziologie, Sonderheft* 24, 219–249.

Kern, M. and Schumann, M. (1984): *Das Ende der Arbeitsteilung? Rationalisierung in der industriellen Produktion,* München: C.H. Beck.

Koch, R. (1984): Elektronische Datenverarbeitung in der Industrieverwaltung, Bundesinstitut für Berufsbildung, Berichte zur beruflichen Bildung No. 68, Berlin.

Lee, D.J. (1981): Skill, Craft and Class: A Theoretical Critique and a Critical Case, *Sociology*, 15, 1: 56–77.

Littler, C.R. (1982): *The Development of the Labour Process in Capitalist Societies*, London: Heinemann.

Müller-Jentsch, W. (1983): Kollektive Interessenvertretung: Das System der industriellen Beziehungen, In W. Littek, W. Rammert, G. Wachtler (eds.), *Einführung in die Arbeits- und Industriesoziologie*, Frankfurt and London: Campus.

Manwaring, T. and Wood, S. (1985): The Ghost in the Labour Process, In: Knights, D. et al. (eds.), *Job Redesign. Critical Perspectives on the Labour Process*, Aldershot: Gower.

Part IV
The State and Self-Management

Introduction

Paul Blyton

Despite the essentially decentralised nature of self-management, the state has several critical roles to play in providing a facilitative context in which industrial democracy can develop. We have already discussed (in Part III) the importance of an educational infrastructure through which workers can develop the necessary competence needed to take on the full role of industrial citizens (with all the responsibilities and decision-making rights which that entails). In non-market economies, the state as both legislator and employer has the direct responsibility for developing forms of industrial democracy which reflect the basic tenets of socialism. But even in market economies, the state is a major employer either directly (e. g. the civil service) or indirectly (e. g. nationalised industries); thus, in all industrial economies, there are important public as well as private sector arenas for the development of industrial democracy. While in terms of the conditions needed for industrial democracy to develop the two sectors have many aspects in common, the nature of the employer in the public sector, and the diverse spheres of activity in which it operates, also raise distinct questions for the effective development of more democratic forms of organisation.

As the legislature, the state has another key role to play. The IDE (1979) study is now one of several which have pointed to the extent to which the presence of a legal framework supporting workers' decision-making rights is associated with levels of shared influence actually practised at the workplace (that is, that *de jure* participation has a direct bearing on levels of *de facto* participation). In addition, following Pateman (1970), it can be argued that democracy in the community is a precondition for industrial democracy – that participatory efficacy gained in one sphere can form the basis of greater shared influence in another. Hence, in terms of the development of self-management and industrial democracy, states have both a direct role to play in terms of establishing the legislative context, as well as indirect roles such as providing the educational infrastructure and sustaining a living form of civil democracy within their own territories.

The three contributions in this section illustrate a number of aspects of the state's role. In his examination of community decision-making in Hungary, Sajó takes our analysis beyond industrial boundaries and in so doing points to the shortage of expert decision-makers in small communities. The result is seen to be a poor articulation of local needs with the result that power gravitates towards state officials. Sekulić also examines the relationship between local activity and the broader political structure, drawing on the Yugoslav case. By using concepts of power and meta-power, Sekulić outlines some of the basic issues and dilemmas facing a society seeking to overcome the competence gaps which hinder the full democratisation of work organisations.

In her study of an Algerian community, Dominelli illustrates how state actions can severely curtail the practical development of workers' control, reinforcing the hierarchical tendencies already present in a production system based around distinct categories of permanent and seasonal workers, and where all the work community's office-holding posts are filled by members of the former group. In pointing to the relevance of this dual labour market, Dominelli also underlines the point made earlier by Drache that labour force segmentation has important implications for the full development of more democratic forms of work organisation.

References

IDE (Industrial Democracy in Europe) (1979): 'Participation: formal rules, influence and involvement', *Industrial Relations*, Vol. 18, pp. 273–294.
Pateman, C. (1970): *Participation and Democratic Theory*, Cambridge: Cambridge University Press.

Chapter 14
Limited Expertise and Local Autonomy

András Sajó

Introduction

In this chapter a few remarks are presented on the role and functioning of experts in public administration and self-government. These remarks are based on Hungarian survey data and case studies of local public administration and self-government efforts especially in small villages. These remarks emphasize those elements which are particularly relevant for industrial self-management. Whatever the differences between self-management and local self-government, expert monopoly or limited access to expert knowledge are considered in both cases as a major hindrance. In the case of Hungarian small villages, self-management and self-government are intertwined since the local agricultural co-operative as a more or less self-managing community – in the legal sense – embraces the majority of the families living in the locality. On the other hand, the "expertise" embodied in the public administration poses similar problems to industrial or agricultural firms and to villages and other territorial units.[1]

It should be added that self-management is understood as a part of a complex system which consists of the firm or bureaucratic organization and its environment. Self-management will remain partial while it remains intra-organizational. Public bureaucracies are increasingly substantial elements of the environment. The present paper focuses on the theoretical problem of administrative expertise vis-à-vis local self-government. Therefore we do not deal here with the actual realization of

---

[1] For a similar comparison based on different considerations see Peterson (1979: 159): "Because cities must protect their economic interests in an uncertain environment, their decision-making process is analogous to that of the private firm in a competitive market." The problem of Hungarian villages is that they have no power to behave as self-supporting economic actors.

self-government. According to Hungarian law, local councils (elected bodies) are "fulfilling the tasks of self-government in their territory." They control most of the public administration in their territory. Notwithstanding considerable advances in this respect one can see from the discussion below that actual village administration cannot be characterized as self-government in the sociological or ordinary dictionary sense of "government of a group by the action of its own members." However, a number of decisions are formally passed locally and local influences or interests prevail on a certain number of questions.

It should be added that some ideas of earlier rural self-government are no longer viable.

While members of communities in the form of villages or towns within a non-mechanized agrarian social field must and can take decisions among themselves for a wide range of problems, the scope for decisions at the community level shrinks in proportion to the growth and the effectiveness and control at higher state levels (Elias 1974: XXV–XXVI).

The problem dealt with here is that of expertise: is expert knowledge theoretically a limit to self-government? According to the Weberian tradition,

direct democracy could ... only operate in local organizations – and the growing complexity of administrative tasks and the sheer expansion of their scope resulted in the technical superiority of those with training and experience. This last argument has been repeatedly corroborated in studies of the operation of participatory democracy (Poole 1982: 187).

What kind of power or powers stand behind the apparently neutral label of technical or expert knowledge which is applied as a legitimate "natural limit" to self-government? There is, however, a more fundamental question that needs to be examined before considering this classic dilemma: is it bureaucratic expertise which really delimits the possibilities for self-government?

Data and Background

Our reflections are based primarily on research conducted in small villages. Case studies of development decisions and implementation in smaller towns are also used. Another source of data for the present analysis was a special survey of public administration personnel (especially the data on professional qualification).

Villages – Councils – Communes

Roughly 44 per cent of the Hungarian population lives in villages. It should be added that "town" is a technical term of the public administration: some towns have no more than 9000 inhabitants. The administrative unit for the village is the commune ("Gemeinde" in German). It is the commune which has its elected representative council. The council controls the organs of public administration. Under the present system some communes are under the public administrative control of a nearby town, but most depend on the *county council*. As a consequence, a village is not necessarily a public administration unit or commune. Only about half of the villages have their own council, others have so-called joint councils. This is due to the fact that many villages are considered as being too small to be self-supporting.

There are about 1600 villages without their own public administration on site. Public services and the representative of the public administration visit these localities once or twice a week. Small villages are considered as not self-supporting and/or the centralization of services is considered as more economic. More than 60 per cent of all the villages were and are considered as declining or unstable; there are 1500 villages with less than 1000 inhabitants. Most of these villages are considered by the higher public authorities as declining, and consequently local public services have been partly withdrawn from them, and they have been obliged to form joint communes with other villages. Partly as a result of this evaluation, undertaken by a central expert institute working under the auspices of the Ministry of Building and Town Development, migration from these villages has increased. The concerned communes have no power to apply for revision: only the elderly have remained in these ghost villages, and their situation is aggravated as a result of this central policy.

In the last 30 years a considerable number of smaller villages have lost their administrative "independence" and have joined another council operated in another village. This often means that these villages will deteriorate further as the other, larger villages, where the joint council of the commune has its seat, take advantage of their position to the detriment of the smaller villages. For example, the school is operated from the larger village, often no public transport is operated to the smaller village, and the financial resources of the village council become more and more restricted as no taxable activity takes place.

As in Britain (and Germany) the dominant argument in favour of such changes has been first that socio-economic development patterns required rationalization of a pre-industrial local government map, and second that economies of scale could be secured (Johnson 1979: 245.)

It is only recently that the government has recognized the inconveniences of this settlement policy. The main inconveniences include increased pressure on urban settlements and the social problems of elderly village populations.

The chances of self-government are greater where there is a *community*. Theoretically speaking, smaller villages as – once upon a time – organic communities are closer to this ideal. It is obvious therefore that the above trend is unfavourable to the establishment of feasible local self-government. It should be added that as long as these more or less closed villages were rural entities with common pasturing, land use, etc., there were common functions in the village community which required self-government. Some of the elements of self-government were accepted in the system of bourgeois public administration which has otherwise been rather centralistic – and it applied its control in all matters which were considered as politically delicate. We will see that during the socialist transformation nearly all the problems or functions of the village, including economic activities, were considered as being of political importance and were treated accordingly. It should be added that pre-socialist local self-government was rather limited, too, and it perpetuated the class differences and local powers which existed in the rural communities.[2]

In order to understand the deterioration of villages and the limits to commune self-government, at least two socio-economic factors should be taken into consideration. First, village dwellers are not necessarily working in the village. There is a general backwardness in urbanization in Hungary: according to official estimates the national level of urbanization is lagging 15 per cent behind the level of industrialization (using international comparisons as a standard). The settlement structure of Hungary reflects the traditional pattern of agricultural production. 50 per cent of the working class live in villages; 1.3 million people travel daily or weekly to towns or greater villages from their domicile (25 per cent of the total workforce). A considerable percentage of village dwellers therefore have only limited contact with their locality. Social taxes are limited.

---

[2] It is extremely important to study the power relations and dominance involved in self-government; it requires a good deal of political and sociological *naïveté* to overlook the stratificational consequences and sources of that system of government. Unfortunately lack of space does not permit that analysis in this chapter. The above consideration applies to self-management, too.

Localities are financially dependent on the agricultural or industrial firms operating in their territories, yet the indirect financial contribution of many of their inhabitants goes to other, larger towns. Daily or weekly migrants make use of the public services of their workplace towns, and they are less interested in local development plans. On the other hand, a considerable number of city dwellers have small plots or rest houses in the villages: they are consumers of local services but do not make a considerable contribution towards them, and they do not have the opportunity to participate in local development.

A second important factor is to be found in the system of financing localities. It is obvious – and it is, of course, not a Hungarian peculiarity – that local resources are insufficient to support most villages. Given the incongruence between workplace and dwelling, then even under a system of local taxation most villages and smaller, non-industrialized towns would be unable to support and develop themselves. Presently only 10 per cent of a commune's budget is covered from local resources, including direct financing by locally operated firms or co-operatives and voluntary work and other contributions by the inhabitants. The remaining 90 per cent comes to the village from central government, including nearly all the development fund. This would not be fundamentally different from what one can observe in some Western European countries. This means that the county council – or in practice the planning and finance department of the county public administration in collaboration with the central planning agencies – establishes those groups of tasks, or even single projects, for which the money can be used. Obviously this determination is not a unilateral act: it follows the suggestions and requests of the localities to some extent. It should be added, however, that this financial redistribution is unequal and it follows its own preferences: it has territorial preferences (and the localities have no formal say against that) and it also follows topical preferences which partly reflect central developmental preferences. Big towns receive a larger share; some regions seem to be preferred due to their political ties, and some territories or communes in regions receive preferential treatment by the region. The legitimating ideology of this practice uses technocratic and value arguments: it is emphasized that national plans (i. e. a systematic unit imperceptible at the village level) must have priority.

Resulting inequalities have been considerable: 90 per cent of all development investments decided by the county formerly went to towns. (The ratio decreased to 80 : 20 in 1985.) Second, and related to this, is that because of the scarcity of resources, centralized use and selectiveconcentrative policies are unavoidable. Thirdly, the value of equality is stressed. It means in this respect that territorial differences which result in inequalities in standards of living shall be abolished in the long run and presently diminished. A given region or village may receive preferential treatment (a bigger share), especially as far as development programs are concerned. The budget which covers existing services is more or less normatively established, though there is a constant danger that the "rationality" of the service will be queried.

Consequently the problem of expertise for local self-government emerges in two respects:

a) Development projects, including projects which are presented by different economic actors and which, due to their location, concern the village. The commune may be interested to favour industrial plants in its territory, or a nearby located plant may cause pollution. The problem is especially delicate if the investment has been decided by governmental authorities, e. g. nuclear power plants.

b) Maintenance of existing public services. In socialist countries most public services depend on the council public administration. Services which are provided by market forces in Western economies are either administratively produced and distributed or depend on the public administration, e. g. it is no simple matter for the regional marketing co-operative to close an unprofitable shop if this is the only one in a given village.

The expertise in question may concern engineering, public sanitation, or economic matters: it may also include legal and administrative knowledge.

The Organization of Expertise and the Experts

Professionals in the Council

One of the favourite arguments in the system of financing and decision-making for referring local problems to the jurisdiction and competence of higher territorial units (counties or cities) is that villages and their councils lack sufficient expertise. Facts corroborate this without corroborating the given distribution of power. Only 2 per cent of the population living in villages are professionals (e. g. teachers, local physicians, agronomists employed in the local co-operative, etc.). Though they are overrepresented in local councils, their professional expertise is limited and it is inadequate for the problems facing self-government, especially as they do not have sufficient administrative expertise. Or, to be more precise, their expertise often does not fit the problems as defined by the laws and the public administration (e. g. given the complicated fiscal and budget system even a slight modification in development plans involves accounting problems). In many cases we observed only limited involvement by professional councillors. Many of the activities of the councils take place in special commissions: the commissions may elect as full members professionals living in the commune. In this way, too, the local physician, the local social worker, or one of the local teachers is involved in the activities of the council. They may offer expertise to the specific commission, yet this is a rather contradictory contribution as they are involved in a process which should, amongst other things, control their own contribution. Formally the professionals are *generally* employed by the commune, though their professional supervision is undertaken by *specialized* public administration departments of the county public administration.

The Functionaries

There are two functionaries in the council who may have administrative expertise: the president of the local council and the secretary. The president is elected – he may not have a formal qualification, though generally he is a local politician who holds this function for several electoral periods. The secretary is nominated by the county, and must be qualified (with either a law degree or College for Public Administration degree).

Whose Experts Are They?

The president and the secretary are dependent on the county public administration. It is this same county department or the executive committee of the county council which exercises employers' rights. The extent of power of the county public administrative organs is extreme vis-à-vis the local functionaries. One should also take into account the role of fiscal revisions. These are carried out from time to time by another county department. In the majority of our interviews with local council presidents they commented that they had to infringe one or another rule if they did not want to be completely ineffective. A revisor can be sent any time. Therefore it is important to co-operative with the county adminis-tration.

They will know that I break rules when I use the renovation fund for the construction of a new health center; but if we (the village) do not build it we will be left without medical service. They like our development but I have to cope with their suggestions otherwise I am lost. (extract from interview with a local council president, who had been president for twelve years)

The great majority of these officials is working hard for their communes, though one can hardly say that their orientation is either "local" or "cosmopolitan": they often reflect the point of view of the county public administration, and consequently they use elements of a bureaucratic expertise which is alien to self-government. This is, however, only part of the story. In many cases they initiate local actions and actively shape local interests in those expert (generalist) terms which enable the local community to communicate with the experts at the county level or in other public administrations.

Given their background, the officials' capacity to formulate technical problems is rather limited (see below). The most characteristic feature of their role is that their activity cannot be evaluated in terms of technical expertise. What they have to sell to the *community* is a brand of county policy. A typical example: as mentioned above, most of the financial resources of the commune comes from the county; traditionally the county supports development projects located at the county capital or development projects which conform to its development concepts. An average president, after trying unsuccessfully to convince the county planners and developers about the necessity of some local development project, has to "sell" what is offered by the county – which means a considerably reduced budget.

It has been a cornerstone of the Hungarian rural policy in the socialist transition period that the center has to have "its man" as head of the local administration in every village. It is only recently that this political concept has been revised. Following the 1985 local elections (in the course of which many local council presidents were not re-elected due to their non-local orientation), one can expect some changes to occur:

a) the redistribution of allowances etc. will follow normative per capita quotas;

b) the local council president will not depend on the county; his/her employer will be the council.

The Expertise of the Local Public Administration Staff

There is a small professional staff under the control of the commune council. This staff deals with problems of local public administration (e. g. taxes, civil registry, building authorization, etc.). The level of expertise of these civil servants is considered to be very low, especially in smaller communes where there is no division of administrative labour. Secondary education is acceptable (although 20 per cent are actually without that), and only a formal exam in public administration has to be passed. Given the low prestige and salary of this job, one can hardly find professional civil servants at the commune level. The expertise concentrated in this organization cannot be characterized either as a monopoly of knowledge which would restrict self-government or as offering expert help to the council. Public services, such as medical provision etc. are provided by professionals, and they depend on the council only formally. Given the poor capabilities of the local public authority, a number of activities are carried out by independent agencies (public sanitation, fire protection, land registry) or belong to the jurisdiction of higher authorities (county public administration or the more specialized and better qualified professional bodies of the nearby town).

Given the present system of competencies and jurisdictions, one may wonder if there is any important relation between local self-government (if there is any left) and expertise represented by the public administration. The local council is not in a position to formulate development policies or projects in expert terms. These decisions (e. g. the budget) are presented generally as propositions, drafts, etc. by the local commune secretary or president and are generally accepted by the local council without further debate. Obviously experts at the county public administration review the various proposals advanced by the local council according to technical criteria; at this level, however, the local council has no say. It is mainly through political (especially party) channels that county decisions can be influenced: the arguments used are mainly non-technical and do not require professional expertise. Expertise acts only as a filter: the main priorities are decided according to "political" criteria which are affected by lobbying, personal contacts, or social policy arguments and considerations.

In the actual system of national planning and central development policy even technical problems are subject to interest and power relations which means that professional logic cannot prevail even at that level. It should also be added that even the professional knowledge accumulated in the bureaucracies of the county public administration seems to be rather modest.

"Politicization" of local needs is the most common way of making local council claims effective. This articulation is, however, often the action of some influential local leader, such as the president of the co-operative, and is not related to any formal council action or resolution. On the other hand, decisions of the administration which are erroneous or difficult to justify on professional grounds are often labeled and protected as "political" decisions. Mannheim (1952: 102) said that it is a conservative feature of the bureaucracy to treat a political problem as an administrative one. Revolutionary ideology seems to lead to the opposite: here the bureaucracy is inclined to define administrative or technical problems as being politically relevant.

It would be erroneous, however, to believe that the council has no direct contact with "classical" bureaucratic expertise. Laws and regulations prescribe a considerable number of cases in which the local council or its public authorities are obliged to use experts, although the council or the civil servant is not always formally bound by what is suggested by the experts. Most of these experts are state-owned firms with no public authority – though they often enjoy a legal monopoly over a particular area of expertise. Of particular importance for local development is the so-called "local settlement/land use plan." (This is somewhat similar to the US zoning plan.) This has to be elaborated by the Central Physical Planning Bureau. The Bureau rountinely plans settlement projects and sends the bill to the council. The council has to accept the plan except in the case of solutions that break the law. It has to be added that the discretionary power of the Bureau is limited as the Ministry for Building and Town Development has elaborated an extremely detailed technical code for settlement plans. The Council may also initiate modifications at the obligatory revision which takes place every five years. This process which may be fundamental for the village obviously requires technical expertise; there is, at least in extraordinary cases, some money available to ask for expert review or alternative plans from another planning office.

Self-Government – The Last Resort

Somewhat unexpectedly in 1984 the Party revised the settlement policy which had led to unhealthy migration from smaller villages. As mentioned above, many of those villages which had to join other villages under a joint council rapidly deteriorated due to this fact.[3] Not only did the limited development funds generally go to the other village which was the seat of the council, but the population felt itself neglected.[4] They had no influence whatsoever on most everyday aspects of life in their community.

Given the lack of resources, no central solution to the considerable social problems in these villages (especially problems related to aging) seemed viable. Therefore the legislature decided to offer some opportunities for local self-government initiatives. The council members elected in the village form a so-called *local board*. In questions concerning their village the local board as a group has veto power in the local council. What seems to be more important is that the local board disposes autonomously of certain funds and of so-called "other local contributions." The latter is particularly important as it makes it possible for a local co-operative or branch of the agricultural co-operative to collaborate and directly intervene with its material services in the life of the locality with which it has "organic" ties. This may seem a trifle but it may solve a number of problems. The local board may without any restriction use its money, rather than, as mentioned above, being subject to regulations and the county administration, which in the past have strictly delimited the field of action of the commune council. For example, the local board can easily convert an old building into an "old people's club" and the co-operative which is cooking for its members can easily afford to send lunch and dinner by lorry to the "club." The local board is entitled to accept that contribution: both parties being actors in the same community. Both parties are influenced by the same public opinion and informal pressures. Finally the local board has real power of control and supervision over local public services, including the employment of teachers.

It is easy to grasp the importance of this solution for self-government. The local board operates under the direct control of the community (its sessions are open to the public); board members are directly responsible to and depend only on their constituency; they have to take into consideration and face local influences daily. They have enough knowledge of the local relations and needs to take action to deal with local problems. Social workers or council members living in other villages

---

[3] The problems associated with the reduction of local authorities are present all over the world; see Johnson (1979: 245).

[4] The ratio of per capita "development money" between "site" and "non-site" villages varies from county to county, and was observed to be between 1 : 3 and 1 : 9.

cannot have this relevant information. It remains a matter for the future, however, whether this possibility for self-government, created by pressing necessity, will be efficient in solving the problems of degraded and deteriorating villages.

Discussion: Theoretical Implications

The political tradition which shaped the present social structures and some of the ideology in Hungary favoured centralization. Lack of resources (the economy of scarcity) contributed to that; consequently the possibilities for local self-government were and are limited – though it has been accepted theoretically.

It is not surprising that in the given political and local social system self-government is residual: it covers issues which are considered not worth handling elsewhere or where other solutions are too costly. Some degree of local power seems desirable, however, even for a centralized system; otherwise the locality will disintegrate. This seems to create a "natural" need for self-government – it depends on the socio-political *environment* whether this is recognized in time. The phenomenon is once again not uniquely Hungarian: "Absence from the locality of power points or organizations associated with major subsystems may result in the destruction of the local social system and even also physical destruction" (Stacy 1974: 22).

As to industrial self-management in Hungary nowadays it is strategic decision-making which is considered as the proper matter for self-management, while daily operative management is a privilege of the executive. In the case of the local self-government of villages, it is the daily operative management which is left to self-government. Daily operative management is more a question of being locally well *informed* than a matter of expert *knowledge*.

It is not a simple matter, of course, deciding *what* issues require expert knowledge. By establishing a long list of issues which have to be dealt with by experts (e. g. plans elaborated by specially qualified professionals or semi-monopolized expert bureaus) it is possible for experts to *dominate* decision processes. As McKinlay writes:

One should perhaps add that this dependency on professionals cannot be regarded as a natural outcome of technological development since the dominant professions usually do not have knowledge in these areas – it is only imputed to them. Having an established power base in society they manage those with expert knowledge of the technology (McKinlay 1973: 72).

The Hungarian case suggests that it is not only, or principally, the professionals who establish a kind of technocratic control over the society, but also the political power holders who use the legitimated requirement of expertise to advance and consolidate their power through professional control. It is obvious that this partly artificially elaborated need for expertise will not allow those active in local village self-government to solve or even successfully articulate their problems.

Following the Weberian vision of the expert bureaucracy dominating democracy, it is now commonplace to state that public administration not only carries out policy, but makes the policy. Formal decision-making bodies – including local councils – are captives of the information and drafts elaborated by their bureaucracies. Public bureaucracies in Eastern Europe are, however, to a great extent constrained in their choices by their political environment.

As to local self-government in villages, where the presence of elements of community increases the chances of self-government, it seems as if the Weberian model should not apply. The decision-makers are not captives of their bureaucracies, as the bureaucracies do not possess enough expertise.

It must be left to further discussion to consider whether Weberian bureaucracy does or does not produce the level of efficiency attributed to it by the adherents of the Weberian tradition. Under normal circumstances, at least in the case of local public administration; there is an absence of those factors which are considered as natural causes or sources of efficiency, namely high qualification, formal training, knowledge, skills, and technical competence of bureaucrats, and the rational and systematic structuring of decision-making that is assumed to exist in bureaucratic organization (Breton and Wintrobe 1982: 33). Expertise is concentrated in different bureaucratic organizations including those of higher level public administration. The local commune, however, has only limited contacts with these bodies: its council receives "solutions" elaborated by these bodies. These suggestions are treated as "political" decisions – and it is through politicizing local needs that the local commune may receive some support. The central government, or its professional departments on the other hand (partly as a necessary tactical weapon in their struggle against the regions), prefer technical regulation which turns even ordinary problems into problems which require professional expertise and knowledge. The Fire Inspectorate, for example, did not have enough money to efficiently supervise what happened in its territory: it had to give up a considerable part of its jurisdiction to county public administration; consequently the Inspectorate has tightened its binding safety standards. The same lesson may be learned in the administration of public education where the Ministry of Education increased its normative regulations and professional standards after the takeover of the financial and personal supervision of schools by the counties. We have cited the case of local settlement plans, too. Central agencies exert control through increased reliance on professional criteria: consequently they prefer professional criteria to directly "political" or "interest group" considerations.

By becoming a gatekeeper to what is popularly valued, the professional gains the additional sanction of being able to make taking his advice a prerequisite for obtaining a good or service valued independently of his service (Freidson 1970: 117).

The meaning of all this has to be understood in an environment where expert knowledge is a scarce resource – and is artificially monopolized. The Weberian model does not apply to the problem of self-government of villages, as these villages reflect a pre-Weberian stage. Somewhat surprisingly the very tragic process of the disappearance of these "pre-Weberian" villages with rural community traditions has offered once more a chance for the revival of village self-government which deals with problems which are transformed neither into professional-technical problems nor into "political" problems. (Problems are termed "political" if they either require professional competence or concern a greater territorial unit.)

The extent of self-government seems to be only partially related to inherent barriers of expertise, especially because expertise itself is an "artificial" construction defined by the power holders. Recent studies on industrial democracy emphasize the importance of

general cultural, ideological and value patterns, the structure of bargaining, complexities in the relationships of power between the state, employers and trade unions, and the exercise of strategic choices in conditions which constrain rather than determine actual outcomes (Poole 1982: 195).

In the Hungarian case of local self-government it is clearly the power of actors in central government and at the higher levels of public administration that primarily shape the objectives, morphology, and institutional structure of both industrial and local democracy.

References

Breton, A. and Wintrobe, R. (1982): *The Logic of Bureaucratic Conduct. An Economic Analysis of Competition, Change, and Efficiency in Private and Public Organizations*, Cambridge: Cambridge University Press.

Elias, N. (1974): Towards a Theory of Communities, In: Bell, C. and Newby, H. (eds.), *The Sociology of Community*, London: Cass.

Freidson, E. (1970): *Professional Dominance: The Social Structure of Medical Care*, New York: Atherton.

Johnson, N. (1979): Some Effects of Decentralization in the Federal Republic of Germany, In: Sharpe, L.J. (ed.), *Decentralist Trends in Western Democracies*, London: Sage.

Mannheim, K. (1952): *Ideologie und Utopie*, 3. Aufl., Frankfurt/Main: Schulte-Bulmke.

McKinley, J.B. (1973): On the Professional Regulation of Change, In: Halmos, P. (ed.), *Professionalisation and Social Change*. University of Keele: The Sociological Review, Monograph 20.

Peterson, P. (1979): Redistributive Policies and Patterns of Citizen Participation in Local Politics in the USA, In: Sharpe, L.J. (ed.), *Decentralist Trends in Western Democracies*, London: Sage.

Poole, M. (1982): Theories of Industrial Democracy: The Emerging Synthesis, *Sociological Review*, 30: 177–203.

Stacey, M. (1974): The Myth of Community Studies, In: Bell, C. and Newby, H. (eds.), *The Sociology of Community*, London: Cass.

Chapter 15
Organizations and Society: On Power Relationships

Dusko Sekulić

Introduction

One of the basic philosophical ideas of the self-management system is the equalization of power in society. Thus self-management principles, such as the abolition of mediation and political professionalism, are all means directed towards the goal of the abolition of inequality among individuals in the sphere of politics. This philosophy evolved directly as a counter-attack on the Stalinistic variant of the theory and practice of socialism, and it leans on the fruitful tradition of philosophical concepts within the workers' movement before its Stalinistic "calcification." In this chapter there is no intention of systematically describing what self-management philosophy is, and what it ought to realize. Rather what we are interested in here is the historical and social context in which the idea was born and continues to evolve and the specific ways in which this context is influencing the development of the idea of self-management. The specific area of social practice in which the analysis is focused is the relationships of organizations to the political environment.

Framework of Analysis

The historical scene of post-revolutionary Yugoslavia is characterized by a markedly asymmetrical distribution of power that was the result of the specific circumstances in which all the potential centres of opposition disintegrated, mainly because of collaboration with the enemy during the war, but also because of the strategy of the revolutionary leadership which held that in the new system there was no need even for "loyal" opposition. Thus,

...leadership of the CPY had almost unlimited potentiality for establishing the policy of socio-political development of Yugoslavia. In history it is very rare to find such strong and unshared power in the hands of one revolutionary movement... Such conditions offered to the Communist Party an opportunity to, almost undisturbed by organized opponents, create relationships in society which would insure the rapid and many sided development of the country... In fact, the general staff for managing the war and revolution, which had unlimited prerogatives, continued to manage society in the post-war period without reducing those prerogatives. The global social system – with its subsystems – the political system, the economic system and so on – was an indivisible monolith, organized on the basis of a revolutionary democratic hierarchy in which the lower levels submitted themselves completely to the directives and decisions of the higher levels (Bilandzic 1978: 101–102).

Such an asymmetrical power distribution in society had at the same time a high level of legitimacy, which prevented the demonstration of this power in the sense of coercion by those who had the power over those who did not. Thus potential power was not actualized in the sense of coercion towards the people (or groups), but only in the sense of the prestructuration of system characteristics with the support of all relevant groups. This asymmetry begins to manifest itself in increasing levels of coercion at the moment when the conceptions of the power holders regarding further social development begin to differ from the conceptions of those who do not have power. This began to occur in Yugoslavia with the start of the "ossification" of the statist structure, or for example, with the hurried land collectivization begun in 1949, which provoked resistance from the peasantry and forced the power holders to apply force.

The existing tendencies of increasing the amount of coercion within the system were stopped because of the preorientation of development in the direction of self-management. This preorientation again generated significant support from different groups. According to Bilandzic (1971), this widespread support was forthcoming because:
- the working class saw the opportunity to maintain power and to become the hegemony of future development;
- the peasantry saw it as a victory in the fight against the imposition of collective farming;
- the intelligentsia preferred democratic means of development;
- the nationalities were opposed to Stalinism because it restricted national freedom;
- the war participants were defending their honour against external attack.
However, this increased legitimacy of the system did not erase the

asymmetrical distribution of power, it only made it "less visible" or more latent than it was initially.

As stated above, the power holders restructured the system in accordance with their concepts of desirability. But now, an integral part of that desirable state included a conception of the elimination of differences in the degree of power held by different groups. This is what is meant by the "socialization" of politics. It means a completely new situation where the actor in a system who is structuring the "rules of the game" creates those rules in such a way that his own power may be eliminated. But the situation is not quite so simple. If we remained only within the conceptual framework applied until now, then we would be forced into simplistic conclusions about the development of power relationships in the course of social development in Yugoslavia. We would be forced into a simplified "either-or" framework: either the goal of democratization is achieved, so the power centre would cease to exist, or this would be only an illusion, with the existing distribution of power remaining intact.

However, in order to be able to describe a complex picture of development it is necessary to introduce a conceptual differentiation between meta-power and power (Baumgartner et al. 1976). Until now we have discussed the concept of power only in the "manifest-latent" dimension. Now we must consider the hierarchical dimension. Every social action exists under some defined framework which acts to place limits on the action, outcomes, and actor-orientation. Meta-power is this framework. On the other hand, we speak of power when some actors, within a framework or rules of the game, have a greater ability to select preferred outcomes than other actors. For example, an organization can have power in an economic system due to a monopolistic position, but it does not mean it has meta-power, which implies an ability to restructure the entire economic system. Of course, the concentration of power in the hands of one actor may very soon arouse "appetite" for the transformation of power to meta-power. Such an example would be multinational corporations restructuring the political systems of underdeveloped nations.

This analogy can help us describe what has happened in Yugoslav development. Holders of absolute power in all spheres of society (of meta-power and power) are consciously proclaiming the "socialization" of power: in other words, their own withdrawal from the political scene. This is the concrete process which marks the withdrawal of the party from the day-to-day management of society and transforms it into an ideational and orientational force. This process was more precisely defined by the VI Congress of 1952 and the VII Congress of 1958. This means that pluralism appeared in the sphere of power (this receives theoretical elaboration in Kardelj's (1978) work on pluralism and self-management), but in practice the sphere of meta-power remained intact. However, the process of system structuring in the sphere of power generates the birth of new groups, which, on certain levels of development begin to aspire towards the attainment of meta-power. So we have the situation where official ideology prefers the entropy of power and meta-power relations through the "socialization" of politics, but the differentiation of the system creates new groups and movements which aspire towards restructuring the framework of the institutional system. This confronts metapower holders with a dilemma: either to stand by and let the system develop in an undesirable direction (the structure of meta-power will be complicated); or to intervene and manifest latent meta-power and act contrary to their own perceptions of desirable behaviour, and to reorient further development in a desired direction. In the historical period just passed, there were several such situations, but here we will concentrate only on certain of them and within these situations only on some of their dimensions. The first dimension involves the power relations between organizations and the environment and other power relationships within organizations.

Organizations and the Power Structures

In the statist period, organizations were a constituent part of the bureaucratic hierarchy which begins at the top with the AOR (administrative operational management), and ends on the bottom with the executor (organization). Lines of command and communications proceed from the top to the bottom. In that period, although legally independent, the organizations were in fact dependent elements in the state machinery.

Introduction of self-management meant significant changes in three basic dimensions:
a) the relationship of the organization toward the state;
b) the relationships between organizations;
c) the relationships within organizations.
These three dimensions are of course interrelated and their separation is only for analytical purposes.

The introduction of self-management meant the discontinuation of lines of control from the top of the state pyramid to the bottom (organization), by means of the introduction of the "boundary" in the relationship toward the environment. As the boundary becomes more marked, the organizations become more and more independent. The state, however, played an important role for a long period primarily through control over accumulation, but also through the director's role. In short, the director kept for an extended period of time the "double role" of the state "agent" on the one hand and the representative of the "working collectives" on the other, with a gradual tendency towards decreasing the first and increasing the second.

In the second dimension the introduction of self-management results in a different type of communication between organizations. While in the statist system it was characteristic for communication between organizations to be mediated through "higher instances", it later became common for communication to be direct, first through the market, and later through new forms of self-management agreements and social compacts.

In the third dimension we can divide the power relations (which are at the same time potential or realized conflicts) into vertical and horizontal dimensions. The horizontal dimension represents relationships between organizational units ("economic units" as they were called in the early sixties and now, according to the new constitution, "basic organizations of associated labour"). With the strengthening of organizational independence, we find also the strengthening of organizational parts in their relationship with the organization as a whole. This produced in some cases strong horizontal conflicts and disruptive tendencies within the organizations.

The vertical dimension is crystallized in the management-workers relationship. This is the only basic conflict relationship considered here because we are interested in how it is later reflected in the relationship towards the environment, although the "power games" within organizations are often much more subtle and complicated (involving, for example, conflicts among specific groups of workers; skilled and semiskilled; or between managers and experts, and so on).

The management-worker conflict dimension has become the main target of institutional changes directed towards the democratization of organizations, but it also becomes evident in strikes and other open conflicts.

Power Structure in the Society

Autonomization of the organizations in relation to the broader social environment is often regarded as an "indicator" of self-management development. This simplification has gone so far that income distribution in favour of organizations was taken as a direct measure of self-management realization. We do not want to negate the thesis that income redistribution is important for the development of self-management. But one should be aware that this does not present the entire story. Organizations are also part of the total social system and in them all societal conflicts are reflected. So the redistribution of funds will not automatically produce the type of behaviour expected by the creators of the system because of the very structure of relationships within the organization.

Most likely motivated by this discussion, Zupanov (1975) has introduced a conceptual distinction between self-management and workers' management. According to him, self-management represents the autonomy of organizations towards the state, and workers' management the influence of workers on enterprise management. But in prior situations, increased self-management (increased autonomy of organizations towards the state) was completely equated with workers' management (i.e. with the influence of the workers on the management of the enterprise). Such a simplistic assumption does not take into account the existing real power structure within the organization – a priori taking it as "self-managerial."

If we start with the proposition of workers' influence on the investment decisions in the organization, and, based on this proposition, we transfer investment funds from the state to the organization expecting then a certain type of organizational behaviour, a discrepancy between real and presumed manners of behaviour could result either from the fact that the workers do not behave in the presumed way or that they do not have the expected influence. Knowing the power distribution in our organizations, we can freely assert that it is the second case. Also, as we know, our organizations do not possess any significant influence on macro-economic decision-making.

One decision of meta-power holders, which was based on the wrong estimation of power relationships within the system, has had significant implications for the further structuring of socio-economic relations. This was the Banking Law of 1964. Meta-power holders believed that transferring state capital into the hands of the banks meant strengthening the position of the "economy," of which the banking system is only a part. This decision, as is obvious from today's perspective, became the basis for what is popularly called the "independent position of banking capital," and a significant part of the processes which are behind the creation of "independent sources of power." The fact was that the complex relationships existing between and within the elements of the economic system were not adequatly conceptualized, so the decision led to the accumulation of inequalities in the sense that the banks were accumulating power on behalf of industrial organizations and other parts of the economic sector. This power accumulation within the economic system created among certain social groups a strong desire for a meta-power position, which played an important, but not well-explained role in the political movements in Yugoslavia at the end of the 1960s.

Some Contradictions in Ongoing Development

System creators, who actually possess meta-power, have among their goals self-management (autonomy of organizations) and workers' management (democratization of organizations), both of which are perceived as inseparable. But the disparities in the realization of these goals has led in past periods to a process which tended towards the redistribution of power within the global system, and consequently towards the redistribution of meta-power.

One of these processes was the creation of a technostructure and its tendency to play a more important role in the broader social scene. This tendency ran contrary to the intentions of the system creators because their action was intended to increase the power of the workers through increasing the autonomy of organizations. But increasing the autonomy of organizations (what is very often simplisticly regarded as the strengthening of self-management), brought onto the scene a new social group – the technostructure. The concept is perhaps not the most adequate one, because the Yugoslav technostructure has many characteristics which make it somewhat different from similar groups in Western industrialized societies.

The evolution of the system from statism towards a "socialist market economy" and self-management also implies the simultaneous process of a rising technostructure. In the earlier period of statism, economic management was a constituent part of the political elite. To become a manager meant to fulfil the party duty, the directive. The same principle held for all other positions in all other sectors of society. The process of the introduction of self-management meant the evolution of a new basis of legitimate authority. Thus in addition to the state, the workers' collective became a source of authority. In fact, with the increasing influence of the market the workers' collective became a more important source than the state. Of course, the connections of management with the state apparatus retained importance as long as the terms of "business making" remained dependent upon the state administration.

With this evolution one also begins to detect changes in the perceptions and expectations of the role performed by the director. In a survey made during the economic reform process it was found that people perceived the role of the business manager as much more important than the role of the political functionary (Zupanov 1969). A prevailing attitude had developed which held that the management of the enterprise should become a separate profession. For example, in the same study, about 90 % of the surveyed managers, when in a situation of conflict between the political and professional role of the business leader, chose behaviour in accordance with the latter. About the same percentage of non-directors displayed a similar attitude. But even more interesting was the fact of heavy stress being placed on education in the process of selecting managers. This means that in addition to political criteria, educational criteria became important.

The relatively increased influence of the collective on the election of managers, demands for adequate education, and various demands arising from the functioning of the market economy, have all led to the professionalization of management. Thus something very similar to the technostructures of the West began to arise. The main imperative of technostructure behaviour, according to Galbraith (1967), is the demand for autonomy. The same demand also appears among Yugoslav technocrats, but it occurs within the context of a general tendency towards the autonomization of organizations. Empirical research during the 1960s demonstrates that when an asymmetric distribution of power exists within an organization, the autonomization of organizations leads to an increase in the power of the technocrats within them. An important development in this regard was Amendment XV to the Constitution, which legitimized this process. Thus certain processes, originally intended to lead to equalization of power within organizations, have actually led to even greater asymmetry.

At the same time, this process had a great influence on the power structure at the societal level. The technostructure, establishing its power within organizations, began to make its influence felt on the broader social scene. On the one hand, this influence developed in the process of the creation of close relationships with the political elite – but based on the presumption that they are two distinct groups. This process culminated at the end of the 1960s, although it took different forms in different Republics. In Croatia it arose out of the connectedness of managers of the larger companies with the political leadership in the fight against the centralization of capital outside of Croatia; in Slovenia it appeared in the orientation towards Western Europe; in Serbia it was part of the concept of the "bearer of development". On the other hand, this process can be seen in the autonomous advancement of the technostructure in the direction of seizing meta-power. This is exemplified in the composition of the economic chamber of the parliament and the increasing role of this chamber in economic and political decision-making.

The political conflicts of the late 1960s and early 1970s led to the defeat of these tendencies, which were in many cases closely connected with nationalist movements (especially in Croatia). The defeat came through the direct intervention of existing meta-power holders through their restructuring of the system. The technostructure was defeated in its attempt to acquire a position of meta-power.

We will now discuss some of the basic dimensions involved in the structuring of the system towards decreasing the power of the technostructure and increasing the power of the workers both within enterprises and in the wider society. This restructuring had its institutional base in the new Constitution of 1974 and a number of subsequent laws (for example, the Associated Labour Act of 1976).

The first dimension is the increased role of the political subsystem which was designed as a counterprocess to the depolitization of the system. This depolitization enabled other groups, and not only the traditional political elite, to play a more important role in the system restructuring. A very clear elaboration of this can be found in Kardelj (1978):

Some time we very rightly dissolved the personal union between the Party and the state executive apparatus, because it was the real cause of the bureaucratization of society and of the Communist Party. Today there is very little danger of such a union ever occuring again. However there is another danger; namely, that in the system in which the centers of political power have definitely shifted from the state apparatus to the self-managing communities, the League of Communists might remain on the sideline of events within the system of self-managing, socio-economic relations of associated labour and in the delegate system, which would weaken its ties with the working masses. ... If the League of Communists were to remain outside the self-management institutions, there is the danger that they would fall under the influence of other forces, and even other political factors seeking to squeeze the League of Communists out of the system, as was advocated by the pettybourgeois liberalist school of thought and advocates of pluralism of political parties, or else the League of Communists might be compelled to reverse its policy and hand down the decisions from above (Kardelj 1978: 213–214, 215).

It is evident that Kardelj understands as "other forces" and "other factors" those groups which may tend to endanger the existing meta-power structure. In "reversing the policy" and "decisions from above" he obviously means what we have described as the activization of meta-power holders in the system restructuring.

The second dimension is the prevention of the technostructure from becoming an independent source of power within the political system. One of the main sources of autonomous political action for the technostructure on the broad social scene, the Economic Chamber of the Parliament (or the Directors Chamber as it was called in political jargon), was dissolved, and the Council of Associated Labour as its successor comes under the general rules of the delegate system according to which managers from all levels cannot be elected. Of course, directors are still members of different delegations within the political system, but they are now "filtered" through the delegations of various political organizations.

The last two dimensions are directed towards the democratization of organizations: the deautonomization of organizations and the accentuation of workers' management. The deautonomization of organizations means dismantling the barriers established by the organizations against the environment. The organization is no longer regarded as the market element in constant antagonistic relations with other elements following the income maximization principle. The general concept of organization switched from the group entrepreneurial model towards the self-managerial (class) model, to use Zupanov's (1975) terminology.

In this global self-managerial model, contrary to the organizational autonomy model, organizations are treated as links in the chain of associated labour; no links means completely autonomous, but where no decision can be imposed on any element in the chain. Autonomous decisions are based on self-management agreements and social compacts.

The second manner in which the organization is conceptualized is that it does not realize its market goals without regard to the interests of other organizations. Rather, these goals are always incorporated in some broader framework (agreement and compacts). In other words, entrepreneurial behaviour is limited by class solidarity, and market coordination by self-management agreements and social compacts.

Regarding the problem of power relationships, one aspect is of special interest because it directly affects the sphere under consideration here. The institutional changes which underlie all the restructuring of the economic and political systems were not in fact initiated by the economic subsystem:

Self-management agreements and social compacts originated and developed as part of the socialist self-management relationships more from the political system and practice than from the needs of economic development. Because of that fact, self-management agreements and social compacts are realized in day-to-day social and economic practice mainly through political actions and normativistic approaches, and much less on the basis of some economic and social need (Kalogjera 1975).

Because there is no movement from the bottom demanding the introduction of agreements and compacts, we can treat this as the action of the system creators (meta-power holders) in the direction of system democratization and toward resistance to tendencies which might endanger their own meta-power.

The second important process is accentuation of workers' management which is the cornerstone of the "BOAL-ization" process. It is based on the proposition that the creation of smaller organizational units will enable workers to participate more directly in the decision-making process. Also, with the same goals in mind, the competency of the workers assembly will be increased.

Some Conclusions on the Strategy of Democratization

If we start from the assumption that the gap has been narrowed in the power distribution in organizations following the latest institutional changes (about which we can only more or less surmise since in the strained political system of the 1970s and in the current unfavourable economic situation the doors of work organizations have been completely closed for empirical research on such sensitive problems as power), we can pose the question of what this means for power distribution in the wider society.

One of the hypotheses which we can make is that in the three-member relationship of bureaucracy-technocracy-workers, an increase in the power of the first at the expense of the second does not immediately mean an increase in influence of the third. In other words, the bureaucracy has again perhaps remained "alone on the battlefield" halting its main competitor, the technocracy, but without a simultaneously significant increase in the power of workers as a third group. Or, stated in yet a third way, a destratification of power in organizations does not automatically mean a destratification of power in the society; on the contrary, it can mean an even more distinctly unequal distribution of power in the society. Accordingly, we could describe the present moment as yet another contradictory situation in which the bureaucracy finds itself attempting to negate the unequal distribution of power in the society (and by doing so, its own monopoly of power). To achieve this, it must draw back considerably, utilizing its meta-power to prevent the uneven structuration of power in the society and, by doing so, again increase the difference between itself and the other groups.

Why does a decrease in the power of the technocracy not automatically mean an increase in the power of workers inside the organization? If in organizations (as in other social systems) we had a "zero-sum" relation in effect as far the power relations among groups are concerned, then a decrease in power of one group would automatically mean an increase in the power of the others (in this case, a decrease of the power of the technocracy would mean an increase in the power of workers). However, most authors believe that the total amount of power in organizations is flexible, and thus, a reduction of power of management does not automatically mean an increase of power of subordinates.

We can pose the hypothesis that a reduction of power of management in a concrete case does not essentially increase the power of workers. In other words, the total amount of control in the organization declines. This is quite consistent with the fact that the autonomy of the enterprise has decreased in relation with the environment (it is essential in this case that the decrease in autonomy does not occur at the expense of the state but rather through self-managing forms of integration – e.g. self-management agreements and compacts). Through a reduction of autonomy occurs a reduction of the "territory of control" from which power is drawn, so that a reduction in the amount of power in the hands of the technostructure goes to the "environment" and not automatically to an increase in the power of workers – that is, to groups opposed to it in the organization.

Thus, an ever greater area of decision-making relevant to the organization is found in the environment where political organizations are still functioning as autonomous regulators. Political organizations become a filter which admits the technostructure into the environment in which decisions are made.

A Contradiction in the Position of the Working Class

The intention of holders of meta-power is to increase the power of the working class in work organizations and, by doing so, also in the society. However, the strategy which can be discerned behind the institutional changes (I am not thinking here that someone consciously recommends this strategy but that it is a result of the unintended consequence of a series of actions) is that greater emphasis is placed on the individual and less on the group. For example, self-management agreements on pooling labour are signed by individuals and not groups. The contradiction of this strategy appears in the fact that such an action is limited to a redistribution of power in the organization with the belief that this automatically increases power in the society.

However, perhaps even with an increase in power in the society we can achieve a change in the structure of power in organizations. Perhaps the autonomous action of the union can be a pre-condition for the redistribution of the structure of power in the organization. Of course, we have examples of situations of democracy in society in the sense of a strong influence of the working class but in which autocratic relations are well preserved in the organization (e.g. in Sweden). Or the reverse, the example of democratic relations in micro-units of society within ultimately non-democratic societal relations (e.g. self-management in some Basque organizations or the tradition of local self-management in countries under various foreign conquerors). What I proposed above – democratization of the workplace as a pre-condition to democratization of the organization – perhaps applies in the situation where there is a strong working class tradition in the form of powerful unions and a democratic tradition in the society. In a situation where such traditions do not exist, perhaps it is illusory to expect that a strategy of change at the lowest levels of society will initiate changes at some middle level. Perhaps the struggle for democratization of the organization is possible only through a struggle for democracy in the society. In this we must warn that the democratization of society is not limited to the control of surplus labour as is often assumed today in Yugoslavia. Autonomous political action and the raising of consciousness about one's own position in society are much more complex than control in the economic sphere.

From this, we can draw conclusions which may be important for the strategy of self-management and the democratization of work organizations:

1. There is probably no "universal way" to democratize work organizations which can be concluded from a reading of the literature. Democratization "from above" or "from below" or in some "convergent" form can be variously successful in various systems.

2. Ahead lies the concrete problem to work out a strategy for the democratization of organizations in our self-managing systems. The first wave of "theoretical critiques" has gone in the direction of demonstrating that democratization does not emerge sufficiently "from below," from the level of the workplace. I would formulate a second proposal: that perhaps exactly the reverse is the case; namely, that it is necessary to begin with democratization "from above" in order to succeed essentially to restructure the unequal distribution of power in the organization.

Such democratization "from above" can be approached in two different ways. The first one proceeds from a proposition regarding the conflict generated within the system. Beginning with a proposition advocating the usefulness of conflict for the stability of the system, a system of institutionalized conflicts on a societal level can be developed. Among other things, this should result in the accelerated democratization both of society and organizations. The key idea within this proposition is the legitimization of management power and the unionization of workers' power (Zupanov 1971).

This political democratization model differs from the approach which advocates maximizing individual economic participation in the system (Rus 1975). In that approach there is a decrease in the existing sphere of decision-making for members of organizations, but an increase of decision-making powers at the societal level of economic processes. However, both models have similar consequences: management professionalization and the recognition of the need for an educated technostructure. An increase in the power of management should always be checked by the creation of centres of counter power.

References

Baumgartner, T., Buckley, W., Burns, T. R., and Schuster, P. (1976): Meta-power and the Structuring of Social Hierarchies, In: Burns, T. and Buckley, W. (eds.), *Power and Control*, London: Sage.

Bilandzic, D. (1971): O Nekim Karakteristikama Danasnjeg Drustvenog Razvoja Jugoslavije, *Nase Teme*, 11–12.

Bilandzic, D. (1978): *Historija Socijalisticke Federativne Republike Jugoslavije*, Zagreb: Glavni Pravci, Skolska knjiga.

Galbraith, J. K. (1967): *The New Industrial State*, Harmondsworth: Penguin.

Kalogjera, D. (1975): Samoupravni Sporazumi I Drusteni Dogovori – Mehanizmi Samoupravne Integracije Udruzenog Rada, *Ekonomski Pregled*, 3–4.

Kardelj, E. (1978): *Democracy and Socialism*, (original title: Pravci razvoja politickog sistema socijalistickog samoupravljanja), Beograd: Stp.

Rus, V. (1975): Novi model samoupravljanja i njegova relevantna okolina, In: *Sistem i Covjek*, Vol. 4, Zagreb: Proizvodne organizacije i samoupravljanje, Odsjek za Sociologiju.

Zupanov, J. (1969): Da li se rukovodjenje poduzecem profesionalizira?, In: J. Zupanov (ed.), *Samoupravljanje i drustvena moc*, Zagreb: *Nase Teme*.

Zupaov, J. (1971): Samoupravljanje i drustvena moc u radnoj organizaciji, In: J. Jerovsek (ed.), *Industrijska sociologija*, Zagreb: *Nase Teme*.

Zupanov, J. (1975): Evolucija i involucija samoupravnog poduzeca – jedan nacrt ta tipolosku analizu, In: *Sistem i Covjek*, Vol. 4. Zagreb: Proizvodne organizacije i samoupravljanje, Odsjek za Sociologiju.

Chapter 16
The Impact of State Intervention on Workers' Control: A Case Study of Autogestion in Algeria

Lena Dominelli

Autogestion is the Algerian form of workers' control. It arose spontaneously in the fields which were vacated by the European colonists when Algeria was granted independence by France in the summer of 1962, when the Algerian agricultural workers decided to maintain food production in the aftermath of a chaotic war situation (Blair 1969). The workers were moved into adopting this course of action out of: sheer necessity – to produce food for survival; a need to make the most of state support in this initiative when it launched "Operations Labourer;" and a commitment to their union, the UGTA (the Union Générale des Travailleurs Algériens), which was organising its financial and material resources in favour of the workers' drive to control their farms.

This chapter looks at the results achieved by these workers ten years later by examining the results of interviews which were administered on a domain in Boufarik in the spring of 1972. The research project, of which these interviews were part, was based on fieldwork spanning the period of one year's work before that.

The interview-questionnaires were given to all the permanent workers on the domain, and to a 10% random sample of seasonal workers working on the domain at the time. Spring was the peak season for the employment of seasonal workers as they were needed to harvest the citrus fruits which formed the bulk of the domain's production. This resulted in 105 permanent and 57 seasonal workers being interviewed.

The domain was a medium-sized holding of 567 hectares which produced mainly oranges, though it also grew other citrus fruits, such as clementines, lemons, and grapefruit. It also had a few acres which had been turned over into market gardening and had introduced livestock into its activities. These last two areas had been introduced in the post-colonial period. Otherwise, its production plan followed the lines set by its previous colonial owners. In this respect, the domain was typical of many in the autogestion sector as a whole.

The domain workers had been extensively involved in the liberation struggle. Also, it had many former FLN (Front de Libération National) supporters and militants within its ranks (Dominelli 1979). Two of its key workers, the President, and the Production Foreman, were leading lights in the liberation struggle. In fact, they owed their initial rise to their positions of power to the major roles they played in that struggle.

The spring of 1972 was a watershed in Algerian autogestion. For, at that time, Boumediene's Agrarian Reform began to shift the regime's interest irrevocably away from autogestion as part of state collectivised production and push reforms inexorably towards individualised and privatised forms of agricultural production. Autogestion and co-operative forms of production remained important at the rhetorical level. But, the rhetoric was cold comfort to the agricultural workers who had seen the demise of their dream – to see socialism flourish in Algeria. Autogestion to them had been a first step in this process. They were now caught in watching Boumediene preside over an onslaught on the physical size of autogestion and an attack on all trade union activists.

Autogestion in the agricultural sector had passed its peak by 1972. At that point, it encompassed 2.3 million hectares of land, having lost 300,000 hectares to the co-operatives which Boumediene had initiated for former guerrilla fighters. These were called CAMs. The land for CAMs had been expropriated from the autogestion sector despite workers' protests. There were approximately 150,000 permanent workers and more than 250,000 seasonal workers employed in autogestion. Private landowners also found many of their former parcels of land returned, as cabinet ministers expropriated additional autogestion lands (Blair 1969).

Unlike agricultural autogestion which had encompassed all colonial lands, industrial autogestion had never reached the heights of involving all the former colonial enterprises. Industrial autogestion reached its peak in 1965 when it covered 507 enterprises, employing 15,000 workers. Boumediene's policy of reducing the industrial autogestion sector in favour of the state-run *sociétés nationales* in order to give the government control of the important sectors of the economy, resulted in its being reduced to 350 firms employing 9,000 workers in 1972. In Boufarik at that time, there were 8,800 hectares in the autogestion sector, 500 hectares in the CAMs, and 235 hectares were in private ownership (Dominelli 1979).

Table 1: Domain Workers' Occupational Stratification

Occupational Description	Number According to Workers' Status		
	Permanent	Seasonal	Total
Top Management (TM)			
Director	1		1
President	1		1
Total Top Management	2		2
Middle Management (MM)*			
Line Management Office (LMO)			
Head accountant	1		1
Sales representative	1		1
Union organiser	1		1
Timekeeper	1		1
Line Management Field (LMF)			
Production foreman	3		3
Gang foreman	2		2
Total Line Management	9		9
Qualified Worker Office (QWO)			
Shopkeeper	1		1
Assistant shopkeeper	1		1
Typist	1		1
Clerical worker	2		2
Qualified Worker Field (QWF)			
Lorry driver	2		2
Wheel tractor driver	1		1
Caterpillar tractor driver	3		3
Pruner	7	1	8
Bricklayer	1		1
Milker	1		1
Cowhand	4		4
Night watchman	4		4
Day-night watchman	7		10
Gardener	3		3
Mechanic	1		1
Grafter	1		1
Total Qualified Worker	40	4	44
Unqualified Worker Office (UWO)*			
Unqualified Worker Field (UWF)			
Unskilled Agricultural Worker	54	53	107
Total Labour Force	105	57	162

* No workers in this category at time of interview.
Source: Own data.

Life on the Ground

According to the majority of workers, life on the domain was a "hard, poor life." The government's physical attack on autogestion through the expropriation of its lands, the government's lack of real interest in the sector, and its failure to invest in autogestion because of its emphasis on exploiting the production of oil and diverting most of its resources to that end, meant that autogestion was starved of the resources it needed to expand and influence other sectors of the economy if it were to achieve its socialist ambitions. The fact that neither the UGTA nor the workers had the resources to develop and expand autogestion also contributed to the tough conditions prevailing in that sector after a decade of independence. In addition, the regime's attack on working class activists and trade union leaders, as well as its control of the UGTA, meant that there was no independently organised working class machinery through which workers could defend their earlier gains in autogestion (Dominelli 1979).

Moreover, the workforce in the domains themselves were divided along permanent and seasonal lines. Permanent workers held the bulk of the "controlling" position on the domain – the presidency, the director-ship. They had a job security which was denied the seasonal workers, many of whom had worked on the domains for years but who had never quite met the criteria for becoming permanent workers. Yet, job security was of major significance in a country where unemployment and underemployment levels were extremely high.

The permanent workers also held the decision-making posts at the local level. Seasonal workers were barred by law from attending the general assembly through which the workers collective was, at least theoretically, entitled to make decisions about production plans and elect its leaders. Those holding positions in the works council and in the management committee were therefore permanent workers. The state had promulgated laws excluding seasonal workers from the decision-making apparatus in the domains as early as the March Decrees of 1963. Yet, the present research indicated that the bulk of the work measured in terms of labour time carried out on the domain was performed by seasonal workers. Thus, we have the position in which those who were extensively involved in the operation of the enterprise were legally barred from exercising any influence in its decision-making processes. Democracy, a major tenet of socialism, was therefore denied to a significant constituent group in the domain workforce. Moreover, we will discover later that democracy does not exist for a significant proportion of the permanent labour force as well. Many permanent and seasonal workers resented this state of affairs. However, they felt powerless to change the situation in a way which conferred full rights to seasonal workers on the domain. For although the majority of permanent workers shared a fraternal solidarity with their seasonal colleagues, they felt that only the state held the power to accord seasonal workers full status as autogestion workers.

The labour process on the domains had been changing over time. By 1972, it was evident that the cheaper labour of the seasonal workers was being substituted for the more expensive labour of the permanent workers, particularly at the unskilled levels. The use of seasonal workers to reduce labour costs was consonant with the state's concern to preserve financial resources for the exploitation of petroleum reserves.

The research project indicated that the use of seasonal workers had increased between 1966 and 1972. At the beginning of that period, for every 100 working days performed by permanent workers, seasonal workers contributed 105. At the end of that period, seasonal workers were working 150 working days for every 100 put in by permanent workers. Whilst this was happening, the proportion of seasonal workers in the workforce doubled; they rose from forming 33 % of the workforce to 67 %. Moveover, seasonal workers lost ground in the jobs they were allowed to hold during that period. In 1966, they used to be employed in the more skilled jobs and managerially-oriented ranks like the chef de gestion and the production foremen, but by 1972, this had ceased. At that time, seasonal workers performed mainly unskilled tasks. Seasonal workers were locked into being exploited in this way because there were so few other employment opportunities for them. As one seasonal worker put it, "Where else can I go? I need to work. I have to feed my family." Another said, "I'd like to work for SONATRACH (the *société nationale* for petroleum). But they would never employ anyone like me. I'm illiterate. I can only do what I do. But life is hard. I'm lucky to have any work at all."

Yet, the division between the permanent workers and seasonal workers is not as divisive as it could be. The reason for this is that both permanent and seasonal workers are extremely poor. Even the director, the highest paid worker, who remains employed by the state instead of the workers' collective and is paid monthly, earns less than 3 times the wages of the unskilled workers. Thus, 69 % of the workforce (70 % of permanent workers and 65 % of seasonal workers) in the research project wanted to ensure that the domain's wealth was evenly distributed amongst all workers.

A large proportion of the workers blamed the state for their unsatisfactory situation. If one includes the Director, who was seen as the state's representative at the local level, 42 % of the permanent workers and 36 % of the seasonal workers subscribed to this view. Yet, they felt powerless before it. The state was seen as remote and outside of their control. They did not have a powerful workers' organisation or union which could oppose the state's dictates.

The Director was considered unapproachable because of his high status. Hence, what he said was bound to be accepted rather than challenged. In another sense, the way in which the state had organised decision-making at the local level, through a series of mediating bodies and circulars, meant that it had succeeded in depoliticising decision-making on the domains and had also made directors feel powerless before its dictates. The agencies with which domains were compelled by the state to do business, refused to act with alacrity, nor did they take demands coming from domain directors seriously. The Director on this particular domain, for example, had been trying for 9 months to get the local accounting agency to release the domain's production figures for the previous year to him. His requests for new machinery and repairs were similarly ignored.

The hard life that workers on the domain had to endure ensured that the majority of them disliked living there. In a context in which their only other alternative was that of being unemployed, it was the lesser of two evils. There were 59 % of the permanent workers and 49 % of seasonal workers who wished they lived elsewhere. As one worker expressed himself, "Everything is dead. I don't like it at all. I live a hard life. I'm very poor. I don't earn enough money." Another, feeling more depressed about his situation, said, "I weep so that Allah (God) may hear. What else can I do?"

Workers' Participation in the Domain's Decision-Making Organs

The majority of workers did not feel that they owned and operated the enterprise. As the majority of them complained, "We're just ordinary wage-earners." In other words, they were at the receiving end of managerial decisions which were made at state level. Their workers had no representation on any of the national and regional bodies controlling autogestion. The Ministry of Agriculture (MARA) which had overall responsibility for the sector, the state agencies, and the marketing boards were autonomous decision-making bodies which had no workers' or trade union representation on them. Edicts were handed from high. These were then put into circulars which reached the domains with worrying regularity. Often, there were no provisions even to ensure that the circulars were understood. Political education either in favour of or against autogestion was non-existent.

Within the framework of local decision-making at the level of the domain, little real democracy prevailed, even amongst the permanent workers who were entitled to membership in its machinery. Unskilled permanent workers were least likely to have had any involvement in the decision-making apparatus. Only 12 % of permanent workers had ever been members of the management committee. Most of those who had done so were located amongst the managerial ranks. None of the unskilled workers had ever been elected to the management committee, and only 20 % of the skilled workers had ever reached this level.

The works council had succeeded in involving 25 % of the permanent workforce at some time or other. Yet, even here, the unskilled workers were least likely to have served on this body. There were 18 % of them who had done so. Slightly more of the skilled workers (23 %) had been members of the works council. But the higher up in the labour hierarchy one went, the more likely the worker was to have participated in the domain's important decision-making bodies. The works council was, therefore, no different from the workers' management committee in this respect. Even in relation to the general assembly, only 73 % of the permanent workforce claimed to have participated in this body. Again, the unskilled workers were least likely to have done so. The skilled workers shared this position with them. Thus, we have a situation in which the assembly is the most democratic of these organs; but it is also the least powerful body.

Top management, which constituted 2 % of the permanent workforce, held 15 % of the posts in the workers' management committee, 8 % of those in the works council and 3 % of those in the general assembly. "Line management office" made up 4 % of the permanent workforce; but it occupied 15 % of the seats on the management committee, 4 % of those on the works council, and 3 % of those in the general assembly. Workers in "line management field" made up 5 % of the permanent workers. They held 8 % of the posts in the workers' management committee, 12 % of the places on the works council, and 6 % of those in the general assembly. "Qualified workers office" comprised 5 % of the permanent labour force.

They held 8 % of the posts in the workers' management committee, 8 % of the seats in the works council, and 4 % of those in the general assembly. "Qualified workers field" constituted 33 % of the permanent workers. They held 54 % of the seats on the workers' management committee, 31 % of those on the works council, and 34 % of those on the general assembly. The unskilled workers ("unqualified workers field") made up 51 % of the permanent workforce, but they were unrepresented in the workers' management committee, held 38 % of the seats on the works council, and 52 % of those in the general assembly.

Thus, these figures reveal that decision-making on the domains was conducted in an extremely hierarchical way, with management exercising its power over the workforce. The workers' management committee, the domain's most powerful body, was the least democratic, whilst the workers' general assembly, its least powerful body, was the most democratic. However, the workers' management committee was not seen as having the power to supercede that of the state. Thus, the state's local representative, the director, was able to exercise considerable authority over the workers' management committee. Or, as one worker complained:

I'm very unhappy about our workers' management committee. The workers are not allowed to express their personal opinions in it. Only the director's decision counts.

Moreover, the state did not intervene in this situation, even though it knew that the legally endorsed requirements concerning the holding of meetings and democratic decision-making on the domain were being flouted.

The existence of hierarchical decision-making on the domain was a source of discontent for a large number of workers. It made them feel they were simply wage-labourers who had no control over either the labour process or the domain's production activities. This was true for workers who held "powerfull" positions on the domain as well as for those who were uninvolved in decision-making structures. One worker who was extremely involved in the domain's decision-making apparatus expressed his dissatisfaction with the situation as follows:

As a Gang Foreman, I would like to leave the Domain. I've had no overtime payment for three months. I need the money to make up for my low wages. Even we do not get enough money to live a decent life. I think it's better to be a simple agricultural worker than to have responsibility with no power. I attract the hostility of others because of my position, but I have no advantages to make up for it. I realise that autogestion is the policy of my country, but I only get paid for the work I do. Yet, I am part of the management of the Domain.

The fact that "management" was drawn from the workers' ranks further complicated the situation. Workers felt even less likely to mount substantial criticisms against their fellow workers. As one worker put it:

How could we argue against them? They decided when to call the meetings. They had all the facts, we didn't. They worked hard. We had to trust them. Even when we didn't agree what equipment we should buy, we knew they were right. We had to support them.

It is clear from this that autogestion failed to meet the workers' aspirations for a particularly Algerian form of socialism. The state was responsible for curtailing the growth of autogestion by physically cutting its size, destroying working class organisation, and diverting resources to the petroleum sector. Moreover, the bureaucratic structures it introduced through the 1972 Agrarian Reforms increased centralised control of the autogestion sector's activities at the expense of democratic decision-making by workers, even at the level of the domain.

References

Blair, Thomas (1969): *The Land to Those who Work it: Algeria's Experiment in Workers' Management*, New York: Doubleday and Company.
Dominelli, Lena (1979): A Structural Analysis of the Effects of Social Turmoil on Socially Dislocated Groups: The Algerian Peasant Workforce on an Autogestion Domain, Brighton: The University of Sussex, unpublished Ph D.

Part V
Education and Competence

Introduction

Paul Blyton

It is self-evident that competence is primarily gained through education, be it formal education and training or the self-education of direct experience and reflection. There are various conditions necessary to foster workers' competence, and these include a national commitment not only to resourcing schools adequately, but also to post-school education and to encouraging the access of workers to that education. The subjects relevant to this post-schooling include not only those which reflect particular aspects of organisational life (knowledge of finance and accountancy, technology, business systems, and so on) but also ones less conventionally included in curricula, such as social skills training, necessary for operating effectively in group decision-making settings.

There are a multiplicity of issues concerning education and competence, and we can only endeavour here to indicate this breadth and choose a few of the issues to examine in detail. To this end, the chapters in this section examine aspects of worker education in three diverse national settings: a socialist economy (Yugoslavia), a developing economy (India), and a Western market economy (Federal Republic of Germany).

In the first of these, Rus examines the question of skills and competence from the viewpoint of the relationship between school and work. In Yugoslavia, this relationship has been under pressure to change, partly as a result of high and continuing levels of unemployment and partly due to the increased professionalisation of those occupations much sought after in more technologically complex environments. Rus develops his argument by reference to the Yugoslav case, highlighting the changes in policy which have taken place in efforts to match the production of education with its utility in the economic sphere. These efforts so far have not been without their critics, since they pose important questions about maintaining a balance between freedom of choice within education and providing skills training to deliver a competent and fully employable labour force.

In her chapter, Avasthi assesses the development of national policies on workers' education in India since that country's independence in 1947. The level of technological change taking place is seen to place considerable demands on workers' traditional educational needs; a much greater emphasis on education (both formal education and in-house training) is seen to be required if workers are to play a significant role in the determination of choices about future patterns of work organisation. In the latter part of her chapter, Avasthi moves to a different level of analysis drawing on two studies of workers' participation to identify the scale of the problem of developing participatory competence in countries where the basic level of literacy remains relatively low.

In the third chapter in this section, Edgar Einemann discusses how universities are generally geared towards serving the material needs of capital rather than labour. However, using the case of the University of Bremen, Einemann demonstrates how it is possible to establish an educational and research base which acts to build up workers' competence within their work setting by, for example, providing them with relevant research findings, acting as advisors on technical matters, and establishing tailored educational courses. This case is an example of the use of external advisors as a means of augmenting the level of internal competence among a workforce. The point is also made that if such a partnership is to be fruitful in the long term, traditional academic boundaries (for example, between engineering, computing, and the social sciences) must be broken down to provide a more adequate picture of the situations confronting worker organisations as they seek to increase their influence over broader areas of organisational decision-making.

Chapter 17
An Inter-Organizational Analysis of Competence

Veljko Rus

Introduction

In this paper I am trying to develop a structural analysis of knowledge implementation. I am neither occupied by psychological processes of knowledge generation nor with socio-psychological processes of its dissemination but with the sociological analysis of inter-organizational relations among those organizations which are involved in the implementation of knowledge.

The most appropriate framework for such a structural analysis is the employment system which functions as a bridge between school and work. Through this alone does the social function of the school become visible since it is defined as an agent of manpower regulation and not just as an educational entity.

Global Trend: Professionalization of Manpower

In spite of the fact that in East European countries there is no unemployment, the growing mismatch between labour potentialities (manpower supply) and available jobs (manpower demand) is present both in East and West Europe: in all industrial countries there is a growing gap between the abilities of the younger generations and the quality of available jobs.[1] This commonality suggests the existence of structural

---

[1] This gap is quite well-documented by a recent cross-cultural research project entitled "Transition from School to Work." In this research 6 East European countries, 7 West European countries, an Yugoslavia are involved. The research is steered by the European Coordination Centre for Research and Documentation in Social Sciences, 1984–1986.

similarities between all industrially developed countries that are more relevant for employment processes than the known structural divergencies like private versus public ownership, state versus market regulation, etc.

The similarities relevant for employment processes in both sets of countries are:
- a steady transfer of the labour force from primary to secondary and tertiary sectors of economic activity;
- school as an increasingly important channel of vertical mobility;
- steady prolongation of schooling;
- a higher educational level of the younger generations;
- the growing aspirations of youth concerning the quality of jobs (new work aesthetics);
- greater professionalization of manpower;
- substratification within the working class itself;
- an increasingly meritocratic differentiation of manpower between central and marginal groups (and decreasing class differentiation based on privilege);
- the growing participation of women in the labour market and decreasing sex discrimination.

Among the above-mentioned trends the most important is, according to our hypothesis, the *professionalization of manpower*. Usually it is observed that there is a growing intellectualization only, or higher skill level of manpower, as a crucial trend of contemporary societies. We do not deny this, but at the same time we would like to stress that it is only one component of professionalization. Professionalization involves, besides certain systems of knowledge, a specific socialization process, professional ethics, and subculture (Greenwood 1962). By professionalization we might tentatively explain the growing work ethics (and aesthetics) documented by many empirical studies which have been done in different East and West European countries (Hartmann 1985, Knapp 1985, Vitečkova 1985, Yankelowich 1979). The increasing centrality of work in life, the increasing intrinsic motivation for it, the growing co-operation and decreasing competitive relations among employees, etc., are signs of growing professional ethics.

However, professionalization not only changes the relationship of an employee towards work and his colleagues, but also his relationship to the enterprise. A professionalized employee is no longer a good "company man", since he is more committed to the profession than to the enterprise (Toffler 1971). Another important implication of professionalization is the growing importance of a life-long career: professionals are less interested in particular jobs and more in the career as a meaningful sequence of jobs. The main problem which industrial democracy has to address is no longer alienation from the job and workplace, but rather a non-erratic lifelong career.

With the central role of career an employee's time dimension is changed: short-term interests are substituted by long-term interests, wages by promotion. In addition, professional associations become more important than organizational coalitions and the labour market is more important than the enterprise. The quality of working life is no longer primarily a function of the quality of the work environment but the quality of employment.

The growing professionalization of manpower increases the horizontal and decreases the vertical or scalar differentiation within the enterprise. There is a continuous trend toward substratification of blue-collar workers on one hand (Form 1976) and diminished status differences between blue- and white-collar workers. White-collar work already accounts for more than a half of GNP in developed industrial countries (Kahn 1982).

Obsolete Social Systems

The obsolescence of social systems can be found in all industrial societies, East and West. Many institutions of industrial societies are out-dated primarily because they were established for the regulation of unskilled manpower which prevailed during the early period of industrialization. This statement might be applicable to all institutions which regulate manpower in industrial societies: schools, work organizations, unions, and employment services. In schools the passive reception of knowledge still prevails; in work organizations a strict division can still be detected between those that work with their "heads" and those that work with their "hands;" in employment services jobs are still standardized according to the needs of the main "breadwinners" (who now represent less than a quarter of the total active population); in unions, branch rather than professional organization prevails. These common obsolescent features impose much greater limits on social development than those differences which come from ideology, type of ownership, or the kind of economic regulation (Kerr 1983).

In addition to the obsolescence of the internal arrangements of the institutions for regulating manpower mentioned above, we would like to make critical oservations about the relationships between these institutions. Not only are the internal structures of schools, enterprises, etc. obsolete, but so are *relations between these institutions*, since they do not create sufficient opportunities for the participative self-employment of professional manpower.

The relations between these institutions are dominated by economic goals. The first consequence of this domination is the subordination of the supply side (e.g. school) to the demand side of the labour market (e.g. enterprises). Domination of economic over non-economic organizations is a common occurrence in all industrial societies, be they in the West or East. In all industrial societies knowledge has only economic value, therefore the demand side regulation of manpower should be the dominant pattern of regulation in them. These economic criteria of regulation are paradoxical in East European countries since they suppose that the labour market and the price of labour time as the main regulators should be abolished.

However, the professionalization of manpower is not just a product of economic growth. It is encouraged by the growth of knowledge intensive technologies which exercise a constant pressure on the supply side of the employment system (new technologies influence, to some extent, educational programs). Beside technology, political systems exercise growing pressure on the professionalization of manpower. Governmental agencies as the main employers within the tertiary sector encourage social promotion through professional channels. These factors stimulate longer and higher-level schooling among the younger generations.

The third factor which encourages professionalization of young generations is social mobility. The cumulative effect of all three factors together is a redundancy of manpower supply which is seen in the so-called over-educated and unemployed youth.

The relations between the various social agents regulating manpower are shown in Figure 1. The first thing that we find in this figure is a whole set of missing links. There is, especially, a weak connection between schools providing skilled labour and other institutions regulating the absorption of this labour. Schools are not directly influenced by the market or employment systems. The demand side is connected with schools only indirectly through state regulation. This is one of the structural weakness in matching supply and demand of labour.

The exclusive role of the state in the regulation of the educational

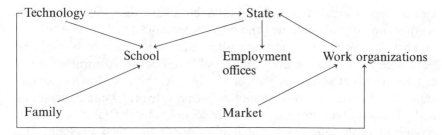

Figure 1: Relations between social agents dealing with manpower regulation

system produces restrictive policies: it tries to prevent redundancy of labour potentialities by financial restrictions and by imposing a *"numerus clausus."* Where an active employment policy is developed (like in Scandinavian countries), "redundancy planning" is established as a corporate regulatory system. This involves co-ordination between the state, work organizations, and employment offices. Redundancy planning does not mutually adjust demand and supply, but only adjusts supply of manpower to the needs of work organizations. Although most of the mismatch between demand and supply of labour is a product of economic goals, the means by which the mismatch can be reduced are not congruent with these goals (i.e. prolonged apprenticeship, additional schooling, youth schemes, compulsory hiring of graduates, etc.). As a result, these forms of regulation may be treated as artificial and temporary.

Such artificial regulation is to some extent the outcome of the fact that the state by its own nature cannot play the role of an alternative regulator. However, if we want to establish a more creative, less restrictive, and less artificial matching between the supply of and demand for labour, we should introduce some other institutions into this transition from school to work, which would be better able to deal with the increasing complexity of the labour force: professional associations, chambers of commerce, and unions. Professional associations have some regulative function only in England and the USA, while the other two do not have any formal role in employment policy. Giving these three agencies the social responsibility for employment might only be achieved through their legal involvement in the system. As a result, the nature of state regulation would be changed: it would become clearly neo-corporatist and no longer authoritative.

While the introduction of new agencies by way of some kind of neo-corporatist regulation of manpower seems to be quite a feasible systems' response to the growing complexity of employment issues, caused by steady professionalization, we should be aware that this response is neither the only possible nor the most acceptable one.

There are perhaps some other alternative solutions which might be both acceptable (democratic) and feasible (efficient). According to our criteria, the best solutions are those which act as a system of conflict resolution between partly or completely opposite professional, personal, and job demands in the transition from school to work (Volanen 1984). If economic goals and market demands dominate, then personal and professional needs are more or less neglected. The alienation of employees and the destruction of professional ethics is the outcome of such employment regulation.

The most acceptable transfer from school to work might be established through self-employment systems – i.e. through the initiative of individuals themselves. Only through the active participation of labour might contradictions between personal, professional, and economic needs be resolved in an optimal way. However, this resolution cannot be achieved by individuals on their own, since the employment process is becoming too complex. Support from all other social agencies is necessary for successful transfer from school to work. This mechanism could be called *guided self-employment*.

In addition to the above-mentioned neo-corporatist regulation of employment and guided self-employment, some other feasible but not acceptable solutions are available. One possibility is to eliminate labour markets altogether and to reduce the regulation of employment to the state plan. This trend exists in East European countries, but it is only a trend. The full implementation of this solution would presuppose the complete elimination of freedom concerning choice of school and choice of work organization by individuals. Although there are substantial restrictions on the free choice of schooling and employment in all East European countries, we cannot talk about complete restriction of individual freedoms. Therefore we might find rudiments of labour markets even in Eastern countries.

"Reaganomics" with its demands on state deregulation of employment represents an opposite solution. It might be a feasible, but it is certainly not an acceptable solution, since the market (of capital and goods) has been shown historically to be a poor regulator producing cyclic unemployment and a steady growth of structural unemployment during the last decades (which is mainly a result of the growing professionalization of manpower).

Japanese systems of industrial relations (called the "Z" system by

Ouchi (1982)) seems to be another feasible and acceptable solution. It is acceptable because it offers lifelong employment, steady education, and steady promotion. With these three processes it meets basic demands of professionalized manpower. However, this system of industrial relations does not seem to be a general solution for the country. It only operates for labour in the primary labour market (which accounts for about a third of the labour force in Japan), while the majority is submitted to an extremely deregulated labour market of the Reaganomic type.

All the above mechanisms for regulating the transfer from school to work assume the domination of economic goals. These have dominated during early industrialization which is usually accompanied by an unskilled or low-skilled labour force. With the increasing professionalization of manpower, human capital becomes a dominant factor of productivity and profitability. As a result, financial capital becomes increasingly dependent on intellectual capital (Bell 1973). This leads to a trend towards the "humanization" of the economy, which means that in employment policy human goals will be at least equally important as economic ones. The humanization of labour force regulation will be, in the near future, the outcome of the increasing bargaining power of professionals. This humanization will certainly change the relations between institutions involved in labour force regulation. The so-called supply side will have greater influence on these processes, as is shown in Figure 2.

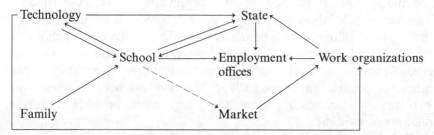

Figure 2: Expected future relations between labour market agents dealing with more professionalized manpower

The more the supply side prevails over the demand side, the more socio-technical regulation of manpower will prevail over economic regulation. When socio-technical regulation becomes dominant, economic goals will only be part of more complex goals used to regulate the labour force. It is quite possible that quality of life (or quality of working life, or quality of family life, or quality of leisure) will become equally important goals. If this happens, then economic goals will no longer represent the limit for human resource development; the phenomenon of redundancy of the labour force or over-educated youth will disappear by itself.

Post-economic regulation of the labour force will be oriented towards the maximum development of labour potentials, which means that the limits of human potentialities will be the only limits for the regulation of the labour force. The limits will come only from the supply side; these will be the limits imposed by technology, by limited aspirations, by limited capacities of schooling, etc. Reduction of all limits to the supply side regulation of the labour force would mean the humanization and democratization of employment policy, and an increase of economic democracy as well.

The Yugoslav Case

Immediately after the Second World War school leavers in Yugoslavia were allocated to work by a state decree. The labour force was regulated by the state plan during the first post-war decade, which means even after the introduction of self-management in 1950. During the short period of five years (1950–1955) Yugoslavia created an unusual system in which self-management and state regulation of the labour force co-existed.

After 1955 the labour market was fully established. Individuals became the "owners" of their own labour and had unlimited freedom of choice of schooling and employment. This exclusively individual ownership over labour power coincided with predominantly public ownership of the means of production (Tanko 1985). The conflicts between these two structural parameters represent the basic framework for Yugoslav manpower regulation.

The most visible outcome of the individual ownership of labour power is bargaining for maximal individual rewards. Within the enterprise there is a fight for maximization of wages, while at the inter-organizational level it is a fight for profit maximization of the enterprise to assure high wages and/or high market power of the enterprise (and by this high job security).

Since the means of production are almost exclusively managed by the workforce collectively, individuals can maximize their own rewards only through their participation in collective decision-making. In this way work collectives become the main regulators of the labour force and the main actors in the labour market as well. They try to maximize their own particular interests by collective appropriation of goods on the basis of their own work contribution, but also by monopoly prices, technical rents, natural rents, etc. This collective profit-sharing system creates great differences in the labour market and contributes to anarchic regulation of the latter. For example, there are great wage differences between enterprises for the same quality and quantity of work (Korošič 1985), segmented labour markets with uneven regional rates of unemployment, and increasing inter-generational employment descrimination (Drobnič 1984).

The segmentation of the labour market caused by the self-interests of work collectives is even more damaging than the uncontrolled wage discrimination. The employment policy of work collectives tries to maximize job security of their own members through capital intensive investment, restrictive hiring, domination of internal promotion, and absence of firing. In periods of recession such a policy of work collectives becomes particularly damaging, because it practically closes the door for school leavers and creates high under-employment within organizations.

Because of these mentioned dysfunctions the resocialization of the labour market became unavoidable. The recession in West European countries was an additional reason for changes because economic emigration was stopped and the problems of the surplus labour force became more critical. After 1973 the rate of unemployment has grown remarkably, particularly among educated youth, and within the less developed regions of Yugoslavia.

The resocialization of the labour market started with two changes:
a. the introduction of Self-Management Associations of Interests (SAI); and
b. the reform of secondary education.

The first change was a structural one. SAI are combined bodies of two assemblies: one assembly is composed of delegates who represent the interests of those work organizations producing certain services, and the other assembly consists of delegates who represent those organizations which are the main potential users of these services. Both assemblies together should create yearly contracts about the program of educational activity and yearly budgets for its implementation. SAI should therefore become the institution for the direct contractual regulation of the labour force; SAI should replace the state plan and the market as regulators. According to the theory and formal rules, the regulation of the labour force after establishing the SAI should look like it is presented in Figure 3.

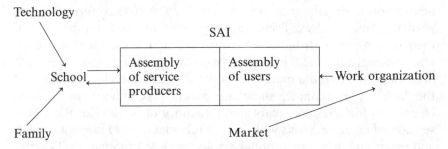

Figure 3: SAI as a System for Regulating the Labour Force

However, during the last ten years SAI has demonstrated quite a lot of weaknesses. Direct contractual regulation between the school and workplace, obviously, cannot completely replace market and state plan regulators. Work organizations are still interested in maximizing their own profit, therefore they try to externalize costs for education and also costs for other social services. The result of this are under-financed social services, especially schools. On the other hand, schools do not like to restrict their programs and capacities to the actual needs of work organizations, since they believe that their function is not only to provide work organizations with labour, but to reproduce the national culture as well. Work organizations, however, are not willing to finance this.

The school reform, initiated by the League of Communists of Yugoslavia at the Xth Congress in 1975, is another change which should help to socialize the labour market. The reform of secondary education abolished the preparatory secondary schools like gymnasiums. The main goal of this reform was that all secondary schools should prepare pupils for certain vocations. At the same time, the apprenticeship system or the so-called "double system" was abolished, too. In all secondary schools a new standardized program of general education was established for the first year of secondary schooling. After the first year programs are oriented towards preparation for certain skills. It was expected that around 80% of secondary school leavers would be employed after leaving secondary school, and that only 20% of them will continue their education in colleges or universities.

The reform of secondary schools was supposed to create a more standardized general education and to decrease cultural differences that arose from the old gymnasiums and vocational schools. Beside greater equalization, the school reform should make secondary schools more responsive to the needs of work organizations by preparing vocational profiles which could be immediately useful for work organizations. This school reform provoked general revolt among parents, school teachers, and intellectuals all over the country. It was seen as an anachronistic reform trying to carry out the re-industrialization of schooling at a time when industrialization as a way of modernization had already demonstrated negative rather than positive effects.

The consequences of the school reform have been, in fact, predominantly negative: the school reform has not created cultural destratification but has made it more painful since it is now exercised within a particular school. The re-orientation of school programs to vocational training increases the costs of schooling (because of the extreme variety of programs), increases structural unemployment, decreases elasticity of manpower, and decreases the number of those who enter colleges and universities.

The first reaction to these dysfunctions is increasing intervention by the state into the school and employment systems. Approaches aimed at overcoming these problems are pollarized in two directions. One approach is to abolish the individual ownership of labour power, or at least to substantially restrict the individual's freedom of schooling and jobs. It is argued that these restrictions would reduce the "anarchic" behaviour of the labour force and the common goals of employment policy would be better achieved (Šuvar 1977). The opposite approach attacks this suggestion as incompatible with the liberal nature of Yugoslav socialism and suggests the deindustrialization of schooling with the reintroduction of general secondary education and the transfer of vocational training to the work organization (Rus 1985).

Beside the dysfunction of the school reform, the problem of the overall regulation of the labour force is also unresolved. Temporary state intervention which tries to overcome dysfunctions of the SAI is not a satisfactory solution. A clear split between the roles of SAI and governmental bodies should be achieved (for instance, state agencies should assure minimal programs and take care of marginal or handicapped groups). In addition, SAI will need external support from unions, chambers of commerce, and professional associations. These agencies have extensive bargaining power and could revitalize the whole employment system. Their participation in bargaining might contribute to more qualitative agreements between the assembly of "users" and the assembly of "producers" within SAI.

References

Bell, D. (1973): *The Coming of Post-Industrial Society*, New York: Basic Books.

Drobnič, S. (1984): Strukturne spremembe v brezposelnosti, (Structural Changes of Unemployment), In: Antončič, Drobnič, Rus, Svetlik (eds.), *Trends of Employment*, Kranj: Moderna organizacija.

Form, W.H. (1976): *Blue-Collar Stratification*, Princeton: Princeton University Press.

Greenwood, E. (1962): Attributes of Profession, In: W. Form and S. Nosow (eds.), *Work and Society*, New York: Basic Books.

Hartmann, J. (1985): *Transition from School to Work in Sweden*, Paper presented at the conference Transition from School to Work in Castelgandolfo, Rome.

Kahn, H. (1982): *The Coming Boom*, New York: Simon and Schuster.

Kerr, C. (1983): *The Future of Industrial Societies*, Cambridge, MA: Harvard Univ. Press.

Knapp, I. (1985): *Transition from School to Work*, Paper presented at the conference Transition from School to Work in Castelgandolfo, Rome.

Korošič, M. (1985): *Neki problemi usmjeravanja raspodjele dohodka*, (Problems of Regulation of Income Allocation). Paper presented at Workshop on Contradiction of Social Ownership, Skopje.

Ouchi, W. (1982): *Theory Z*, New York: Avon.

Rus, V. (1985): Kriza izobraževanja in zaposlovanja, (The Crisis of Education and Employment), In: Jerošvek, Rus, Zupanov (eds.), *Kriza jugoslovenskog društva*, Zagreb: Globus.

Šuvar, S. (1977): *Škola i tvornica*, (The School and the Factory), Zagreb: Pedagoška biblioteka.

Tanko, Z. (1985): *Teoretsko opredeljivanje društvene svojine*, (Theoretical Definition of Public Ownership), Paper presented at Workshop on Contradictions of Social Ownership, Skopje.

Toffler, A. (1971): *The Future Shock*, London: Pan Books.

Vitečkova, J. (1985): *Transition from School to Work in Czechoslovakia*, Paper presented at the Conference Transition from School to Work, Castelgandolfo, Rome.

Volanen, M. (1984): *How Does the Young Adult Settle Down in a Vocation*, Paper presented at Sofia meeting on Transition from School to Work.

Yankelowich, D. (1979): Work Values and New Breed, In: C. Kerr and M. Rosow (eds.), *Work in America, the Decade Ahead*, New York: Van Nostrand and Reinhold.

Chapter 18
The Prospects of Industrial Democracy in the Context of the Proposed New Educational Policy in India

Abha Avasthi

Introduction

Of the different themes addressed in this book, the present chapter focuses on the area of "Education and Competence" and particularly on workers' educational policy, as implemented by the ruling party. I have attempted primarily to focus attention on the contemporary Indian scene and then, as far as possible, examine the validity of the present norms. Subsequently, I will attempt a critique of the medieval Indian pattern of workers' continuing education in their guild (Sathe 1984). It was the responsibility of the master craftsman of the guild to educate the worker in a manner which would make him better educated and acquire a higher level of skills. Then came the trauma of the British conquest of India. The first Industrial Revolution converted my countrymen to a class of producers of raw materials, selling them at the arbitrary rates fixed by our imperialist masters. In this introduction two further aspects of Indian history need emphasis, particulary the economic and industrial history of India. From the earliest days of civilization and inter-continental trade, India along with China was the world's greatest exporting country and in return imported gold from the Egyptians and Romans. The Portuguese, French, Dutch, and the British in the sixteenth century came to India to purchase spices, silks and cotton textiles such as the legendary Dhaka muslin. Other favourite commodities exported were chintz, ivory, precious jewels, and artistically worked ornaments of gold and silver. The European traders begged the Mughal Emperors to allow them to establish godowns or "factories" from where they could transport the precious items by the newly discovered sea route. Gradually their operations assumed the form of the flag following the trade, to be further followed by Christian missionaries with a view to converting the heathens.

After the industrial revolution the master craftsmen and workers were reduced to the level of growers of raw cotton and raw silk which, having passed through the new machines in England, were exported to India at exorbitant rates. Thus began the colonial era which later assumed imperial dimensions. The net result was the total destruction of the ages-old traditional handicrafts and ruthless exploitation of India as a whole.

The second aspect of my country's history which needs clarification is that historians differ as to whether the end of the medieval era was the mid-eighteenth century or 1857, the year of the revolt (termed by the British as the mutiny, and by some Indian historians as the first war of Indian independence). Hence, in contrast to Western Europe, modernisation came to India about three to four centuries later.

It is in this perspective that I have chosen to analyse India after her independence in 1947 and the evolution of workers' education and their competence to date, when we are on the threshold of an era of rapid modernisation, after having already constructed an infra-structure of industry and education which in numerical terms rivals the United States and the Soviet Union. India has the highest numbers of engineers, doctors, and technocrats in the world. It is a major exporter not only of cotton textiles, iron ore, manganese, and cut diamonds, but also of heavy basic machinery, railway engines and coaches, bridges, and high rise building complex technology and expertise.

In the late 1980s, India is gearing up to enter the twenty-first century as one of the world's major powers, achieving its proposed goals by acquiring, adopting, and innovating the highest technology, and oriented towards the expanding horizons of the Third Industrial Revolution, based upon electronics, microchips, and seventh generation computers. It would only be emphasizing the obvious by stating that a key need in this ever-spreading development is education. It would again be tautological to state that any integrated policy of education should involve all groups from the shop-floor to the peaks of planning, management, and production (Agarwal 1973, Srivastava 1976) synthesing at all levels and not just bringing some kind of symbiosis between the worker and the manager as though they belonged to two separate species.

Historical Developments

To take an overview of the Indian panorama from the first year of independence in 1947, when the country did not even produce a sewing needle, the first faltering steps were taken to spell out the direction of development, in the Industrial Disputes Act of 1947. The motivation behind this legislation was the philosophy of India's first Prime Minister, Jawaharial Nehru, universally regarded as the architect of modern India. Yet this Act had serious limitations: it failed to define its scope and jurisdiction in concrete terms (Saini 1983).

The Nehruvian model of industrial and agricultural development was based on the ethos of planning, each plan telescoped into five years. The First Five Year Plan (1952) only casually touched upon worker-employer participation through works committees, acting as advisory committees for discussing matters relating to the workers' welfare; greater stress was laid on discipline and manufacture of high quality products, rather than providing for any kind of workers' education.

It was in the Second Five Year Plan (perhaps the most successful so far) that it was specifically stated that industrial democracy was a prerequisite to the establishment of a socialist, egalitarian, secular, and modern state. In 1956 the industrial framework noted that "in democracy, labour is a partner in the common task of development and should participate in it with enthusiasm." Hence, joint management councils were created for developing healthier industrial relations (Planning Commission 1956: 49). In 1958 it was realized that any meaningful participation would *ab initio* require the education of workers. Participation is just not possible unless the workers make a big dent in management's armour. Thus came into existence the Central Board of Workers' Education. However, the rubric of workers' education was defined as the development of effective trade unions with more enlightened membership to encourage the emergence of leadership ability among them, to give organised labour its legitimate place in a democratic society and promote among this class a greater understanding of the industrial and economic environment of the country.

The concept of a mixed economy was defined as one in which the public sector would occupy the commanding heights of industrial development, while the private sector was limited to consumer oriented industries. Maximum emphasis in this model was placed on the self-sacrifice of the workers for building India into a strong welfare state.[1] The earlier advisory councils were replaced by a National Labour Commission. The Commission was concerned only with the inculcation of a sense of discipline and responsibility and commitment among the workers for nation building. This was the dimension of workers' education, and the earlier stress on their becoming more enlightened members of trade unions was more or less abandoned.

This kind of educational programme was inherently unsatisfactory, as the goals laid down for the workers were proposed to be achieved without even perfunctory consideration given to their demand for changing the content of the education syllabus. The scheme was bound to fail, and hence a review committee went into the reasons for its failure. This committee redefined the educational objectives as, (i) to equip all sections of workers including farm labourers for their positive participation in the social and economic development; (ii) to make the workers aware of their milieu, their rights and obligations as equal citizens; (iii) to raise the level of trade unions by the induction of educated workers; (iv) to construct a democratic model by giving equal share to traditional values and the current industrial culture, and (v) to prepare the trade unions for becoming the instrument of implementing these educational requirements.

The new incentives and ideals of the changed concept of workers' education were formulated by the the Chairman of the N.L.C., G. Ramanujam, Secretary of the Indian National Trade Union Congress (INTUC), an ancillary trade union organisation of the Indian National Congress which has remained the major ruling party since 1947 (the three years, 1977–1980 of the Janata interregnum were just a passing phase).

However, the change from the 1958 model to the one defined by the Central Board of Workers' Education (CBWE) in 1975 was only a shift in emphasis. The hope that the trade unions by themselves would assume the charge of academics' imparting education to the workers proved non-productive because, under this structure, the only "responsible" union was the INTUC alone. Long before the foundation of the INTUC in 1948 there was the All India Trade Union Congress (AITUC), a Marxist-oriented organisation, wedded to the concept of class-struggle and economic "dialectics." Some other trade unions, such as the Centre of Industrial Trade Union (CITU), were born after the split in the

---

[1] The emphasis on the self-sacrifice of workers alone was as utopian as the trusteeship concept of Gandhian economics.

Communist Party of India. The more radicals called themselves CPI-Marxist (CPI-M), the moderates remaining within the CPI, and the pro-Mao Zedong factions were labelled as CPI-ML (Marxist-Leninist). However, because of continuing infighting among these factions they could never establish their own trade union organisation. Then there were unions of the Railwaymen, Dock Workers, and others, being the offshoots of the Indian Socialist Party, with George Farnandes commanding the maximum influence (however temporary and that too confined to Bombay); the Textile Unions; the Hind Mazdoor Sabha (HMS), a left of centre socialist union; and the pro-bourgeoise trade unions led by the Hindu organisation, the Bhartiya Jan Sangh, which had only peripheral influence. Yet these trade unions had an anti-Congress outlook. Hence, among the ruling circles these unions were never regarded as "responsible" trade unions, as conceptualised by the CBWE. The multiplicity of trade unions claiming recognition (often on the basis of a very large number of bogus members) was a major constraint in the implementation of Ramanujam's goals. On the whole, the level of education remained stagnant and ineffective (Ramaswamy 1983).

In 1981 the CBWE gained a new Chairman who in conformity with the prevailing norms has been repeatedly stressing the "responsible" and the "responsive" role of the workers rather than educating them for an awareness of their rights. Although after 1958 there was no broad shift in the workers' education policy, the new Chairman addressing a conference of regional directors of CBWE remarked,

Education by the Board so far has laid greater emphasis on the right of workmen and trade union... There were of course references to responsibilities of workers, but then that was just nominal. The result is that there has been a lop-sided development – directed more towards their rights, than about their responsibilities. One of the new directions should therefore be, equal if not greater emphasis on the obligations of the workers.

The *summum bonum* of the address was

that the primary obligation of the worker was towards the country, that they should be taught about the economy of India where 52 % of the people were living below the poverty line. These undefined sections have equal rights ... hence it is the responsibility of the organized sector workers to give greater attention to their weaker brothers and the new direction of the educational policy should be an adoption of a national approach (CBWE 1981).

The major theme of the address was that workers' education should give new thrust to labour's role as the house-keepers of the nation. That they should assume upon themselves the duties of a house-wife who feeds all the members of the family first and takes her turn last. Hence labour should serve the country first and resign itself to the remnant crumbs of food (sic).

Thus was the Chairman's audacity, to orient the workers' education more or less towards the equivalent of what is euphemistically called Domestic Science; or just to keep on adhering to the code evolved by Manu, in which on the one hand the housewife was goddess Lakshmi, the goddess of plenty incarnate, yet in actuality she was to be the slave of her father, then her husband, and in her old age, the servant of her son. If her husband predeceased her, she was to be burnt alive along with the corpse of her lord and master and thence to be venerated as "sati."[2] In this era of women's lib women all over the world (including India) are agitating for equal rights and equal pay for equal work.[3]

Obviously, the logic behind the workers' education policy was to divorce him from the more militant trade unions. It is just human and natural that the worker would reject this code which was formerly regarded as valid. Now the parameters of the new educational policy are clearly based on a format of education of workers to equip them for an age of rapid technological change and an electronic revolution.

The New Educational Policy

Prime Minister Rajiv Gandhi, in a national broadcast, placed education as his first priority, his object being to prepare India for her projected role as one of the major powers by the turn of this century. This could be achieved only by the adoption of the latest technology and the computer culture. For this, the need of the working class was for a much higher educational level and competence. And this was required immediately. Hence, a national debate is currently taking place on structuring an

---

[2] Sati – sate was a custom in which a widow was forcibly to burn herself on the pyre of her deceased husband until it was legally abolished by the British Governor General, Lord William Bentinck in 1829. However, even today if a widow voluntarily burns herself alive at the funeral pyre of her husband, the Hindu is respectful towards this "sati."

[3] Manu – The law giver of the eighth century A.D. defining the respective roles of man and woman in which woman is at all times subordinate. The code laid down by Manu was followed by Hindu society until the passing of the Hindu Code Bill (1955). This Act gave women the right of divorce, share in the property of her deceased father and that of her husband, and made strict monogamy the norm.

integral system of education from the primary to the highest level, and de-coupling jobs from university degress. Over 150 universities in India are churning out, year after year, thousands of semi-literate B.A.s and M.A.s. Except for the top 5% of the students the rest are only able to come up to the level of Macaulay's mould of education shops, producing "Babus" (Clerks) to work the lower rungs of British administration. These white-collared workers from peons to high-grade bureaucrats and the semi-literate or unlettered blue-collar industrial workers were to gradually fade away; they already belonged to a prehistoric era.

Sri K.C. Pant, the Union Education Minister, during the course of a recent parliamentary debate over sanctioning the grants for his ministry, made a number of pertinent observations. To stress just a few of these points: "our vision of educational system should not be unidimensional." He rejected the prevailing colonial system of education where the changes during the last 150 years were only marginal. Instead, he said, we now require two things as the essential bases of our education: first, vocational education without having any terminal point, meaning that education would be a continuous process leading to the higher levels of formal and technological education. Secondly, after de-coupling academic degrees from jobs, it is a must that at a given point of educational achievement, it is possible to move in the direction of vocational training where jobs must be immediately available, so that the new vocational education does not work as a disincentive. In the sphere of workers' education from ground level, the principle should be that a worker could climb on and on to the summit, provided he has the necessary mental equipment and aptitude (Lok Sabha proceedings: April 8, 1985).

This educational structure can also cover the managerial sector. Central Minister Vasant Sathe stated in clear terms that in the Public Sector there would be no employer and no employee. All the managers, technocrats, and workers would be equal partners. This pronouncement would remain an unattainable utopia unless workers are sufficiently educated to comprehend their rights and responsibilities and have incentive-oriented programmes with the aim of producing more and better quality of goods. The major problem in about 60% of Public Sector enterprises is the increasing quantum of losses reaching billions of rupees. The much trumpeted virtues of the private sector by the vested interests in reality is equally grim. About 70,000 of the factories and mills come in the category of "sick" mills. Thus, the educational model spelt out in this paper is equally valid for the two major organised sectors.

By adopting a slightly different structure, the problem of drop out children, even during the primary level education, could be resolved as K.C. Pant said during the debate in Parliament by a programme of informal education. This will cover both the drop outs and the illiterate adults who also need to be educated.

The Issue of Competence

It is in the above context that the national debate is underway for providing a viable model which has to be relevant to Indian conditions. Hence, at this juncture, while placing India in the perspective of other industrially developed societies and the patterns of education and competence as concomitant and component parts of workers' overall education level, competence needs to be further investigated.

To define "competence," I refer to Heller (1983) who states that "the term 'competence' includes experience, skill and know-how and access to information." Thus "competence" can be taken both as a subjective and an objective phenomenon, since both are important in developing democratic behaviour in organisations. The term "competence" therefore draws a distinction between political and individual efficacy, but there is also a basic line of similarity. Political efficacy encapsulates change through the process of political structure, and from this flows increased political efficacy eventually giving the "competent" the control of levers of political power. In this process of broader political efficacy aimed at overall control, the concept of the individual cannot be wished away. Thus any emphasis on the individual comes within the controversial arena of "elitism," which has the potential to exclude the lower "competence" level worker. Indeed, it can be postulated that the term "competence" can have elitist-authoritarian overtones, and thus "competence" is a suspect value concept.

This contra-distinction has the ingredient of synthesising individual "competence" and "collective competence," because they both are species of the same "genre." Further, there are three basic reasons why a democratic efficiency theory involving "competence" can be structured. Firstly, recent empirical researches support the importance of "competence" variables while participating in power-sharing (Heller 1983). Secondly, sociological interpretation of research evidence has often misinterpreted "competence" dimensions. Attempt has been made to remove this error in a paper read at the first International Sociological

Conference on "Participation and Self-Management" (Heller and Rose 1973). The conclusion drawn is that employees participating in determining their own working process – based on shared knowledge and experience even with different levels of "competence" – can manage any enterprise if their sum total of knowledge or skill or "competence" is not of a lower order. Finally, the basic contention of this argument is that the competence-efficacy factor need not be seen only in elitist terms, and does not exclude workers or their representatives with assumed lowers level of "competence" from participating in the decision-making process (Pateman 1970).

In this context I now wish to draw on my own limited experience in this area. In 1982, I had made a study of workers' participation in two important industries: one a subsidiary of the giant multinational Union Carbide, The Eveready Flashlight Company (TEFCO) in the private sector. In Lucknow TEFCO manufactures flashlight torches. The second study concerned a major public sector enterprise: the Hindustan Aeronautics Limited (HAL) where complete aircraft are assembled and components for indigenous or imported aircrafts are produced.

In the private sector multinational, a majority of workers (57%) were either illiterate or just nominally literate, while 71% had no technical training. Hence, they possessed little "competence." This subaltern class was treated as outcasts even by their foremen, and their relationship to the lower level of supervisors was secondary, formal, and socially distant. The level of decision-making or managerial bureaucracy was beyond their horizon.

Contrarily, in the public sector HAL, 90% workers had the minimum qualification of secondary education level achieved in High School examinations. They engaged in informal relations with supervisory cadres, (e.g. both sharing the lunch hour meal), and their access to the managerial level was always available. These workers also had additional technical training to their credit. In spite of such basic differences in the two industries, they had similar structural and functional bureaucracies and a "high tech" managerial model as defined by Scheinder (1969; also Joshi 1982). In the private sector TEFCO there was a multiplicity of trade unions working at cross purposes, while in the HAL there were accredited trade unions. Moreover, in the former all of the executive positions in the trade unions were occupied by outsiders, i.e. by the so-called labour leaders, whereas in the latter all the top office-bearers were drawn from its own work force (Srimali 1969, Walker 1973). One interesting discovery in this study was that the better educated workers with college and university degrees (10%) comprised the most dissatisfied sector. They would rather have preferred to be low level white-collar clerks than, out of economic compulsions, getting employment in a factory. They were misfits because their academic culture had made them outsiders in the company's industrial culture.

In the global context and more specifically in the Asian context the Japanese model is the most relevant for India. In Japan professional and formal education is not yet a major aspect of the higher educational system. The Japanese universities and colleges provide a highly discipline-segmented basic education exclusively for whole-time students. Out of nearly 400,000 graduates, 76% get employment in industries where very little professional and continuing education is offered. But, once employed in the industrial sector, the Japanese workers have ample scope for better job opportunities by training themselves and absorbing skills which come within their "competence" sphere. Thus, they have no need to go back to school for advanced technological education, as is typical in the American system. The key element in upgrading the labour force of Japan (which is largely a lifetime employment-oriented concern) is the emphasis on vocational and managerial training (Nagata 1983). Hence, taking Vasant Sathe's (1984) as our point of reference, the Japanese model is suitable for Indian workers who, at least theoretically, are to become the owners of the factories where they work.

Concluding Remarks

In the context of contemporary industrial economic democracies, India in the new era is compelled to restructure its educational policy. This policy has to have the basic component of high level "competence" involving a working knowledge of the electronic mode of production, building on a formal academic course in basic science disciplines comprising natural sciences, life sciences, earth sciences, and the new field of space sciences. This model has to adapt itself to a mix of formal intramural education, and on-the-spot education to achieve a multi-dimensional level of expertise. This integrated educational structure needs to realize a 100% rate of free compulsory primary education for all citizens in India (as enshrined in the Directive Principles of India's Constitution) and from this level to move forward to a viable, interdisciplinary course of higher education. The two main streams in this (i) high academic theoretical and applied research and (ii) higher level of secondary vocational-technological education, would together become an integral part of the national educational policy framework. At the same time this structure has to resolve harmoniously a number of competing pressures including those of the centre versus the states, and the regions versus the local communities.

References

Agarwal, Pratap C. (1973): Cultural Milieu in India and participatory Management, In: Thakur, C.P. and Sethi, K.C. (eds.) *Industrial democracy. Some issues and experiences*, New Dehli: Sri Ram Centre for Industrial Relations and Human Resources.

Avasthi, Abha (1982): Participational Lag in India – A Perspective, Paper presented at Xth World Congress of Sociology (R.C. 10) in Mexico.

Central Board for Workers' Education (1981): *New Dimensions of Workers' Education*, New Delhi: CBWE.

Cherns, A.B. (1973): Conditions for an Effective Management Philosophy of Participation, In: Thakur and Sethi (eds.) *op.cit.*

Drenth, P.J.D. et al. (1979): Participative Decision-Making in Organizations: A Three Country Comparative Study, *Industrial Relations*, 18: 295–309.

Emery, F. (1982): New Perspectives on the World of Work: Sociotechnical Foundations for a New Social Order, *Human Relations*, 35: 1096–1122.

Heller, Frank A. (1983): *The Role of Competence in Democratic Organizations*, London: Tavistock Institute.

Joseph, Cherian (1978): Workers' Participation in Industry: A Comparative Study and Critiques, In: Ramaswamy, E.A. (ed.), *Industrial Relations in India*, New Delhi: MacMillan.

Joshi, P.C. (1982): Bureaucratic Functioning of Industries in the Private and Public Sectors, Unpublished Ph.D. Thesis, Department of Sociology, University of Lucknow, India.

Manu (1888): Manusmriti, *Sacred Books of East, Vol.XXV*, Ed. Max Muller, Oxford: Claredon Press.

Nagata, Kiyoshi (1983): Stress in Japan Still on Learning by Doing, *Capital: A Management Journal*, Vol.189 No. 4744: 21–27.

National Commission on Labour (1969): *Report of the National Commission on Labour*, New Delhi: Government of India.

Pateman, Carole (1970): *Participation and Democratic Theory*, Cambridge: Cambridge University Press.

Planning Commission (1956): *Second Five Year Plan*, New Delhi: Government of India.

Ramaswamy, E.A. (Ed.) (1978): *Industrial Relations in India*, New Delhi: Mac Millan.

Ramaswamy, E. A. (1983): What Education do Workers' Need, *Economic and Political Weekly*, 18, 9: 4–11.

Saini, Debi S. (1983): Industrial Democracy: Law and Challenges in India, *Indian Journal of Industrial Relations*, 19, 2: 191–205.

Sathe, V. (1984): *Towards Social Revolution: A Case of Economic Democracy*, New Dehli: Vikas Publications.

Scheinder, E. V. (1969): *Industrial Sociology*, New York: McGraw-Hill.

Srimali, P. D. (1969): *Implementation of Labour Laws in Uttah Pradesh*, Labour Research Centre, Department of Economics, University of Lucknow, India.

Srivastava, A. K. (1976): Why Blue-Collar Workers Do not Put Efforts, *Indian Journal of Industrial Relations*, 12, 2: 201–211.

Walker, Kenneth F. (1973): Workers' Participation in Management in Practice: An International Perspective, In: Thakur and Sethi (eds.), *op. cit.*

Whetras, V. G. (1966): *Labour Participation in Management: An Experiment in India*, Bombay: Manaktalas.

Chapter 19
Cooperation Between Universities and Unions

Edgar Einemann

Background

A process of increasing scientification of society can be observed. Development and research is taking place in businesses, institutes, and universities, separated from the immediate production process. The conditions in a capitalistic industrial society result in private entrepreneurs being, on the whole, able to decide the content and tasks of scientific work and dispose of the results. This applies not only to the research carried on in businesses and to studies done by many consultant-academics, but also to the apparently neutral and publicly financed science. The necessity of good cooperation with the "business world," for example in order to ensure access to the business and to sources of money, or to further the career chances of graduates, place a large section of the universities in a direct or indirect capitalistic connection.

Criticism of the content and tendency of the prevailing science has been voiced in universities, institutes, and businesses: for instance, the fact that the study of industrial management is orientated only towards a mono-economic rationality and not towards a social rationality (as a result of which, the requirements and problems of the worker are not sufficiently catered for in the development of technologies). This exacerbates the problem that the political economy offers inhuman concepts as political advice and the law contributes to the cementation of the socially dominating conditions. Objections are also raised both against the specific use of the results of scientific work, e. g. in order to control people or to build up military destroying potential as well as against the ignoring of human and ecological aspects. Criticism is also made of the internal scientific distribution of work, which allows little scope for multi-disciplinary ideas. The contradiction between the public financing of a section of science and the private-capitalistic use of the results is a further starting point in the demands for alternative scientific approaches which are orientated not only towards social processes of change, but also towards the interests of those involved and those employed in dependent positions.

A critical science which aims to orientate itself towards those employed in a dependent position and which wants to work at changing the socially dominating structures, should try to establish a relationship with worker organisation, namely the unions (Katterle and Krahn 1980). Local union organisations as well as national union boards could be partners in cooperation with a worker-oriented science. This cooperation must be of a critical and unanimous nature. The independence and self-reliance of science should also be capable of producing results which may not at first meet with the approval of the unions (e.g. as regards ecological problems).

The German trade unions, which are strongly centralised, recognised at an early stage their need for social research in order to strengthen strategic decisions. For example, the analysis of the development and distribution of income, the assessment of global economic development, and the evaluation of legal factors have considerable influence on tariff and other policies. Likewise, unions are forced to react to the use of new technologies and changes in social security.

The conservative traditions of the universities as well as the interest in possessing their "own" scientific resources have led the unions to build up an "internal social science." The basis of these systems are staff members and departments at the respective directorates, the research institute of the DGB (formerly the WWI and now the WSI), which has economic, sociological, and legal competence, and the Hans-Böckler-Stiftung of the DGB, which besides bestowing annual grants also provide several million DM for research support. Although these projects are carried out by research teams outside the unions, a close bond with the unions is ensured by the financing, terms of reference, appraisal, and accompanying conditions, as well as the compulsion of passing on the research results. Over and above this, the union directorates have joint research programs supported by the Ministry of Research and Technology. They have succeeded in gaining involvement in projects supported by considerable personnel and material, e.g. projects for utilising research findings, projects for disseminating information concerning humanising initiatives, for advising workers, for the development of educational material, and for the assessment of the consequences of the use of technology.

Two negative aspects must be mentioned, however:

a) The scientific analysis of social structural changes and political-strategic perspectives hardly play a part. A self-critical politising does not seem to be of primary interest to those responsible in the unions.

b) The scientific potential is for the most part centralised, that is, adapted to the requirements of central bodies.

Collaboration Between Unions and Universities

In order to expand quantitatively and to overcome the mentioned deficiencies, the unions have to utilise external resources. Over and above the cooperation practised with some academics and institutes, a broader cooperation with the universities must be started. This must not only be anchored in worker-oriented thinking in teaching, but must also encourage union-oriented social research (Bamberg et al. 1979). The availability of resources for such research, based on practice and interests, as well as the institutionalising of cooperation with the unions, must be required of the scientific institutions.

On the part of the union, the use of such joint cooperation assumes the articulation of factual interests on political-strategic questions, the opening up of their structures for external scientists, an understanding of time periods and the special terminology used in research, and the ability to cope with criticism.

Worker-oriented social science in cooperation with the unions is only a part of the necessary critical science which calls for change in the prevailing society. This science is oriented towards the interests of people who are employed in a dependent position in businesses or administration, or who have founded cooperatives. While concentrating on problems in the business field, the social associations should not be neglected, which becomes clear when handling medical-ecological problems (health, work safety, environment protection), or political problems (e. g. the production of socially useful goods). Interacting with worker interests requires overcoming the traditional academic division of tasks and the cooperation of different disciplines (Franz 1985).

Possible areas of work for the universities within a cooperative relation with the unions include:

a) carrying out research projects;

b) writing appraisals, e. g. in connection with legal and labour-scientific questions;

c) disseminating scientific results through publications, work conferences, and seminars;
d) setting up advisory bodies for workers and their representatives, e. g. to
   assess the consequences and options concerning technical changes;
e) the provision of further education courses, which should also allow the
   university education of workers who do not have matriculation
   qualifications;
f) the development of seminars for adult education and for the training of
   team leaders;
g) influencing the university itself in connection with worker-oriented
   instruction.

The central requirement for the opening-up of universities as institutions
is a firm cooperation with the unions and the material provision of
cooperation areas with lecturers, colleagues, and material which are
financed in the long-term budget of the university. The short-term
creation of cooperation areas staffed with one or two scientific workers
may increase the possibility of the unions to use scientific results, but
cannot fill the gap as substitute for a change in the scientific work.

The Case of Bremen University

An area of cooperation which is adequately supplied with personnel and
money, and whose destiny is determined half-and-half by representatives
of the university and the unions, exists at Bremen University in the
Federal Republic of Germany, which places 5 % of its resources at their
disposal. The newly-founded Reformed University of Bremen signed a
cooperation contract in 1971 with the Worker's Chamber in Bremen to
bring to realisation a "Science in the Interests of the Worker" and to
interlock its activities with ordinary workers. The Worker's Chamber is a
public institution founded after the Second World War, of which all
workers in Bremen are members and whose activities are determined by
the unions. In order to carry out the joint work, a special department was
set up in the university, called the Cooperation Area University/Worker's
Chamber, staffed initially with 6 scientific workers and one professor. The
work of this group began with a long-term research project concerning
work in the ports, the making of films, the organisation of work seminars,
and the development and testing of concepts for worker education.
Research, which was poorly developed at the university, together with the

aim of the cooperation-area to factual contributions, led to the extension of the department in the early seventies as a social-scientific research institute, with 6 professors assigned to research and a growing number of scientific workers, some of which were financed from outside. Projects were carried out concerning the use of robots in industry, problems in union education work, and the developments in dock work (Einemann 1979).

The shipyard study (Schumann et al. 1982) was carried out under the leadership of the industrial sociologist Michael Schumann from 1975 to 1981 and was well received. A general achievement of this project was the further development of worker-oriented social research through the reporting of objective structures and the analysis of the "worker perspective," in which workers were taken seriously as subjects and in which their complex outlook was comprehensively represented. However, in the course of the project work three problems for the cooperative relationship were raised:

a) Difficult research problems forced an extension of the project which resulted in a final report being published 5 years after the start of the work, and consisting of more than 1,000 pages – a time and product structure for which production workers and union members interested in the use of the results could not show great understanding.

b) The power of the company management prevented access to the place of work, so that the project was forced to seek access in other regions. This meant that the contact with Bremen shop floor workers and union members was not as intense as was wished and was necessary.

c) The utilisation of the results which was planned at the outset via a direct feedback with the workers concerned in the study and the recording of the experiences gained in this joint discussion of the research results had to be excluded because of lack of time.

Interim results of the shipyard study were disseminated in a worker education project under the leadership of Adolf Brock (Brock and Einemann 1983). From 1976 until 1980 continuous work-relevant educational work was carried out with shipyard workers, within which a "research of those concerned" could be realised. Ideas regarding a humanising of the work soon concentrated on those conditions of work which caused illness. Frequent occurrence of certain illnesses in work groups were identified. The existing work safety system was also identified, regarded as insufficient and worthy of supplementation. The worker experts drew up a questionnaire in the seminars to examine the concerns of the worker. These questionnaires were handed out by shop stewards in the shipyards. The evaluation of the questionnaire was carried out in a seminar and led to the publication of a small brochure, which formed the basis of discussions in the shipyards. With this self-questioning the workers not only became subjects or research, but also made a considerable contribution to strengthening their consciousness at work. The debates triggered off by the questionnaires also influenced the behaviour of worker groups, e.g. when refusing to carry out specific dangerous work in spite of the economic crisis in the shipyards. A problem was connected with the project, however: the "interference" of the cooperation department in the union works politics met with the criticism of the union after the majority faction in the works council left the education project. The union regarded the continuation of the project work as strengthening internal union opposition.

Before the end of the projects, the cooperation department was subject to severe pressure from the unions, who had serious discussions about withdrawal from the contract. The local union organisation had problems with the political-strategic research and the critical educational work which, from their point of view, revealed a lack of union interest and showed deficiencies in the practical relations with the cooperation department.

A compromise was found involving a positive change in union criticism: parallel to the research work, an institution more strongly oriented towards service was established, with the task of taking care of the more intensive transfer of scientific results, advising shop stewards and unions, and increasing the range of worker education courses. The discussions thus resulted in the restructuring of the cooperation department into a research department and a department concerned with dissemination, media production, and worker education.

In the first half of the 1980s three integrated educational and research projects were carried out by 6 scientific staff members of the worker education sector. Seminars, which were built up in accordance with the one week annual study leave guaranteed by law in Bremen, were carried out jointly with union educational institutions. Within the project "Crisis, Rationalisation, Humanisation" (Einemann and Lübbing 1985), continuous education work closely connected with practice was carried out from 1981 until 1985 with employees in the aviation industry. Altogether 66 employees, among them many engineers, took part in a total of 7 weekly and 7 weekend seminars. In 1982 a factory working group for alternative production was founded, which demanded the conversion of production to manufacturing socially useful goods instead of the reduction of jobs and the production of armaments. Monthly meetings of an organizational group and working groups (including ones concerned with specific technological areas) were introduced.

The main working group, together with the works council, planned a poll in the employee seminars and evaluated the responses. Through the distribution of questionnaires and the presentation of the results, a considerable internal discussion was triggered. A small brochure concerning the aims and activities of the working group was compiled and distributed (Fischer et al. 1984). In addition, the evaluation of all works newspapers distributed in recent years led to the listing of over 80 examples of useful civil products developed in the business concern. The working group now has contacts with similar groups in other factories and also with local initiatives, e.g. in the fields of health, environment protection, and peace. It has also taken part in several talks held in universities, churches, political parties, and unions. Initiated by the working group, meetings of the cooperation department arranged in conjunction with professors on the theme "Alternative Production" and with theoreticians and practitioners concerning the theme "Jobs Through Regional Energy Concepts" were organised.

Conclusions

On the whole, we can argue that a successful and intensive cooperation between science and unions has been achieved, in which a worker-orientated social science has been realised. This form of cooperation differs from concepts of action research in that the scientists have confined themselves to a supporting role, without using their status as publicly paid and secure research workers to gain leading political positions.

At the beginning of 1985, a further re-structuring of the cooperation department was decided upon. Austerity measures by the government and the changing of political majorities within the university in favour of conservative tendencies brought the department once more to the limits of its existence. The result of the discussions has been the laying down of an average of about 5% of the university budget for the University/Worker's Chamber Centre, which, since mid-1985 has consisted of:
a) a research centre at the university, open to all lecturers, and which does not allow exemption from teaching;

b) a legally independent media institute which has the task of finding new sources of finance;

c) a transfer department to support university research "cooperation" and to supply scientific results to the unions;

d) an Academy for work and politics, which offers long-term courses for workers (without matriculation qualifications), lectures, and seminars held by scientists.

The future will show whether the new structures will lead to the optimal cooperation of university and unions, whether they will meet the requirements of a worker-oriented social science, and whether the development of research of the people involved is possible. A number of important lessons can be learnt from the "Bremen Model." It would be desirable, for example, to integrate more strongly the engineering sciences and medicine, as well as strengthening the interdisciplinary cooperation. The cooperation of critical science and workers can at the same time make a politically important contribution to the understanding between different cultures and to cement the union of traditional and new social movements.

Hard work awaits the scientists involved, however, as has been identified by Gerhard Leminsky (in Franz 1985) of the Hans-Böckler-Stiftung of the DGB, using a project as an example:

Hereby it is made clear, how varying changing relationships between "research" in the strict sense and meetings, publications, and various transposition forms are developed, which lay open new dimensions for the work of the social research worker. At the same time, however, they demand qualifications which the usual discipline-oriented scientific work does not provide, and which are frequently not rewarded in an academic career, such as the connection and transmission of research, integrated ways of thinking concerning several disciplines, and research management."

References

Bamberg, H.-D., Kröger, H.J. and Kuhlmann, R. (1979): *Hochschulen und Gewerkschaften*, Köln: Bund-Verlag.

Brock, A. and Einemann, E. (1983): Lernen am Konflikt, In: Görs, D. (ed.): *Arbeiten und Lernen*, München: Max Hueber Verlag.

Der Senator für Bildung, Wissenschaft und Kunst der Freien Hansestadt Bremen (ed.) (1985): *Arbeit und Technik als politische Gestaltungsaufgabe*, (authors: Fricke/Krahn/Spitzley and Schröder) Bonn: Verlag Neue Gesellschaft.

Einemann, E. (1979): Zur Institutionalisierung der Kooperation zwischen Wissenschaft und Gewerkschaften, *Arbeitshefte der Juso-Hochschulgruppen*, (Bonn) Nr. 21, May 21: 36–58.

Einemann, E. and Lübbing, E. (1985): *Anders produzieren. Alternative Strategien in Betrieb und Region*, Marburg: SP-Verlag.

Einemann, E. and Lübbing, E. (1987): *Politisches Lernen und Handeln im Betrieb*, Marburg: SP-Verlag.

Fischer, J., Ladewig, L., Einemann, E., and Lobbing, E. (1984): *Alternative Produktion statt Arbeitsplatzabbau und Aufrüstung*, Universität Bremen.

Franz, H.-W. (Ed.) (1985): *22. Deutscher Soziologentag 1984: Soziologie und gesellschaftliche Entwicklung*, Opladen: Westdeutscher Verlag.

Katterle, S. and Krahn, K. (Eds.) (1980): *Wissenschaft und Arbeitnehmerinteressen*, Köln.

Schumann, M., Einemann, D., Siebel-Rebell, Ch. and Wittemann, K.P. (1982): *Rationalisierung, Krise, Arbeiter*, Frankfurt: Europäische Verlagsanstalt.

Conclusion

Chapter 20
Competence and Organizational Democracy: Concluding Reflections

Cornelius Lammers

What can one infer from the foregoing chapters as to the state of our knowledge concerning the interrelations between competence on the one hand, and participation, workers' control, and self-management, on the other? First of all, a short discourse on the central concept of competence is in order. Then follow some observations on participation, workers' control, and self-management. For the sake of convenience, but not without theoretical justification, I will subsume these three under the heading of "organizational democracy." The next two sections are dedicated to the nature of democratic competence in organizations and the connections between various kinds of competence, on the one hand, and organizational democracy, on the other. After that I will pay attention to the organizational and societal context of competence and organizational democracy. Finally I will comment on the range of views evinced by the authors as to the viability of various kinds of organizational democracy. Is the struggle for a measure of self-determination by people in work organizations a lost cause, a kind of Sisyphean labor, or an ongoing emancipation process?

Competence

Let us take as our starting point Heller's definition of competence: "experience, skill and know-how and access to information" (quoted by Avasthi in Chapter 18 on p. 322). Given the enormous variety of fields of competence, one should discuss competence*s* (plural) rather than competence (singular). In the contributions reviewed here we meet with several types of competence, such as: technical, administrative, social, political, and economic competence.

Several authors (Avasthi, Dominelli, Heisig/Littek, Rus, Sajó) refer to the level of education or training (e. g. skilled versus unskilled workers) and then have people's *technical* competence, their know-how, experience, and skills with respect to their job, trade, or profession in mind. When the discussion centers around bargaining skills, quite a different sort of competence of employees is meant (Bernoux, Briefs, Heisig/Littek, Sajó, Teulings). I will conceive of such skills as indicative of (micro-) *political* competence, for no doubt both formal negotiations of unionists or works councillors with employers and "informal effort bargaining" (a term of Lee, quoted by Heisig/Littek, Chapter 13 on p. 236) rest on knowledge about, and experience with, tactics and countertactics in organizational or inter-organizational transactions, insight and access to information on power and authority relations, on legal and other formal arrangements, etc.

It stands to reason that political competence shades off into *social*, interpersonal skills, on the one hand, and *administrative* or general organizational skills, on the other. In quite a few contributions, in my impression, these sorts of competence are more or less implied. Avasthi, for example, distinguishes individual and collective competence (efficacy), and obviously the latter type presupposes on the part of those who want to engage in collective action the ability to build and maintain some sort of group solidarity and to organize forms of opposition. Finally, *economic* competence is also referred to, for example by Sajó when he describes the way in which Hungarian employees who are members of work communities make use of their knowledge about market demand for various kinds of services.

Of course, the "whole" of competence is more than the sum of its parts. In the first place, I presume that what matters in the connection between competence and organizational democracy is the degree to which and the ways in which people manage to convert their know-how, experience, and information into skills. But since a "skill" in and by itself is an *ability*, even if we can apply a skill, we may not want, or may not get a chance, to do so. In other words, competence can remain latent, either because people do not know how to apply what they know, or because they do not see fit to use their potential skills in practice. Competence is a force that has to be "turned on," a "factor" which becomes operative only under certain conditions.

In the second place, if competence is not a loose assembly of bits of knowledge, experience, and information, but a sort of purposeful organization of one's experience, know-how, and information with respect to a certain area of action, it follows that we presume a degree of *rationality* on the part of the actors in question. The question then arises: what kind of rationality? In my judgment most authors in this book do attribute to the "competent" actors a measure of what Karl Mannheim called "functional" rationality. This entails the supposition that competence can be used as a (more or less effective) means toward certain ends. Mannheim (1940: 53) contrasts this type of rationality with another one: "substantial rationality," which he describes as: acts of thought "which reveal intelligent insight into the interrelations of events in a given situation."

Admittedly, this Mannheimian concept of substantial rationality is a rather elusive one. Nevertheless, it may very well be a rather crucial notion in connection with the theme of this book, for regardless of the utility of competence as a tool for actors to obtain certain benefits (individually or collectively), competence can also be seen by the actors concerned as something of value in and by itself.

Organizational Democracy

Participation usually stands for participation-in-decision-making and then denotes some form of "upward" influence or power-exertion by subordinates in a hierarchical relationship. Consequently, participation is by definition a form of practice embedded in a non-democratic setting. Nevertheless, hierarchical organizations can very well harbour more or less democratic arrangements or processes. Even in the cold climate of Antarctica it may be warmer in one region than in another one! In similar fashion one can say that among hierarchically structured organizations some are (even) less democratic than others. This simply means that hierarchical organizations vary considerably as to the kind, scope, and amount of participation bestowed on, or gained by, subordinates.

As hinted at in this last sentence, "lower" participants in hierarchical organizations can either "receive" or "wrest" from the powers-that-be chances for upward influence or power-exertion. The latter case of "adversary participation" is often called *workers' control*, a term used by Hancké and Wijgaerts in their contribution about the development of guiding conceptions of self-management in Belgian Unions. Workers' control, in this sense of the term, signifies power on the part of workers or their representatives to check, thwart, prevent, redress, and even veto certain policies, directives, rules, or decisions by management without sharing management's responsibilities.

If participation is the upward exertion of influence or power in a more or less *cooperative* spirit, then workers' control in the ideal typical case stands for upward exertion of influence or power by *opposition*. Of course, the distinction is much clearer in theory than in practice. Parties striving for vastly different goals may nevertheless both have a shared interest in maintaining their relationship; then they either cooperate by opposing each other in institutionalized ways, or engage in struggles contained in, and by, cooperative forms. Although, as Hancké and Wijgaerts point out, participation and workers' control are qualitatively different orientations, the *practice* of these orientations in industrial relations may very well show rather similar variations in workers' power or powerlessness.[1]

The likelihood that dissimilar ideals of organizational democracy can, nevertheless, when they are put in operation, form a continuum in terms of differences of degree of upward influence or power on the part of the rank-and-file, also comes to the fore when one considers the differences between participation and workers' control, on the one hand, and *self-management*, on the other. In principle, self-managed organizations are fully democratized, with all members jointly deciding about all matters of importance, and no one exerting "upward" influence or power. However, as soon as a division of labour comes into being between mere members and office-holders to whom certain powers are delegated, again those "mere members" can and do "participate in," or "contest," the decision-making of those they have allowed to become in some respects more powerful than themselves.

In other words, egalitarian organizations in fact exhibit differences in degree of democracy comparable to those found in hierarchical organizations. If one part of Antarctica is warmer than another one, so in tropical Africa it is here "colder" than there! Egalitarian organizations range from quite to not (so) hierarchical (oligarchic). The only – but by no means negligible – difference between democratically and hierarchically constituted organizations is, that in the former case democracy means the rank-and-file "retaining" or "regaining" their legitimate rights instead of (in the latter case) "receiving" or "wresting" influence or power from their hierarchical superiors.

---

[1] Some of the problems with the realization of workers' control in the practice of Dutch unions are described in Teulings et al. (1981: 300 ff.).

All this leads me to the conclusion that, with an eye towards the empirical study of participation, workers' control, and self-management, it makes sense to look at these forms and processes as probably similar, and anyway in many respects quite comparable. In all three instances one encounters differences in individual or collective self-determination of people's work and working conditions, in the ways in which and the extent to which employees or members can defend or promote their interests with respect to their terms of employment or membership, and in the chances for them to direct or redirect the goals and policies of their organizations. Participation and workers' control are in principle quite divergent ways of power exertion in hierarchical organizations, but can be seen as processes that one also encounters under the regime of self-management.

One final note of caution. Even if one studies participation, workers' control, and self-management in terms of continua that cover two or three of the three types mentioned, it certainly does not follow that they represent "stages" of an evolutionary sequence. In other words, whether or not participation can or will *ceteris paribus* "mature" into workers' control or self-management, and whether or not workers' control has the potential to develop into self-management, are open questions. I will come back to these issues at the end of this chapter.

The Competence of an Organizational Democrat

For a better understanding of the effect of competence on organizational democracy and vice versa, we must have a somewhat more concrete idea what the role of a participant in a QWL (Quality of Work Life)-experiment, a Works Councillor, a shop steward, a member of a Union council, or an officer of a cooperative, entails. To devise a classification (see Table 1), I will take it that "lower" participants in systems of organizational democracy:
– act as solo performers, or *en groupe*;
– speak for themselves, or on behalf of a constituency;
– promote interests (their own and/or those of a constituency), or advise and consent (and sometimes codecide with) leaders on organizational policies.
Altogether one can distinguish eight tasks, one or more of which form the role of an organizational participant exerting some sort of upward influence or power:

Table 1: Elements of the Roles of "Lower Participants" in Forms of Organizational Democracy

	Promote interests	Advise/consent
– as individuals	a	b
– as group members	c	d
– as solo-representatives	e	f
– as representatives, members of a group	g	h

a) promoting one's own interests individually vis-à-vis one's boss;
b) advising one's boss on work or work-related matters;
c) promoting jointly with one's colleagues the interests of oneself and one's group vis-à-vis one's boss;
d) acting jointly with one's colleagues as an advisory group to one's boss on work and work-related matters;
e) representing single-handedly the interests of a constituency vis-à-vis leaders of the organization;
f) acting as a consultant, mandated by a constituency, to leaders of the organization on policy matters;
g) representing jointly with other representatives the interests of a constituency vis-à-vis organizational leaders;
h) acting jointly with other representatives as an advisory group to organizational leaders on policy matters.

In the papers collected in this book one finds examples of roles consisting of one or more of the tasks indicated. The individual white-collar employee described by Heisig and Littek is a soloist trading expert advice for a certain degree of autonomy and other advantages (a + b). Barber and Towers, however, portray workers participating in QWL-projects as people engaged primarily, if not only, in advisory tasks (b), and thus give something for nothing. The French members of "expression groups," appearing in Bernoux' paper, act as a collective consultant to their boss but try at the same time to benefit from their contribution to the welfare of the organization (c + d). Teulings and Briefs discuss works councils, the members of which fulfil to a variable extent both promotion of interest and advise-and-consent functions (g + h). An interesting, but quite different case (at the inter-organizational level) of delegates who must reconcile "upward duties" with "downward loyalties," is depicted by Sekulić. If directors or members of workers' councils of self-managed firms in Yugoslavia are elected to "higher" representative bodies such as a Chamber of Associated Labor, they stand up for the interests of their firms (g) but are also engaged in policy making (h) at the local, sector, regional, or state level.

It is striking that most of the above examples relate to a and b, c and d, e and f, g and h. One wonders if the process of pleading one's cause with higher authorities always, or at any rate frequently, engenders a form of "collaboration." I suspect that indeed the dynamics of representation usually entail a measure of cooperation as the price for the right to voice one's views and requests.

"Lower" participants in systems of organizational democracy can promote their interests, either because they have something to offer – that "something" being: advice, consent, or decision-sharing – or because they can somehow force bosses or organizational leaders to comply with their demands. In the former case the "lower" participants bring positive, in the latter case negative, sanctions to bear on their "uppers." Given the limited supply and disadvantages of negative sanctions at the disposal of the "lower" participants,[2] they tend to resort in many, if not in most, cases (also) to the deployment of positive sanctions to get their way. Consequently, in the practice of organizational democracy, cooperation and opposition often go together, and alternate or exhibit after a while the predominance of cooperation over opposition.

However, I do not want here to go into the vices and virtues of cooperative and oppositional forms of organizational democracy. I point to the interconnection of these task-elements merely because this illustrates neatly that with respect to the role of the "lowers" in organizational democracy, one can say: the whole is more that the sum of its parts. Any particular kind of activity mentioned in Table 1 requires already a specific competence, but the very *combination* of the tasks, for example those of a promoter of interests with those of a consultant, calls forth another type of competence: the ability to strike an effective balance between promoting interests and consulting, to time correctly switches from the one to the other set of tasks, to do one, but not to omit the other thing, to cope with role conflicts, etc.

Similarly in positions of this sort there is often the problem of the somewhat contradictory demands of operating on one's own (a, b, e, and f) and in accord with a group (c, d, g, and h). The solo performer has to be

---

[2] The reasons why negative sanctions in the hands of workers and unions have some "built in" disadvantages are elaborated in IDE (1981: 260–261) and Lammers (1981: 36–41).

self-reliant, ascendant, and pushy, whereas operating in a group requires a measure of interpersonal sensitivity and empathy. Last but not least, there is the perennial dilemma representatives face that in performing their duties (e to h) they unwittingly or wittingly may at the same time serve – or be misguided by – their own interests (a).

The Connection Between Competence and Organizational Democracy

The foregoing survey of ingredients that go into the role of a participant or representative in an organizational or interorganizational setting can be seen as a description of the competence needed to function in systems of organizational democracy. As mentioned already, technical and political competence were frequently designated by various authors in this book as variables explaining the presence or absence of viable forms of participation, workers' control, or self-management. Therefore, we can rephrase the question concerning the connection between competence and organizational democracy in terms of the relationship between technical and political competence on the one hand, and the "democratic" competence required to participate, control, or self-manage, on the other.

Evidently, *political* competence has a more direct impact on the practice of organizational democracy than technical competence. If workers themselves or their representatives have, or obtain temporarily, rights to a say in certain areas of decision-making, it stands to reason that they will be the more capable to avail themselves of these opportunities, the more experience they have in bargaining and contesting, in coalescing with others, and in the art of combining cooperation with opposition. Consequently, inasfar as participants or representatives are already – due to experience in politics, voluntary associations, schools, or jobs – used to bargain or struggle with opponents in lateral or hierarchical relationships, in all likelihood they will be able to transform or transfer these skills (in)to those necessary to fulfil the role of a competent democrat. Thanks to this anticipatory socialization they will not need the same amount of training or learning by trial and error on which their colleagues without such previous experience have to rely.

If the meaning of the term "political competence" is extended sufficiently, one can even conceive of democratic competence as a special kind of political competence. Nevertheless, it makes sense to distinguish between the skills and know-how learned in systems of organizational democracy, and political proficiency acquired in other settings, since these two kinds of skills differ at least in some respects and to some extent. Moreover, these two types of competence can be said to result from experiences taking place at different times, so that one can study the ways in which and the degree to which general political competence affects competence at the level of organizational democracy and vice versa.

Turning now from political to *technical competence*, I note first of all that in general training for, and experience on, a job has a direct bearing on one's capacity to participate, control, or self-manage only with respect to advisory tasks (primarily $b + d$ in Table 1). His or her work qualifications enable the employee in most cases only to participate in decisions about work or work-related matters, to a lesser degree on policy matters $(f + h)^3$ and not at all to act as a defender of interests or spokes(wo)man.

Certainly, there are exceptions to this rule. The salesman's skills in persuading people and bargaining come in handy when he faces a boss who contests the height of his expense account. The staffman of the company in charge of handling labour relations is experienced in keeping at, or bringing to, bay union representatives; he can apply similar tactics when negotiating with management about the interests of his department. In general, however, the technically more qualified employee is not as a result of his (her) work experience or training better equipped to speak up for him (or her)self, for his (or her) colleagues, than the less qualified one.

But even though training and work experience are not directly relevant for promotion-of-interests tasks, technical competence may very well contribute *in*directly to one's fitness to undertake the oppositional (i. e. a, c, e, and g in Table 1) tasks of the role of a participant or representative. In most, if not all, societies education is a major determinant of one's status (in and outside work organizations), so that the more educated person probably feels more self-confident and can count on a better chance to be taken seriously by bosses or managers than his less educated colleague. Observations to this effect occur, for example, in the paper by Avasthi whose research findings indicate that in India in private industry unskilled workers are more likely to be treated as outcasts by their foremen than

---

³ Obviously, the problem for most employees (and their supervisors as well) is that they can see from their own position only part of the policy-picture.

more highly trained employees in public enterprises. Likewise, Bernoux mentions that to be accepted as a social partner is a rather important condition enabling and/or motivating members of "groupes d'expression" to participate.

Of course, not only the *status* of employees, but also their *power* will in all likelihood correlate with their level of training. The higher the job qualifications, the higher in general the chances that the function will be considered as indispensable and that candidates for such a function will be relatively scarce. One gets the impression that, for example, the workers in Hungarian enterprises who see their way clear to start a work-community or enterprise-work-community are those who have not only marketable skills, but also (thereby?) a certain leverage vis-à-vis management.

Systems of organizational democracy obviously require democratic competence not only on the part of "lower," but also on the part of "upper" participants. Most authors in this book treat competence from the "bottom up" perspective, but provide us nonetheless sometimes with hints at the "top down" view. From Bernoux' report on expressive groups in French industry, as well as from various other contributions, one gathers that the sparring partners of participants and representatives have to be quite competent at handling the give-and-take inherent in any form of viable organizational democracy. In general, I suspect that the role of the boss or manager, when in consultation or confrontation with his subordinates or their delegates, exhibits similar ingredients, complexities, intricacies, and dilemmas as the latter's roles.

Nevertheless, given the arguments just brought forward in connection with the correlation between education and democratic competence, it stands to reason that employers and their representatives will by and large be more competent at the game of organizational democracy than those who oppose or advise them. In addition, the work roles of supervisors and executives usually entail a good deal of administrative and social competence. Finally, those occupying leadership positions in work organizations tend to hold far more frequently than the "common" man or woman offices in voluntary associations, political parties, churches, etc., and this experience also diffuses into administrative, political, and social competence.

To conclude, I think it is fair to presume that lack of *willingness* may be far more important than lack of *ability* in the case of "uppers" than in the case of "lowers" as a reason why systems of organizational democracy often do not function (well).

Thus far we have looked at competence as the "independent" variable in relation to organizational democracy, but it is quite feasible to study competence also as "dependent" on the practice of organizational democracy. In this manner Briefs notes that the German system of *Mitbestimmung* may have adversely affected union militancy. Union members and functionaries have grown accustomed to dealing with employers and their representatives within a legal(istic) framework, and this might have fostered a juridical, cooperative kind of competence at the expense of competence at opposition in the traditional style of the labour movement.

The same author also observes a tendency towards the "professionalization of codeterminators," and this reminds us of Avasthi's fears concerning the possible "elitist" overtones of competence. Indeed, as we ought to know following the writings of Michels, democratic competence can become appropriated by an elite of representatives who use their skills in this respect to increase the dependence rather than the independence of their constituents. Another example is found in the paper by Kamdem who tells us of a cooperative in Cameroon where the original nucleus of founders remained the exclusive "proprietors," refusing others who wanted to join and who had the proper qualifications.

Of course, if participation and representation are not privileges of a few, but duties of many, competence at organizational democracy may be strengthened and diffused. Particularly if efforts to democratize the work place meet with success, one is led to believe that democratization is a self-reinforcing process. But what happens in the numerous cases that experiments of this kind die off, or are thwarted?

Participation, workers' control, or self-management imply for most people involved in such activities learning by doing. No doubt, as Barber and Towers repeatedly stress in their treatment of QWL-programs, negative experience with pseudo-democracy is quite discouraging. If workers do not benefit from it, they will not be willing to continue with it. In a similar vein, Bernoux points out that participation fails when the participants do not get a chance to give advice and do some side-bargaining on their own terms. In other words, in such cases participants will be demotivated, but in spite of that they may very well have become more competent at initiating action and defending their interests. In the Netherlands I have come across instances where the failure of a program of humanization of work later on appeared to have sown the seeds of union activity. Previously unorganized employees formed a union shop and became militant as a result of their short-lived experience with workplace democracy and with the ways in which supervisors and managers handled and stopped the experiment.[4]

Frustrated and frustrating efforts at democracy may no doubt lead to many "never again" vows on the part of some participants, but others may become more determined not to endure paternalistic or authoritarian rule in organizations, so that they may be more on the alert than before to search for alternatives, either by way of "voice" or by way of "exit." I do think it a highly interesting and socially quite relevant theme for further research to investigate the after-effects of abortive democratization projects in hierarchical organizations. Under what circumstances and to what extent does diffusion take place not only among those who were involved in experiments of this nature, but also among those who witnessed the project from some distance in adjacent departments or organizations?

Competence and Organizational Democracy in the Organizational and Societal Context

In most of the presentations reviewed here, the interconnections between various kinds of competence and organizational democracy are analyzed as forms or micro-processes situated in the context of organizational settings, while also conditions pertaining to the macro-social environments are seen as impinging on these forms and processes. Let us look at the organizational context first.

In the foregoing discussion it has become clear already that participants and representatives acquire, consolidate, and elaborate their competence to a large extent by interacting with their colleagues and the "uppers" they relate to in the course of participative or representative activities. In addition, management, as well as the unions active on the scene, can provide facilities for training, information gathering, consulting with constituents, expert advice, etc. to increase the level of competence of those involved in shop floor participation, works councils, and the like.

Naturally, the factual support managers and union officials give to such participative projects or to the functioning of representative bodies is probably more decisive than the formal provisions they arrange. Does

---

[4] One such cause is described in *O. R. Blad* (1980).

management heed the advice which comes out of such groups? And does it react in a constructive manner to the use of such channels of upward communication for the airing of views, grievances, and demands "from below"? If the answer to these questions is affirmative and unionists and/or informal strategic groups go along, then there is a reasonable chance that the system of organizational democracy in question will be(come) a going concern and thereby enhance the competence of participants therein. Furthermore, in such a situation both "lower" and "upper" participants are likely to use formal provisions for training, expert consultation, etc. intensely and to urge their extension.

To make a long story short, the general organizational *regime* which is a function not only of the "style of governance of dominant élites" in organization, but also of the "style of organizational effort arising from the norms and tactics of rank-and-file groups" (Lammers and Hickson 1979: 392), is in all likelihood significant for the viability of most forms of organizational democracy and of efforts to increase the level of competence of those involved in it.[5]

Of course, if an enterprise or public agency engages in a program of participation, this does not necessarily imply that unions or militant oppositional groups from within the company, are tolerated in, let alone welcomed to, the arena of organizational democracy. Often enough liberal rulers in organizations manipulate participation as instruments (in the words of Barber) of "union avoidance." But even where there is a certain readiness on the part of management to grant the right of opposition and cooperation within the firm to unions – either because it is forced to do so, or because its style of governance has a touch of the truly democratic spirit – the union may refuse to play ball.

One of the reasons why QC (Quality Circles), QWL, or kindred programs frequently succumb sooner or later may be that they require not only (as Bernoux stresses) supervisors and managers with a sufficient amount of discretion, but also a union or comparable association to see the experiment through.

---

[5] On the basis of the outcome of various research projects on industrial democracy I have been engaged in, I have the impression that, on the whole, participation and other "voluntary" forms of organizational democracy are in their functioning and development more determined by the regime of an organization than codetermination and other arrangements that are legally prescribed or agreed on by collective bargaining. It could very well be that in the latter case the nature of labour relations in the sector, union policies, and other "external" factors are more important than in the former case.

This brings me to the *interorganizational and societal context*, in which the role of external agencies with respect to competence and organizational democracy looms large. In the previous paragraphs the policies and practices of *unions* has already come to the fore. If we scrutinize the chapters in this book containing information on this point, we arrive at quite a varied picture. In France, according to Jansen and Kissler, the unions, with the exception of the CFDT, tend to look askance at democratization of the workplace. Bernoux' account of the unions' policies regarding the Auroux legislation yields a slightly more positive impression.[6]

The U.S. unions, Barber informs us, mostly take a positive stance or adopt a "policy of decentralized neutrality" towards QWL projects. In the case of Germany and The Netherlands (as indicated by Briefs, Einemann, and Teulings) there is evidence of a more positive attitude of unions towards works council activities. Differences in union policy between these latter two countries and the ones mentioned in the previous paragraph, may be due not only to the fact that in The Netherlands and Germany legally established forms of representation, rather than management-initiated experiments of participation, are at stake, but also to differences in union strength.

In other countries, if one goes by the reports in this book (of Blyton on Wales, of Dominelli on Algeria, of Kamdem on Cameroon, of Avasthi on India), unions are too poor or too powerless, or for policy reasons not inclined, to spend much energy on efforts to boost the democratic competence of their members and to support initiatives to introduce, maintain, or enlarge intra-organizational forms of participation and representation.

In general, only unions that are strong enough will be able to afford to take the risks of encouraging efforts at opposition and cooperation within work organizations which may develop into relatively independent power centres. In this connection I think it is relevant to draw attention to the possibility that not only the strength of the unions is in question, but also the strength of the *employers' associations* they have to deal with, which may be a (positive!) factor conducive to the formation of formal arrangements and support of organizational democracy systems.[7] If

---

[6] Perhaps Bernoux reports only, or mainly, on the degree to which unions were ready to negotiate with employers the introduction of "groupes d'expression," and not on the degree to which unions were willing and able to support the functioning and development of such groups.

[7] See on this IDE (1981: ch. 14).

unions consider themselves capable of containing "syndicalist tendencies" and at the same feel they can rely to some extent on employers' associations to keep their members form turning organizational democracy into a anti-union weapon, then they may be willing to engage in enduring commitments to make organizational democracy work.

As hinted already, unions may prefer legally based forms of participation and representation to those that have been bestowed on the lower orders *au bon plaisir du chef*. In the former case there are certain guarantees for the durability of the arrangements, while political parties, government agencies and public opinion may help to enforce the law, at least to some extent. Moreover, as exemplified by the "rationality political" type of works council sketched by Teulings, representatives can sometimes make effective use of legal interventions to force their entrance in the decision-making process.

It goes without saying that the role of the *State* with respect to establishing and supporting forms of organizational democracy is in general by no means of a positive nature. The accounts of Dominelli on Algeria, Kamdem on Cameroon, and Avasthi on India show that governments and their bureaucracies can not only remain inactive, or be active only in rather ineffectual ways, but can even pursue an active policy of dismantling existing forms of self-management.

Perhaps the State and her agencies become a potent sponsor of organizational democracy only, or mainly, if other intermediary organizations more directly involved in the system of labour relations, take and sustain initiatives to this end. In Western parliamentary democracies it will usually be the unions and (albeit somewhat reluctantly and only for strategic reasons) employers' associations that can form such a supportive network, while political parties and the media play a secondary role in this respect. In socialist countries like Hungary in recent years, and Yugoslavia in the early fifties, one surmises that there the party for economic and/or political reasons was the prime mover redirecting state policy to the introduction of worker communities in the one, and self-management in the other case.

Governments and public agencies can do something about organizational democracy evidently not just by legislation, but also by sponsoring activities to enhance the democratic competence of workers. However, as the case of the efforts of the Indian government in this direction show, raising the level of competence of the labour force in and by itself is of little avail. Only in combination with serious legislation and if backed by unions, and accepted or tolerated by employers, do attempts of governments to educate and train people for organizational democracy work. In the latter case, governments will not generally establish, but rather subsidize or co-sponsor organizations especially designed for this purpose.

The *supportive agencies*, which Blyton and Cornforth focus on, perform quite a lot of other functions besides helping participants and representatives to improve their competence. If one looks at the distinction Cornforth makes between external and internal functions of CSO's, one could say that these agencies attempt to legitimate this alternative way of (organizational) life to the outside world and also to build op the organizational and interorganizational competence of the cooperatives. One of the ways to achieve this latter goal is by providing training and information to the cooperators. In other words, improving the competence of individual members of cooperatives is one of the means to improve the competence of the coops and their interorganizational network. Supportive agencies that do not have coops as their clientele, but cater to those involved in more "moderate" forms of organizational democracy, will presumably offer a narrower range of services. These organizations will busy themselves primarily with courses, information, and counselling, that is with competence building at the individual level.

Agencies which contribute in one way or another to competence at organizational democracy can be joint ventures of unions and employers' associations (e.g. the Work in America Institute, mentioned by Barber), constitute departments of, or belong to, unions; or occur as tripartite structures (sponsored by unions, employers' associations, and state agencies). Besides these agencies sailing under the flag of the main actors on the labour relations front, we also notice individuals or organizations operating more or less independently from these actors. In this book we meet with a couple of interesting examples – a German one analyzed by Einemann, and an American one reported by Woodworth – of university-based groups or individuals acting as advisors to unions and workers engaged in organizational democracy projects. In both cases one is struck by the problems which "independence" entails. Even though in both cases the consultants clearly take sides with unions and workers, one gets the impression that in a way the unions are not much less distrustful of their activities than those of the managers.

However, the "labour advocate" (as Woodworth calls him) is like his/her counterpart on the other side, the management consultant, a flexible "competence builder" who can render services tailored to the needs of his or her clients. Unlike trainers or consultants who are employed by agencies under the aegis of unions and/or employers' associations, the "free" agent is not bound by standard programs and organizational policies. Therefore, his/her often dearly maintained independence may enhance the free consultant's credibility and effectivity in the eyes of the participants and representatives with whom he or she works.

Both Cornforth and Woodworth outline two contrasting approaches, the "top down" and the "bottom up" one, to develop people's democratic competence. The problem with the first is that in this way one tries to establish democracy by non-democratic methods. Obviously this kind of imposed democratization confronts those who have to have a go at some form of organizational democracy with the well-known discrepancy between medium and message. However technically correct and expedient for participation, codetermination, or self-management the directives are, the way in which they are delivered often does not breathe the spirit of democracy. To put it in other words, the recommendations may be instrumental for the design and functioning of a democratic *structure*, but the process by which they are conveyed is not expressive of a democratic *culture*.

This dilemma is certainly not confined to the micro-scene of the relation between advisors and advised, but has parallels on other levels. When national unions or governments launch campaigns or enact measures to promote forms of participation, representation, and self-management "from above," there is always the danger that they may succeed in introducing the "mechanics" of the system so forcefully that the norms and values which have to ensure its proper functioning get lost in the process.

In a more general way there is the problem that all the agencies discussed thus far, that make up the interorganizational context of attempts at democratization in most societies, seldom function themselves in a very democratic way. Therefore, even if one finds constellations – rare enough – that make for concerted efforts to initiate or maintain forms of organizational democracy, the dynamics of interorganizational transfer may contribute to individual and organizational competence but at the same time unwittingly undermine the democratic potential of this competence.

The Prospects for Organizational Democracy

In the written contributions to this volume, quite a variety in tenor exists as to the prospects for organizational democracy. Some authors are decidedly more optimistic in this respect (for example, Bernoux, Teulings, Woodworth) and others more pessimistic (for example, Barber, Kamdem, Briefs). What accounts for such differences in view? Obviously, personality, the kind of experience one has gone through, and the overall national situation in which one finds oneself will explain the variations noted to some extent. However, I think that in addition to, or as a result of such factors, the *socio-political outlook* and the *role one adopts as a sociologist*, have a lot to do with *le ton qui fait la musique*.

If one considers organizational democracy as an ideal in the sense that we ought to realize self-management in organizations as an actual, and not only a formal, state of affairs, the prospects look dim indeed. Completely egalitarian organizations can and do exist sometimes for some time, but there is, as far as I know, no historical or empirical evidence that such "states" last, even in the best of circumstances. Therefore, if one concentrates attention on the (enormous) degree to which present levels of organizational democracy deviate from the ideal of a full-fledged system of individual and collective self-determination, pessimism is certainly warranted and realistic. The only sensible role for a sociologist to adopt is the role of the social critic who does not want to forsake his or her ideals, but is convinced that the only thing to do is to maintain and stimulate awareness about the undesirability of the ways in which our organizations are governed, and the imperfection of society at large.

If, however, one conceives of organizational democracy not so much as a goal to be realized, but rather as a road to take, the fact that here and there, in spite of even the worst of circumstances, people make efforts in this direction, is encouraging. Personally, as the reader will have guessed already, I tend towards a certain well-tempered optimism. I do not feel committed to democracy as an attainable endstate, but rather to the goal of working at *democratization*. Satisfactorily functioning systems of organizational democracy occur now and then, but always constitute, in my perception, an episode between two periods in which the degree of power inequality between rulers and ruled was (or eventually became) even larger. To keep the process of democratization going and to keep fighting efforts at de-democratization is in my view a sort of categorical imperative, lest people become even less self-reliant and self-determining than they already are.

Consequently, I do not share Mannheim's hope for a sort of evolutionary macro-process of fundamental democratization, but neither do I view organizational democracy as a lost cause. Yes, working at democratization is perhaps best described as a kind of Sisyphean labour (à la Camus' famous novel), worthwhile as far as it prevents further deterioration of the ways in which we lead our organized lives, and maybe also as far as it has at least as a beneficial side-effect, the enhancement of our political competence in the sense of Mannheim's substantial rationality.

References

Industrial Democracy in Europe (IDE) International Research Group, (1981): *European Industrial Relations*, Oxford: Clarendon Press.

Lammers, C.J. (1981): Industrial Relations from an Interorganizational Perspective, chapter 11 In: A.W.J. Thomas and M. Warner (eds.), *The Behavioural Sciences and Industrial Relations. Some Problems of Integration*, Farnborough: Gower.

Lammers, C.J. and David J. Hickson, (eds.) (1979): *Organizations Alike and Unlike. International and Inter-Institutional Studies in the Sociology of Organizations*, London: Routledge & Kegan Paul.

Mannheim, K. (1940): *Man and Society in an Age of Reconstruction. Studies in Modern Social Structure*, London: Routledge & Kegan Paul.

O.R. Blad (1980): Medezeggenschapsproject: rommelen in de marge, *O.R. Blad*, january: 22–23.

Teulings, A., F. Leijnse, and F. van Waarden (eds.) (1981): *De nieuwe vakbondsstrategie. Problemen en dilemma's in loonpolitiek en werkgelegenheidsbeleid*, Alphen aan den Rijn: Samson.

List of Contributors

Abha Avasthi is Reader in the Department of Sociology, University of Lucknow, India.

Bob Barber is a researcher and organizer, and is currently Research Director for Lee Associates, an Oakland, California-based consulting firm.

Philippe Bernoux is Head of the Groupe Lyonnais de Sociologie Industrielle, Lyon, France.

Paul Blyton is Senior Lecturer in Industrial Relations at the Cardiff Business School, University of Wales, Cardiff, U.K.

Ulrich Briefs is a member of the Parliament (Bundestag) of the Federal Republic of Germany, and senoir researcher at the Economic and Social Science Institute of the German Federation of Trade Unions, Düsseldorf.

Chris Cornforth is Allied Dunbar Lecturer in Voluntary Sector Management at the Open University, Milton Keynes, U.K.

Lena Dominelli teaches Social Work and Social Policy in the Department of Applied Social Studies, University of Warwick, Coventry, U.K.

Daniel Drache is Professor of Political Science, Atkinson College, York University, Toronto, Canada.

Edgar Einemann is a Lecturer in Industrial Sociology at the Academy for Labour and Politics, University of Bremen, Federal Republic of Germany.

Bob Hancké is a Research and Teaching Assistant in the Sociology Department of the Free University of Brussels, Belgium.

Ulrich Heisig is a Senior Researcher at the University of Bremen, Federal Republic of Germany.

Peter Jansen is a Research Assistant in the Political Sociology Department of the FernUniversität, Hagen, Federal Republic of Germany.

Emmanuel Kamdem is a Professor in the Department of Business, Management and Administration in the Pan African Institute for Development in Doula, Cameroon.

Leo Kissler is a Professor of Political Sociology in the Department of Educational and Social Sciences at the FernUniversität, Hagen, Federal Republic of Germany.

Cornelis Lammers is Professor of Sociology at the University of Leiden, The Netherlands.

Wolfgang Littek is Professor of Industrial Sociology and Sociology of Work at the University of Bremen, Federal Republic of Germany.

Veljko Rus is Senior Research Fellow at the Institute of Sociology, University of Ljubljana, Yugoslavia.

András Sajó is a Professor in the Institute for Political and Legal Sciences, Hungarian Academy of Sciences, Budapest, Hungary.

Dusko Sekulić is Professor of Sociology at the University of Zagreb, Yugoslavia.

György Széll is Professor of Sociology, University of Osnabrück, Federal Republic of Germany.

Ad W.M. Teulings is Professor of Sociology of Organizations at the University of Amsterdam and Director, Sociology of Organizations Research Unit.

Rochelle Towers studied Quality of Work Life Programs as part of her work as a union organizer.

Dany Wijgaerts is Deputy-Director for Research, European Centre for Work and Society, Maastricht, Netherlands.

Warner Woodworth is Professor of Organizational Behaviour, Brigham Young University, Provo, Utah, USA.

B. Strümpel (Ed.)
Industrial Societies after the Stagnation of the 1970s – Taking Stock from an Interdisciplinary Perspective
1989. 15.5 x 23 cm. XIV, 313 pages. With 27 figures and 65 tables. Cloth.
ISBN 3 11 011345 7; 0-89925-372-5 (U.S.)

A. Gladstone with **R. Lansbury, J. Stieber, T. Treu, M. Weiss** (Eds.)
Current Issues in Labour Relations: An International Perspective
1989. 17 x 24 cm. X, 380 pages. With 6 illustrations and numerous tables. Cloth.
ISBN 3 11 011653 7; 0-89925-471-3 (U.S.) (A Publication of the International
Industrial Relations Association, IIRA)

G. Dlugos, W. Dorow, K. Weiermair in collaboration with **F. C. Danesy**
(Eds.)
Management Under Differing Labour Market and Employment Systems
1988. 17 x 24 cm. XXVIII, 486 pages. Cloth. ISBN 3 11 010947 6; 0-89925-185-4 (U.S.)

M. Dornstein
Boards of Directors Under Public Ownership: A Comparative Perspective
1988. 15.5 x 23 cm. X, 166 pages. Cloth. ISBN 3 11 011740 1; 0-89925-496-9 (U.S.)
(de Gruyter Studies in Organization, 15)

R. Wolff (Ed.)
Organizing Industrial Development
1986. 15.5 x 23 cm. XII, 391 pages. Cloth. ISBN 3 11 010669 8; 0-89925-168-4 (U.S.)
(de Gruyter Studies in Organization, 7)

C. C. Perrucci, R. Perrucci, D. B. Targ, H. R. Targ
Plant Closings
International Context and Social Costs
1988. 15.5 x 23 cm. X, 193 pages. Cloth. ISBN 3 11 011746 0; 0-202-30338-1 (U.S.);
Paperback ISBN 3 11 011747; 0-202-30339-X (U.S.)
(Social Institutions and Social Change – An Aldine de Gruyter Series of Texts
and Monographs)

de Gruyter · Berlin · New York

Genthiner Strasse 13 · D-1000 Berlin 30 · Tel.: (0 30) 2 60 05-0 · Telex 1 84 027
200 Saw Mill River Road · Hawthorne · N. Y. 10532 · Tel. (914) 747-0110 · Telex 64 66 77